MEMOIRS

OF

GENERAL COUNT RAPP,

FIRST AIDE-DE-CAMP TO NAPOLEON.

Rapp, Général Jean, comte (1771-1821). This much-wounded aide-de-camp of Napoleon was destined as a boy to become a Protestant pastor, but instead joined up in the cavalry in 1788. He was twice woulded in the Army of the Moselle under Hoche in 1793 and was commissioned next year. He was wounded again several times in the Army of the Rhine and was appointed aide to General Desaix. He accompanied him to Egypt, received more wounds, and then returned to France with his general and fought under him at Marengo (1800) where Desaix perished in his arms. The next day he was appointed aide to the First Consul, and in 1801 was charged with raising the Mamelukes of the Guard. In 1803 he was promoted to *général de brjgade*, and in 1805 he captured Prince Repnine at Austerlitz after leading a charge to rout the Russian Imperial Guard, being wounded in the process. In December he was promoted to *général de division*. A number of governorships followed, but he as at Jena, received a further wound at Golymin, and then became governor of Danzig. Made a count in 1809, he led an attack with Mouton to rescue Boudet's division at Aspern-Essling. After a period in disfavor for opposing Napoleon's divorce from Josephine, he served in Russia at Smolensk, Borodino (four wounds), Krasnöe, and the Beresina, where he again was wounded. He defended Danzig throughout 1813, surrendered on terms, but was imprisioned in the Ukraine until 1814. During the Hundred Days he rallied to Napoleon and commanded the tiny Army of the Rhine, winning the combat at La Suffel near Strasbourg ten days after Waterloo had been fought. He lay low until 1817, but thereafter held court posts under Louis XVIII before dying of cancer.

David Chandler: Dictionary of the Napoleonic Wars.

MEMOIRS

OF

GENERAL COUNT RAPP,

FIRST AIDE-DE-CAMP TO NAPOLEON.

WRITTEN BY HIMSELF,

AND PUBLISHED BY HIS FAMILY.

The Naval & Military Press Ltd

Published by

The Naval & Military Press Ltd
Unit 10 Ridgewood Industrial Park,
Uckfield, East Sussex,
TN22 5QE England

Tel: +44 (0) 1825 749494
Fax: +44 (0) 1825 765701

www.naval-military-press.com
www.military-genealogy.com
www.militarymaproom.com

In reprinting in facsimile from the original, any imperfections are inevitably reproduced and the quality may fall short of modern type and cartographic standards.

CONTENTS.

Chapter I.—Commencement of the Author's military career.—His promotion.—Certificate from Desaix.—Good fortune in Egypt.—Introduction to, and character of, Napoleon.—Servile conduct of the old nobility. - - - 1

Chap. II.—Napoleon's temper.—His flatterers.—His clemency. - - - - - - - - 8

Chap. III.—Napoleon's attachment to his family.—Lucien's opposition to the views of Napoleon.—Napoleon's bounty to Rapp.—Rapp's intercession for Requier and Damas.—Is unsuccessful.—Writes to Requier.—Letter intercepted and carried to Napoleon.—The Emperor greatly incensed at it.—Rapp apologizes.—Is restored to favour.—Marries.—Bernadotte's disgrace with the Emperor.—His restoration to favour. - - - - - - - - 12

Chap. IV.—Napoleon's courage.—Infernal machine.—The Emperor's escape. - - - - - - 19

Chap. V.—Napoleon's readiness to receive advice.—His contempt for ignorance.—His partiality to the game of *vingt et un.* - - - - - - - 22

Chap. VI.—The third Austrian war.—The French victorious.—The Austrian army shut up in Ulm.—Summoned to surrender.—Negotiation conducted by M. de Segur.—The enemy surrender.—Napoleon's joy. - - - 26

CONTENTS.

CHAP. VII.—The remainder of the Austrians pursued.—Defeated by Murat.—Werneck's capitulation; disregarded by Count Hohenzollern.—Correspondence.—Napoleon's proclamation. - - - - - - - 40

CHAP. VIII.—The French march towards Vienna —The Russians defeated.—Napoleon's instructions to Murat on the occupation of Vienna. - - - - - 50

CHAP. IX.—Anecdote of the Emperor and Madame de Bunny.—The advance of the French troops.—Stratagem in crossing the Danube.—Austerlitz.—The advance-guard of the French repulsed by the Russians.—The Russians completely defeated.—Rapp wounded.—His promotion.—Napoleon's kindness to him.—His recovery.—The Emperor's instructions to Rapp.—Peace concluded. - 54

CHAP. X.—The conduct of Prussia.—Rapp's mission.—Its object.—His return.—The Grand Duchess of Darmstadt offends the Emperor.—Her punishment.—The French troops attacked by some Prussian detachments.—Rapp's appointment to the command of the military division at Strasburg.—He receives instructions.—The Emperor arrives at Mentz.—Rapp joins him at Wurtzburg.—His mission to the Grand Duke of Baden.—The impatience of the Prussian Generals to commence the war.—Character of Prince Louis.—Demand of Prussia.—Napoleon's proclamation.—Prussians defeated at Schleitz.—Rapp sent to the King of Prussia.—Recalled.—Mission of De Montesquiou.—His treatment. - 66

CHAP. XI.—The calculations of the Duke of Brunswick.—He is disconcerted at the movement of the French.—Manœuvres.—Napoleon issues orders.—Battle of Auerstadt and Jena.—The French victorious.—Rapp instructed to pursue the Russians.—He enters Weimar.—The King of Prussia makes overtures.—Napoleon's conduct.—He sends Duroc to visit the wounded.

—Head-quarters established at Weimar.—Movements of the enemy.—Attacked and routed by Bernadotte at Halle.—Napoleon visits the field of battle.—Goes to Dessau.—His treatment of the old Duke. - - - - 79

Chap. XII.—The Prussians closely pursued by the French.—Surrender of a corps before Magdeburg.—Misfortunes of Prussia.—The French prepare to march on Berlin.—Napoleon's instructions to Davoust. - - - - 89

Chap. XIII.—The French set out for Potsdam.—Anecdote of the Emperor and a female native of Egypt.—State of Potsdam.—Flight of the Court.—Deputations to the Emperor.—Their reception.—Napoleon's observations to the Duke of Brunswick's envoy.—Head-quarters at Charlottemberg.—Napoleon's proclamation. - - - - - 93

Chap. XIV.—Napoleon reviews the third corps.—Effect of the proclamation on the troops.—Surrender of 25,000 Prussians.—The Duke of Weimar abandons his command.—Blucher surrenders.—Napoleon's despatch to General Belliard.—Blucher allowed to retire to Hamburg. - 101

Chap. XV.—Arrest of Prince Hatzfield as a spy.—Napoleon's determination to have him executed.—Intercession for him.—The release of the Prince.—His letter to Count Rapp.—Embassies to the Emperor.—Rapp authorised to settle the affairs of the Court of Weimar.—The Duke permitted to return to his estates.—His letter of thanks to Rapp. - - - - - - - - 107

Chap. XVI.—Surrender of the Prussian fortresses.—Arrest of the Prince of Wurtemberg.—Head-quarters at Posen.—State of Poland.—Entry into Warsaw.—The Emperor's reception.—Anecdotes of the Poles and of the French soldiers.—Passage of the Vistula. - - - - 114

CHAP. XVII.—Affairs with the Russians.—Battle of Pultusk.—Rapp's wounds.—His appointment to the government of Thorn.—Blucher's letter to him.—He intercedes for Blucher.—Is made Governor of Dantzic.—Contributions levied.—Napoleon's dissatisfaction with Prussia. - 124

CHAP. XVIII.—Fourth Austrian war (1809.)—Battle of Esslingen.—Schill's insurrection.—Napoleon's feeling.—Battle of Wagram.—Rapp's accident.—Rapp obtains the pardon of some conspirators. - - - - 136

CHAP. XIX.—Attempt of a young German to assassinate Napoleon.—Conversation and conduct of the assassin. 141

CHAP. XX.—Execution of the young German.—Peace concluded.—Rapp's reception in Munich.—Situation of Bavaria.—Trait of the King of Wurtemberg.—Napoleon's return to Fontainebleau. - - - - - 147

CHAP. XXI.—Divorce of Josephine.—Marriage of Napoleon and Maria-Louisa.—Napoleon displeased with Rapp; sends him to Dantzic.—Rapp at Dantzic—Character of his garrison.—He gives offence to the Russian Resident. 151

CHAP. XXII.—Napoleon's dissatisfaction with Rapp, for evading the anti-commercial decrees.—*Douane* established at Dantzic.—Discontent in the North of Germany.—Rapp's representations.—Napoleon's ignorance of the German Character. - - - - - - 158

CHAP. XXIII.—Napoleon repairs to Dantzic.—Conversation between the Emperor and Rapp. - - - 164

CHAP. XXIV.—Napoleon proceeds to Konigsberg.—His intentions.—The advance of the French troops. Their arrival at Wilna.—Commencement of the Russian war. - - - - - - - - 168

CHAP. XXV.—Flight of the Russians.—Their rear-guard defeated by the King of Naples.—His report of the en-

CONTENTS.

gagement.—Dispute between the King of Westphalia and Vandamme. - - - - - - - 171

CHAP. XXVI.—Rapp leaves Dantzic.—State of the roads.—Arrives at Wilna.—Opening of the Polish Diet.—Speech of the President.—Eloquence and negotiations of the Abbé de Pradt. - - - - - - 176

CHAP. XXVII.—Activity of the Emperor.—His instructions to Hautpoult.—Distress of the army.—Hopes of Napoleon.—The Russian Patriarch's denunciation of the French. 186

CHAP. XXVIII.—Battle of Smolensko.—Escape of the Russian army.—Junot's inactivity.—He is in disgrace with the Emperor.—Intercessions in his favour.—Rapp named for the command of the Westphalian corps, instead of Junot.—Character of Junot.—He is allowed to resume his command.—Irruption of Tormasoff.—Napoleon's instructions to the Duke de Belluno. - - - - - - 190

CHAP. XXIX.—Kutusow takes the command of the Russian army.—His qualifications; his losses.—Rapp sent to reconnoitre.—Napoleon's conversation before the battle of Borodino.—Proclamation. - - - - 197

CHAP. XXX.—Battle of Borodino.—Rapp's wounds. 204

CHAP. XXXI.—Retreat of the Russians.—Occupation and burning of Moscow. - - - - - - 209

CHAP. XXXII.—The Emperor's delay at Moscow; its motives and consequences.—His instructions to the Duke de Belluno.—Deplorable state of the French army.—Rapp's recovery.—The Emperor's anxiety about the wounded. 213

CHAP. XXXIII.—Retreat of the French.—The Emperor's despatch to Mortier.—Battle at Malojaroslawitz.—Napoleon visits the field of battle.—Surprised by some Cossacks.—Rapp's conduct: the Emperor loads him with eulogiums.—General Winzengerode taken prisoner.—His treatment. - - - - - - 221

CONTENTS.

CHAP. XXXIV.—Deplorable condition of the French.—
Mallet's conspiracy.—The Emperor's surprise.—The
French cross the Borysthenes.—Attacked by the Russians.—Retreat of the French.—Marshal Ney's courage. - - - - - - - - 230

CHAP. XXXV.—Continuation of the Retreat.—Capture of
Witepsk.—Loss of the magazines.—State of the weather.
—Disasters of the French.—Attacked by the Cossacks. 235

CHAP. XXXVI.—The Emperor's solicitude for Ney.—
Receives information of his escape from the Russians.—
Embarrassment of the French.—Battle of the Beresina.—
Surrender of Partonneau's division.—Retreat of the French
uponWilna.—Napoleon sets out for Paris.—His instructions.
—Rapp proceeds to Dantzic. - - - - 242

CHAP. XXXVII.—Description of the town and garrison of
Dantzic.—Rapp's preparations.—His difficulties.—Losses
of the garrison by disease.—Scarcity of provisions.—Breaking up of the ice. - - - - - - 254

CHAP. XXXVIII.—Conduct of the Allies.—General Detrées
sent to reconnoitre.—Skirmishes between the French and
Allies.—The Russians defeated at Langfuhr, and Ohra. 262

CHAP. XXXIX.—Destructive ravages of the epidemic.—
Expedition against Quadendorf.—Defeat of the Russians.—
Ignorance of the garrison of the progress of events.—The
epidemic disappears.—The Russian signals set on fire.—
Attempts to seduce the troops of the garrison.—Review of
the garrison on the glacis. - - - - 271

CHAP. XL.—The garrison's efforts to obtain provisions; its
difficulties.—Rapp sends an expedition into the Nerhung.—
Is successful.—He demands a loan from the Dantzickers.—
Accusation against the senator Piegeleau.—Conduct of the
Duke of Wurtemberg.—News of the victories of Lutzen

and Bautzen.—Its effect on the French troops.—The Russians defeated.—The Allies solicit an armistice.—Rapp receives the ribbon of the order of La Réunion.—Napoleon's despatch to Rapp. - - - - - - 282

CHAP. XLI.—Conditions of the armistice.—Duke of Wurtemberg raises obstacles to the fulfilment of them.—His subterfuges.—Rapp's letter to the Prince de Neuchatel.—Scarcity of provisions.—Recommencement of hostilities. 292

CHAP. XLII.—Attempts of the besiegers.—Engagement between the garrison and the Russians at the advanced posts.—Details.—A second engagement.—The Russians take Langfuhr.—Their intentions.—Rapp's preparations.—Ohra put in a state of defence.—The Russians attack Kabrun.—Their fleet fire on the French batteries; but are repulsed.—Overflowing of the Vistula.—Combined attack by the land and sea forces of the besiegers. - - 303

CHAP. XLIII.—Severity of the weather.—Scarcity of provisions.—Attack of the Russians.—Their defeat.—Situation, and plan of operations.—State of Dantzic, the magazines, and the surrounding fortresses.—Condition of the garrison.—Disaffection of the German troops.—Means used to decoy them.—Rapp capitulates.—The Emperor Alexander annuls the capitulation.—Rapp protests and surrenders. - - - - - - - 323

CHAP. XLIV.—The garrison taken prisoners to Kiow.—Their liberation.—The state of France in 1814.—Rapp's treatment at Court.—The return from Elba.—Conversation between Napoleon and Rapp.—Rapp's appointment to the command of the army of the Upper Rhine.—Napoleon's arrangements.—His letter to the allied Sovereigns.—Rapp sets out for Alsace.—State of public feeling.—Enthusiasm of the women at Mulhausen. - - 337

CONTENTS.

Chap. XLV.—Preparations of the Allies.—Napoleon's letter to Rapp.—Rapp receives fresh funds.—The Emperor's despatch to Rapp. - - - - - - 352

Chap. XLVI.—Amount and division of the French troops.—Rapp receives news of the battle of Waterloo.—His determination.—Rapp's advanced posts attacked.—Movements of the Allies.—The success of the French.—Their retreat. - - - - - - - 357

Chap. XLVII.—Effect of the news of the battle of Waterloo.—Disposition of Rapp's troops.—Battle of Lampertheim.—Designs of the Allies.—Rapp throws himself into Strasburg.—Prince of Wurtemberg's conduct.—Military convention signed. - - - - - - - 364

Chap. XLVIII.—Mutiny of the garrison of Strasburg.—A description of their conduct.—Dissolution of the army.—Rapp's letter to the King.—Its effect.—Rapp's death.—Conclusion. - - - - - - - 375

APPENDIX.

Letter from General Rapp to the Duke of Wurtemberg.	405
Answer.	407
Letter from the Duke of Wurtemberg to his Excellency Count Rapp.	409
Answer.	410
Letter from the Duke of Wurtemberg to General Count Rapp.	411
Answer.	413
Letter from the Duke of Wurtemberg to General Rapp.	415
Capitulation of Dantzic.	417
Letter from the Duke of Wurtemberg to General Rapp.	424
Answer.	426
Letter from Count Rapp to the Duke of Wurtemberg.	428
To the same.	430

MEMOIRS

OF

GENERAL RAPP,

FIRST AIDE-DE-CAMP TO NAPOLEON.

CHAPTER I.

I DO not pretend to be an historical character; but I was long near a man who has been the object of base misrepresentations, and I commanded brave troops whose services have been disowned. The former overwhelmed me with favours; the latter would have laid down their lives for me: these things I cannot forget.

I served in the army for several years; and I was successful in some enterprises, though without gaining distinction, as is usual with those who hold subaltern rank. At length I was fortunate enough to engage the attention of General Desaix. Our advance guard, which had been thrown into disorder, was speedily rallied. I hastened forward with a hundred hussars; we charged the Austrians, and succeeded in putting them to flight. We were almost all covered with wounds; but for these we were amply rewarded by the praises that were bestowed on us. The General made me promise to take all requisite care of myself, and he delivered to me the most flattering attestation that ever a soldier obtained. I mention this circumstance, not because it procured me a pair of epaulettes, but because it obtained for me the friendship of that great man, and was the origin of my fortune. The attestation was as follows:

ARMY OF THE RHINE AND THE MOSELLE.

"Head Quarters at Blotsheim, 30th Fructidor, year III. of the French Republic one and indivisible.

"I, the undersigned General of Division, commanding the right wing of the above mentioned army, certify that citizen Jean Rapp, lieutenant in the 10th regiment of Horse Chasseurs, has served under my command with the said regiment during the two last campaigns; that on all occasions he has given proofs of singular intelligence, presence of mind and courage; that he has been wounded three different times; and that, on the

9th Prairial of the year II, at the head of a company of chasseurs, he attacked a column of the enemy's hussars, whose number was five times greater than his own force, with such devoted intrepidity, that he cut them to pieces, covering the retreat of a portion of our troops, and bearing away the honour of the victory. It cannot be too deeply regretted that he has been the victim of his valour, and has been dangerously wounded in such a way as to be deprived of the use of his arm. He is a worthy object of national gratitude, and well deserves to be appointed to some honorable post, should he be rendered incapable of more active service. I attest that citizen Rapp bears with him the friendship and esteem of all who know him. DESAIX."

Having become the aide-de camp of the modest conqueror of Offenburgh, I fought under him in the campaigns of Germany and Egypt. I was made the chief of a squadron at Sediman; where I had the happiness, at the head of two hundred brave troops, to carry off the last remnant of the Turkish artillery, and I was promoted to the rank of Colonel, at Samanhout, near the ruins of Thebes. I was severely wounded in this last affair; but I was honorably mentioned in the dispatches of the General-in-chief.

On the death of the brave Desaix, who was killed at Marengo, at the moment when he had decided the victory, the First Consul deigned to appoint me to a post about his own person. The favour which he would have conferred on the conqueror of Upper Egypt was extended to me. From that time I was in some manner permanently established, and my connexions became more extended.

Zeal, frankness, and some degree of military talent, procured for me the confidence of Napoleon. He frequently remarked to those about him, that few possessed a greater share of natural good sense and discernment than Rapp. These praises were repeated to me, and I must confess I was flattered by them: if this be weakness, I may be excused; every one has some foible. I would have sacrificed my life to prove my gratitude to the First Consul. He knew this; and he often repeated to my friends that I was a grumbler—that I had a poor head but a good heart. He treated both me and Lannes familiarly, using the pronoun *thou* when he spoke to us; if he addressed us by *you* or *Monsieur le General*, we became alarmed, we were sure that we were out of favour. He had the weakness to attach importance to a gossiping police system which for the most part deceived him by false reports. That odious system of police embittered the happiness of his life; it frequently incensed him against his best friends, his relations, and even his wife.

Napoleon attached but little importance to mere courage, which he regarded as an ordinary kind of merit, common to all Frenchmen: he set a higher value on intrepidity; and he was willing to pardon every fault in an intrepid soldier. When any one solicited a favour, either at an audience or a review, he never failed to enquire whether he had been wounded. He declared that every wound was a quarter of nobility. He honoured and rewarded the individuals who were thus distinguished, and he had good reasons for so doing. However, he soon perceived that they did not attend the antichambers, and he opened them to the old nobility. This preference offended us; he remarked this, and was displeased at our taking offence. "I see plainly," said he to me one day, "that these nobles whom I have placed in my household are disagreeable to you." I, however, very well deserved the privilege. I had erased several gentlemen from the list of emigrants; I had procured places for some, and had given money and pensions to others. Some have remembered these favours, but the majority have forgotten them; and consequently my purse has been closed since the return of the King. Though my object was to relieve misfortune, and not to obtain gratitude, yet I did not choose that the emigrants should interpose between us and the great man whom we had raised on the shield.

I had forgotten this disagreeable scene; but Napoleon did not forget any offensive observations that might escape him. In vain he sought to assume the mask of severity; his natural disposition subdued his efforts, and kind feelings always gained the ascendancy. He called me to him: he spoke to me of the nobles and the emigrants; and suddenly recurring to the scene above alluded to, he said: "You think, then, that I have a predilection for these people; but you are mistaken. I employ them, and you know why. Am I connected with nobility? I, who was a poor Corsican gentleman?"—"Neither I nor the army," I replied, "have ever inquired into your origin. Your actions are sufficient for us." I related this conversation to several of my friends, among others to Generals Mouton and Lauriston.

Most of these same nobles, however, allege that they had yielded only to compulsion. Nothing can be more false. I know of only two who received Chamberlain's appointments unsolicited.

Some few declined advantageous offers; but with these exceptions, all solicited, entreated, and importuned. There was a competition of zeal and devotedness altogether unexampled. The meanest employment, the humblest offices, nothing was rejected; it seemed to be an affair of life and death. Should a treacherous hand ever find its way into the portfolios of M.M. Talleyrand, Montesquiou, Segur, Duroc, &c., what ardent expressions may be found to enrich the language of attachment. But the individuals who held this language now vie with each other in giving vent to hatred and invective. If they really felt for Napoleon the profound hatred which they now evince, it must be confessed that, in crouching at his feet for fifteen years, they did strange violence to their feelings. And yet all Europe can bear witness, that from their unrestrained manner, their never-varying smile, and their supple marks of obedience, their services seemed to be of their own free choice, and to cost them but little sacrifice.

CHAPTER II.

MANY persons have described Napoleon as a violent, harsh, and passionate man; this is because they have not known him. Absorbed as he was in important business, opposed in his views, and impeded in his plans, it was certainly natural that he should sometimes evince impatience and inequality of temper. His natural kindness and generosity soon subdued his irritation; but it must be observed that, far from seeking to appease him, his confidents never failed to excite his anger. "Your Majesty is right," they would say, "such a one deserves to be shot or broken, dismissed or disgraced: I have long known him to be your enemy. An example must be made; it is necessary for the maintenance of tranquillity."

If the matter in question had been to levy contributions on the enemy's territory, Napoleon, perhaps, would demand twenty millions; but he would be advised to exact ten millions more. He would be told by those about him, " it is necessary that your Majesty should spare your treasury, that you should maintain your troops at the expense of foreign countries, or leave them to subsist on the territory of the confederation."

If he entertained the idea of levying 200,000 conscripts, he was persuaded to demand 300,000. If he proposed to pay a creditor whose right was unquestionable, doubts were started respecting the legality of the debt. The amount claimed was perhaps reduced to one half, or one third; and it not unfrequently happened that the debt was denied altogether.

If he spoke of commencing war, the bold resolution was applauded. It was said war enriched France; that it was necessary to astonish the world, and to astonish it in a way worthy of the great nation.

Thus, by being excited and urged to enter upon uncertain plans and enterprises, Napoleon was plunged into continual war. Thus it was, that his reign was impressed with an air of violence contrary to his own character and habits, which were perfectly gentle.

Never was there a man more inclined to indulgence, or more ready to listen to the voice of humanity: of this I could mention a thousand examples; but I confine myself to the following.

Georges and his accomplices had been condemned. Josephine interceded for M. M. Polignac, and Murat for M. de Rivière, and both succeeded in their mediation. On the day of execution, the banker Scherer hastened to Saint-Cloud, bathed in tears, and asked to speak with me. He begged of me to solicit the pardon of his brother-in-law, M. de Russillon, an old Swiss Major, who had been implicated in the affair. He was accompanied by some of his countrymen, all relatives of the prisoner. They observed that they were conscious the Major merited his sentence; but that he was the father of a family, and that he was allied to the most distinguished houses in the Canton of Bern. I yielded to their entreaties, and I had no reason to regret having done so.

It was seven in the morning. Napoleon was up and in his closet with Corvisart, when I was announced. "Sire," said I, "it is not long since your Majesty settled the government of Switzerland by your mediation. But you know that the people are not all equally satisfied; the inhabitants of Bern in particular. You have now an opportunity of proving to them your magnanimity and generosity. One of their countrymen is to be executed this day. He is connected with the best families in the country; if you grant his pardon it will certainly produce a great sensation, and procure you many friends."—" Who is this man? What is his name?" inquired Napoleon.—" Russillon," I replied. On hearing this name, he became angry.—" Russillon," said he, " is more guilty than Georges himself."—" I am fully aware of all that your Majesty now does me the honour to tell me; but the people of Switzerland, his family, his children, will bless you. Pardon him, not on his own account, but for the sake of the many brave men who have suffered for his folly."—" Hark ye," said he, turning to Corvisart, while he took the petition from my hand, approved it, and hastily returned it to me; " immediately despatch a courier to suspend the execution." The joy of the family may be easily guessed: to me they testified their gratitude through the medium of the public papers. Russillon was imprisoned along with his accomplices; but he afterwards obtained his liberty. Since the return of the King, he has several times visited Paris, though I have not seen him. He thinks that I attached but little importance to the act of service I rendered him; and he is right.

CHAPTER III.

No man possessed greater sensibility, or evinced more constancy in his affections than Napoleon. He tenderly loved his mother, he adored his wife, and he was fondly attached to his sisters, brothers, and other relatives. All, with the exception of his mother, caused him the bitterest vexation; yet he never ceased to overwhelm them with riches and honours. Of all his relations, his brother Lucien proved himself the most determined opposer of his views and plans. One day, while they were disputing warmly on a subject which has now escaped my recollection, Lucien drew out his watch, and dashing it violently on the ground, he addressed to his brother these remarkable words: " You will destroy yourself, as I have destroyed that watch; and the time will come when your family and friends will not know where to shelter their heads." He married a few days after, without obtaining his brother's consent, or even signifying his intention to him. This, however, did not prevent Napoleon from receiving him in 1815; though it was not without being urged to do so: Lucien was obliged to wait at the out-posts; but he was speedily admitted to the Emperor's presence.

Napoleon did not confine his generosity to his relatives; friendship, services, all met their due reward. On this I can speak from experience. I returned from Egypt, in the rank of aide-de-camp to the brave General Desaix, and with two hundred louis which I had saved, and which constituted my whole fortune. At the time of the abdication, I possessed an income of 400,000 francs, arising out of endowments, appointments, emoluments, extraordinary allowances, &c. I have lost five sixths of this income; but I do not regret it: that which I still possess forms a vast contrast to my early fortune. But what I regret is the glory acquired at the price of so much blood and exertion: it is for ever lost, and for that I am inconsolable.

I was not the only one who shared the bounty of Napoleon; a thousand others were in like manner overwhelmed with favours; and the injury which he suffered, through the misconduct of some, proved no bar to the exercise of his kindness. Whatever might be the depth of these injuries, they were forgotten as soon as he was convinced that the heart had no share in producing them. I could cite a hundred instances of his indulgence in this respect; but the following will suffice.

When he took the title of Emperor, the changes that were made in his household, which had been hitherto exclusively military, gave umbrage to several of us. We had been accustomed to enjoy the intimacy of the great man, and we felt displeased at the reserve imposed upon us by the imperial purple.

Generals Regnier and Damas were at that time in disgrace: I was intimate with both, and I was not in the habit of abandoning my friends in misfortune. I had exerted every effort to remove Napoleon's prejudices against these two general officers; but without success. I one day resumed my intercession in favour of Regnier; and Napoleon becoming impatient and out of humour, told me, dryly, that he wished to hear no more about him. I wrote to inform the brave General, that all my endeavours had proved unavailing: I entreated him to have patience; and added a few phrases dictated by the disappointment of the moment. I was so imprudent as to entrust my letter to the conveyance of the post; and the consequence was, that it was opened and sent to the Emperor. He read it over three or four times, ordered some of my writing to be brought to him for the purpose of comparing it, and could scarcely persuade himself that I had written it. He flew into a violent rage, and despatched a courier from Saint Cloud to the Tuileries, where I was lodged. I thought I was summoned for a mission, and set out immediately. I found Caulincourt in the saloon of the household with Cafarelli, and I asked him what was the news. He had heard the whole affair; he seemed much vexed by it: but he said not a word about it to me. I entered the apartments of Napoleon, who came out of his closet, with the letter in his hand, in a furious rage. He darted upon me those angry glances, which so often excited dismay. "Do you know this writing?" said he.—"Yes, Sire,"—"It is yours?"—"Yes, Sire."—"You are the last person I should have suspected of this. Is it possible that you can hold such language to my enemies? You, whom I have treated so well! You, for whom I have done so much! You, the only one of all my aides-de-camp, whom I lodged in the Tuileries!"—The door of his closet was ajar: he observed this, and he threw it wide open, in order that M. Menneval, one of the secretaries, might hear what passed. "Begone," said he, scanning me from head to foot, "begone; you are an ungrateful man!"—"Sire," I replied, "my heart was never guilty of ingratitude."— "Read this letter," said he, presenting it to me, "and judge whether I accuse you wrongfully."— "Sire, of all the reproaches that you can heap upon me, this is the most severe. Having lost your confidence, I can no longer serve you."— "Yes, you have indeed forfeited my confidence." I bowed respectfully, and withdrew.

I resolved to retire to Alsace, and I was making preparations for my departure, when Josephine sent to desire me to return and make my best apologies to Napoleon. Louis, however, gave me contrary advice, and I was not much inclined to obey the directions of the Empress, as my resolution was formed. Two days elapsed, and I heard no news from Saint Cloud. Some friends, among whom was Marshal Bessieres, called on me. "You are in the wrong," said the Marshal, "you cannot but acknowledge it. The respect and gratitude you owe to the Emperor render it a duty to confess your fault." I yielded to these suggestions. No sooner had Napoleon received my letter, than he desired me to attend him in one of his rides on horseback. He was out of humour with me for some time; but one day he sent for me very early at Saint Cloud. "I am no longer angry with you," said he, with exceeding kindness of manner; "you were guilty of a great piece of folly; but it is all over—I have forgotten it. It is my wish that you should marry." He mentioned two young ladies, either of whom, he said, would suit me. My marriage was brought about; but unfortunately it did not prove a happy one.

Bernadotte was in the deepest disgrace, and he deserved it. I met him at Plombières, whither he had been permitted to go, accompanied by his wife and son, for the benefit of the waters; and I had visited the place for the same purpose. I had always admired Bernadotte's kind and amiable disposition. I saw him frequently at Plombières. He communicated to me the circumstance that most distressed him, and begged that I would use my influence to bring about his reconciliation with the Emperor, whom he said he had never ceased to admire, and who had been prepossessed against him by calumnious reports. On my return I learned that his friends, his brother-in-law, and Madame Julie herself, had uselessly interceded in his behalf. Napoleon would hear nothing they had to say; and his irritation against Bernadotte continually increased. But I had promised to do what I could for him; and I was bound to keep my word. The Emperor was preparing to set out for Villiers, where Murat was to give a *fête:* he was in high good-humour, and I determined to avail myself of this favourable circumstance. I communicated my design to Marshal Bessières, who, with myself, was to attend the Emperor: he tried to dissuade me from my intention. He informed me that Madame Julie had that very morning been at Malmaison, and that she had departed in tears for the ill success of her suit. This circumstance was not calculated to inspire me with confidence; but I nevertheless ventured on my mediation. I informed Napoleon that I had seen Bernadotte at Plombières, that he was dejected and deeply mortified by his disgrace. "He protests," added I, "that he has never failed in his love and devotion for your Majesty."—" Do not speak of him; he deserves to be shot," said Napoleon; and he set off at full gallop. At Murat's *fête*, I met Joseph and his wife; and I told them how unlucky I had been. The affair came to the knowledge of Bernadotte, who thanked me for my good intentions. Notwithstanding his numerous misunderstandings with Bernadotte, Napoleon subsequently forgave all his past offences, and loaded him with wealth and honours. The Prince Royal is now about to ascend the throne, while the author of his fortune is exiled to a rock in the midst of the ocean.

CHAPTER IV.

It has been affirmed that Napoleon was not brave. A man who, from the rank of lieutenant of artillery, rose to be the ruler of a nation like France, could not surely be deficient in courage. Of this his conduct on the 18th Brumaire, on the 5th Nivose, and during the plot of Arena, are sufficient proofs, if proofs were wanting. He was well aware how numerous were his enemies among the jacobins and the chouans; yet every evening he walked out in the streets of Paris, and mingled with the different groups, never accompanied by more than two individuals. Lannes, Duroc, Bessières, or some of his aides-de-camp usually attended him in these nocturnal excursions. This fact was well known throughout Paris.

The affair of the infernal machine has never been properly understood by the public. The police had intimated to Napoleon that an attempt would be made against his life, and cautioned him not to go out. Madame Bonaparte, Mademoiselle

Beauharnais, Madame Murat, Lannes, Bessières, the aide-de-camp on duty, and lieutenant Lebrun, now duke of Placenza, were all assembled in the saloon, while the First Consul was writing in his closet. Haydn's Oratorio was to be performed that evening: the ladies were anxious to hear the music, and we also expressed a wish to that effect. The escort picquet was ordered out; and Lannes requested that Napoleon would join the party. He consented; his carriage was ready, and he took along with him Bessières and the aide-de-camp on duty. I was directed to attend the ladies. Josephine had received a magnificent shawl from Constantinople, and she that evening wore it for the first time. " Allow me to observe, Madame," said I, " that your shawl is not thrown on with your usual elegance." She good humouredly begged that I would fold it after the fashion of the Egyptian ladies. While I was engaged in this operation, we heard Napoleon depart. " Come, sister," said Madame Murat, who was impatient to get to the theatre; " Bonaparte is going." We stepped into the carriage: the First Consul's equipage had already reached the middle of the *Place Carrousel*. We drove after it; but we had scarcely entered the *Place* when the machine exploded. Napoleon escaped by a singular chance.

Saint-Regent, or his French servant, had stationed himself in the middle of the *Rue Nicaise*. A grenadier of the escort, supposing he was really what he appeared to be, a water-carrier, gave him a few blows with the flat of his sabre, and drove him off. The cart was turned round, and the machine exploded between the carriages of Napoleon and Josephine. The ladies shrieked on hearing the report; the carriage windows were broken, and Mademoiselle Beauharnais received a slight hurt on her hand. I alighted, and crossed the *Rue Nicaise*, which was strewed with the bodies of those who had been thrown down, and the fragments of the walls that had been shattered by the explosion. Neither the Consul nor any individual of his suite sustained any serious injury. When I entered the theatre Napoleon was seated in his box, calm and composed, and looking at the audience through his opera-glass. Fouché was beside him. " Josephine," said he, as soon as he observed me. She entered at that moment, and he did not finish his question. " The rascals," said he, very coolly, " wanted to blow me up. Bring me a book of the Oratorio."

The audience soon learned the danger he had escaped, and they saluted him with testimonies of the deepest interest. These, I think, are unequivocal proofs of courage. The men who have followed him on the field of battle, cannot be at a loss to quote many more.

CHAPTER V.

Napoleon, whatever his detractors may say, was neither overbearing nor obstinate in his opinions. He was eager to obtain information, and he wished to hear the opinions of all who were entitled to hold any. Among the members of the Council, the wish to please him sometimes superseded every other consideration; but when he perceived this, he never failed to restore the discussion to its proper tone. "Gentlemen," he would say to his lieutenants, " I summoned you here, not to bring you over to my opinion, but to let me hear your's. Explain to me your views; and I shall see whether the plans which you propose are better than my own.'

While we were at Boulogne, he gave a lesson of this kind to the minister of the Marine. He had proposed some questions, to which M. Decrès replied only by a string of compliments. Napoleon wrote to him thus:—" I beg you will send me, in the course of to-morrow, a memorial on the following question: *In the present state of affairs, what is most proper to be done, should Admiral Villeneuve remain at Cadiz?* Raise your mind to the importance of present circumstances, and the situation in which France and England are placed. Send me no more letters like that which you addressed to me yesterday; they can answer no purpose. I have but one wish, and that is, to succeed; for which, I pray God," &c.

Two days before the battle of Austerlitz, a portion of the army was stationed in an unfavourable position, and the general who occupied it exaggerated its disadvantages. However, when the Council was assembled, he not only admitted that the position was tenable, but he even promised to defend it. "How is this, Marshal?" said the Grand Duke of Berg. "What has become of the doubts you expressed but a short while ago?"— "What signifies flattering, when we have met for the purpose of deliberating?" said Marshal Lannes, in his turn. "We must represent things in their true light to the Emperor; and leave him to do what he may deem expedient."—"You are right," said Napoleon; "those who wish to win my good graces must not deceive me."

But though he was always ready to receive advice from those who were qualified to give it; yet he could not endure remarks made by individuals who might happen to be ignorant of the subject of which they were speaking. Fesch was one day about to make some observations on the Spanish war. He had scarcely uttered two words, when Napoleon, leading him to a window, said, " Do you see that star?"—It was noon, and the archbishop replied that he saw none. " Well," said Napoleon, " so long as I am the only one who perceives it, I will pursue my own course, and will hear no reflections on my conduct."

On his return from the Russian campaign, he was lamenting, with deep emotion, the death of the many brave men, who had been sacrificed, not by Cossack spears, but by the rigours of cold and hunger. A courtier, who wished to throw in his word, said, with a very doleful air, " We have, indeed, sustained a severe loss!"—" Yes," replied Napoleon, " Madame Barilli* is dead."

He always sneered at folly; but he never shewed himself averse either to pleasantry or frankness.

Madame Bachioci one day brought to the Tuileries her relation, M. d'A * * * *. She retired

---

* A celebrated opera singer.

after introducing him to the saloon of the household, and he was left alone with me. This M. d'A * * * *, like many of his countrymen, had a very unprepossessing countenance. I was distrustful of him; but, nevertheless, I informed the Emperor he was waiting, and he was introduced. He had doubtless something important to communicate. Napoleon, by a motion of his hand, directed me to return to the saloon. I pretended not to observe him, and I remained, for I was apprehensive for his safety. He advanced towards me, and said that they wished to be alone. I then withdrew, but I left the door of the chamber partly open.

When Napoleon had dismissed M. d'A * * * *, he asked me why I had been so reluctant to withdraw. "You know," replied I, "that I am not officious; but I must frankly confess that I do not like your Corsicans." He himself related this anecdote, which displeased some of the individuals of his family. However, I am persuaded that he would rather not have heard me speak of his countrymen in this way.

One evening, after the battle of Wagram, we were playing at *vingt-et-un*. Napoleon was very fond of this game: he used to try to deceive those he was playing with, and was much amused at the tricks he played. He had a great quantity of gold spread out upon the table before him. "Rapp," said he, "are not the Germans very fond of these little Napoleons?"—"Yes, Sire, they like them much better than the great one."—"That, I suppose," said he, "is what you call German frankness."

CHAPTER VI.

I was at the camp of Boulogne when the third war with Austria broke out. The French were passing the Rhine. The remnants of the enemy's army, which had been beaten and nearly cut to pieces, shut themselves up in Ulm, and they were immediately summoned to surrender. The account of this negotiation, which was conducted by M. de Segur, so well pourtrays the confusion and anxiety of the unfortunate general, that I cannot refrain from inserting it here. The following is M. de Segur's own statement.

" Yesterday, the 24th of Vendemiaire (16th of Oct.), the Emperor desired me to attend him in his closet. He directed me to proceed to Ulm, and to prevail on General Mack to surrender in five days, or, if he absolutely required six, I was to allow him that time: I received no other instructions. The night was dark; a terrible hurricane arose and the rain poured in torrents: it was necessary to travel by cross roads, and to adopt every precaution for avoiding the marshes, in which man, horse, and mission, might all have come to an untimely end. I had almost reached the gates of the city without finding any of our advanced parties. All had withdrawn: sentinels, videttes, outposts, all had placed themselves under shelter. Even the parks of artillery were abandoned; no fires, no stars were visible. I wandered about for three hours before I could find a general: I passed through several villages, and interrogated all whom I met; but without receiving any satisfactory answer.

"At length I found an artillery trumpeter, beneath a cassoon, half buried in mud, and stiff with cold. We approached the ramparts of Ulm. Our arrival had doubtless been expected; for M. de Latour, an officer, who spoke French very well, presented himself on the first summons. He tied a bandage over my eyes, and made me climb over the fortifications. I remarked to my guide that the extreme darkness of the night rendered it unnecessary to blindfold me; but he replied that it was a custom that could not be dispensed with. We seemed to have walked a considerable way. I entered into conversation with my guide; my object was to ascertain what number of troops were shut up in the city. I inquired whether we were far from the residences of General Mack and the Archduke. 'They are close at hand,' replied my guide. I concluded that all the remains of the Austrian army were in Ulm, and the sequel of the conversation confirmed me in this conjecture. At length we reached the inn where the general-in-chief resided. He was a tall elderly man, and the expression of his pallid countenance denoted a lively imagination. His features were disturbed by a feeling of anxiety which he endeavoured to conceal. After exchanging a few compliments, I told him my name; and then entering upon the subject of my mission, I informed him that the Emperor had sent me to invite him to surrender, and to settle with him the conditions of the capitulation. These words evidently offended him; and at first he seemed disinclined to listen to me further: but I insisted on being heard; and I observed that having been received, I, as well as the Emperor, might naturally suppose that he knew how to appreciate his condition. But he replied, sharply, that his situation would soon be changed, as the Russian army was advancing to his assistance; that we should be placed between two fires, and it would then be our turn to capitulate. I replied, that situated as he was, it was not surprising he should be ignorant of what was passing in Germany; but that I must inform him Marshal Bernadotte was in possession of Ingolstadt and Munich, and that he had his advance posts on the Inn, where the Russians had not yet shewn themselves. 'May I be the greatest ———,' exclaimed General Mack, angrily, 'if I am not positively informed that the Russians are at Dachau! Do you think to impose on me thus? Do you take me for a boy? No, Monsieur de Segur, if I receive not assistance within eight days, I consent to surrender my fortress, on condition that my troops shall be prisoners of war, and my officers prisoners on parole. Eight days will allow time for affording me assistance; and I shall thus fulfil my duty. But I shall receive aid, I am certain!'—' Allow me to repeat, General, that we are masters not only of Dachau, but of Munich also: besides, allowing your supposition to be correct, if the Russians be really at Dachau, five days will enable them to advance and attack us, and these five days his Majesty is willing to grant you.'—'No, Sir,' replied the Marshal, 'I demand eight days. I can listen to no other proposition; I must have eight days; that period is indispensable to my responsibility.'—'Then,' resumed I, 'the whole difficulty consists in settling the difference between five and eight days. But I cannot conceive why your Excellency should attach so much importance to this point, seeing that the Emperor is before you, at the head of 100,000 men; and that the corps of Marshal Bernadotte and General Marmont are sufficient to retard for three days the advance of the Russians, even supposing them to be where they are really very far from being.'—'They are at Dachau,' repeated General Mack.—'Well, Baron! be it so: and even allowing them to be at Augsburgh, we should only be the more ready to come to an agreement with you. Do not force us to carry Ulm by assault; for then, instead of waiting five days, it will be but a morning's work for the Emperor to gain possession of it.'—'Sir,' replied the General-in-chief, 'do not imagine that fifteen thousand men are so easily subdued. The conquest will cost you dear.'—'Perhaps a few hundred men,' I replied; 'while Germany will reproach you with the loss of your army and the destruction of Ulm; in short, with all the horrors of an assault, which his Majesty seeks to prevent, by the proposition which he has charged me to make to you.'— 'Rather say,' exclaimed the Marshal, 'that it will cost you ten thousand men! The strength of Ulm is known.'—'It consists in the heights which surround it, and which are in our possession.'—'Come, come, Sir, it is impossible that you can be ignorant of the strength of Ulm!' — 'Certainly not, Marshal; and I am the better able to appreciate it, now that I am within the walls of the city.'—'Well, Sir,' resumed the unfortunate General, 'you see men ready to defend themselves to the utmost extremity, should your Emperor refuse to grant them an armistice of eight days. I can hold out for a considerable time. Ulm contains 3000 horses, which, rather than surrender, we will eat, with as much pleasure as you would were you in our place.'—'Three thousand horses!' I exclaimed: 'alas, Marshal! you must look forward to dreadful misery before you can think of trusting to so pitiful a resource.'

" The Marshal eagerly assured me, that he had provisions for ten days; but I believed no such thing. Day was beginning to dawn, and the negotiation was no farther advanced than at the commencement of our interview. I might have granted six days; but General Mack so obstinately insisted on eight, that I concluded the concession of a single day would be useless. I would not incur the risk, and I rose to depart, saying, that my instructions required me to return before daylight; and, in case my proposition should be rejected, to transmit to Marshal Ney the order for commencing the attack. Here General Mack complained of the conduct of the Marshal towards one of his flags of truce, whose message he had refused to hear. I availed myself of this circumstance to remark, that the Marshal's temper was hasty, impetuous, and ungovernable; that he commanded the most numerous corps, and that which was nearest the city; that he impatiently awaited the order to commence the assault, which order I was to transmit to him on my departure from Ulm. The old General, however, was not intimidated; he insisted on being allowed an interval of eight days, and urged me to make the proposal to the Emperor.

" Poor General Mack was on the point of signing his own ruin, and that of Austria. But notwithstanding his desperate situation, in which he must have suffered the most cruel anxiety, he still refused to yield: he preserved his presence of mind, and maintained the dispute in an animated way. He defended the only thing that he could defend, namely, time. He sought to retard the fall of Austria, of which he had himself been the cause, and wished to procure her a few days longer for preparation: when lost himself, he still contended for her. His character, which was political rather than military, led him to exert cunning in opposition to power. He was bewildered amidst a crowd of conjectures.

" About nine in the morning of the 25th, I rejoined the Emperor at the Abbey of Elchingen, where I rendered him an account of the negotiation. He appeared quite satisfied; and I left him. He however desired me to attend him again; and finding that I did not come at the very moment, he sent Marshal Berthier to me, with a written copy of the propositions which he wished me to induce General Mack to sign immediately. The Emperor granted the Austrian General eight days, reckoning from the date of the 23d, the first day of the blockade; thus their number was in reality reduced to six, which I might at first have proposed, but which I would not concede.

" However, in case of obstinate refusal, I was authorized to date the eight days from the 25th, and thus the Emperor would still have gained a day by the concession. The object was to enter Ulm speedily, in order to augment the glory of the victory by its rapidity; to reach Vienna before the town should recover from the shock, or the Russian army could be in a situation to act; and, finally, our provisions were beginning to fail us, which was another reason for urging us on.

"Major-General Marshal Berthier intimated to me, that he would approach the town; and that if the conditions were agreed on, he should be glad if I would procure his admittance.

"I returned to Ulm about noon. The precautions which had been observed on my first visit were again repeated; but on this occasion I found General Mack at the gate of the city. I delivered to him the Emperor's ultimatum, and he withdrew to deliberate upon it with several of his Generals, among whom I observed a Prince of Lichtenstein, and Generals Klénau and Ginlay. In about a quarter of an hour, he returned, and again began to dispute with me respecting the date. He mistook some particular point in the written propositions, and this induced him to believe that he would obtain an armistice of eight whole days, reckoning from the 25th. In a singular transport of joy, he exclaimed, "M. de Segur! my dear M. de Segur! I relied on the Emperor's generosity; and I have not been deceived. Tell Marshal Berthier I respect him. Tell the Emperor, that I have only a few trifling observations to make; and that I will sign the propositions you have brought me. But inform his Majesty, that Marshal Ney has behaved ill to me—that he has treated me most disrespectfully. Assure the Emperor, that I relied on his generosity." Then, with increased warmth of feeling, he added, " Monsieur de Segur, I value your esteem: I attach importance to the opinion that you may entertain of me. I wish to show you the paper I had signed; for I assure you my determination was fixed." So saying, he unfolded a sheet of paper, on which were written these words: *Eight days, or death!* signed, *Mack.*

" I was thunderstruck at the joyful expression which animated his countenance. I was unable to account for the puerile triumph he evinced at so vain a concession. When on the point of sinking, to what a frail twig did the poor General cling, in the hope of preserving his own reputation, the honour of his army, and ensuring the safety of Austria! He took my hand, pressed it cordially, and suffered me to depart from Ulm without being blindfolded: he moreover allowed me to introduce Marshal Berthier into the fortress without the observance of the usual formalities; in short, he appeared perfectly delighted. He started, in the presence of Marshal Berthier, another argument respecting the dates. I explained the mistake that had occurred; and the matter was to be referred to the Emperor. In the morning the General assured me that he had provisions for ten days; but I had already intimated to his Majesty, that he appeared to have a very short supply; which, indeed, proved to be the case, for that very day he solicited permission to have provision conveyed to the fortress.

"Mack, on finding that his position was turned, conceived, that by throwing himself into Ulm and remaining there, he would draw the Emperor beneath the ramparts, where he hoped to detain him, and thus favour the flight of his other corps in different directions. He thought he had sacrificed himself, and this idea served to uphold his courage. When I entered upon my negotiations with him, he was of opinion that our army was drawn up before Ulm, and unable to move. He made the Archduke and Werneck secretly quit the city. One division attempted to escape to Memmingen; another was flying to the mountains of Tyrol: all were either actually made prisoners, or were on the point of being taken.

" On the 27th, General Mack came to see the Emperor at Elchingen: all his illusions had vanished.

" His Majesty, to convince him of the uselessness of detaining us longer before Ulm, described to him all the horrors of his situation. He assured him of our success on every point; informed him that Werneck's corps, all his artillery, and eight of his Generals had capitulated; that the Archduke himself was in danger, and that no tidings had been received of the Russians. All this intelligence came like a thunderbolt on the General-in-chief: his strength failed him, and he was obliged to support himself against the wall of the apartment. He was overpowered by the weight of his misfortune. He acknowledged the extremity to which he was reduced; and frankly told us, that the provisions in Ulm were exhausted. He however said, that instead of 15,000 men, there were 24,000 fighting men, and 3000 invalids; but that all were plunged into the deepest confusion, and that every moment augmented the dangers of their situation. He added, that he was convinced all hope had vanished, and he therefore consented to surrender Ulm on the following day (the 28th) at three o'clock.

" On quitting his Majesty's presence, he saw

some of our officers; and I heard him say, 'It is mortifying to be disgraced in the estimation of so many brave men: however, I have in my pocket my opinion, written and signed, in which I refused to have my army parcelled out. But I did not command; the Archduke John was there." It is very possible that Mack was obeyed only with reluctance.

"On the 23th, 33,000 Austrians surrendered themselves prisoners. They defiled before the Emperor. The infantry threw down their arms on the other side of the ditch; the cavalry dismounted, laid down their arms, and delivered up their horses to our cavalry on foot. The troops, while surrendering their arms, shouted 'Vive l'Empereur!' Mack was present: he said to the officers, who had addressed him without knowing who he was, 'You see before you the unfortunate Mack!'"

I was at Elchingen with Generals Mouton and Bertrand when Mack came to present his respects to Napoleon. "I flatter myself, Gentlemen," said he to us, as he passed through the saloon of the aide-de-camp on duty, "that you do not cease to regard me as a brave man, though I have been obliged to capitulate with a force so considerable: it was difficult to resist the manœuvres of your Emperor; his plans have ruined me."

Napoleon, who was overjoyed at his success, sent General Bertrand to examine the returns of the army that was in Ulm. He brought intelligence that there were 21,000 men in the city: the Emperor could not believe this. "You speak their language," said he to me; "go and ascertain the truth." I went; I interrogated the commanders of corps, the generals, and the troops; and, from the information thus collected, I learned that the garrison contained 26,000 men fit for service. Napoleon, on hearing this, said, "I was mad, and that the thing was impossible." However, when the army defiled before us, its number, as M. de Segur had stated, amounted to 33,000 men, and nineteen generals: the cavalry and artillery were superb.

CHAPTER VII.

We had not been able to shut up all the Austrian force in Ulm. Werneck escaped by the way of Heidenheim, and the Archduke hastened after him. They were both in full flight; but Fate had pronounced her decree, and against that there is no appeal. Napoleon being informed, in the middle of the night, that they were advancing on Albeck, immediately summoned the Grandduke. "A division," said he, "has escaped from the garrison, and threatens our rear; pursue and destroy it: let not one escape." The rain descended in torrents, and the roads were in a dreadful condition; but fatigue and danger were forgotten in the triumph of victory. Our troops hastened onward intent on conquest. Murat came up with the enemy, attacked and routed him. He pursued him closely in his flight for the space of two leagues, scarcely allowing him time to take breath. Some masses occupied Erbrectingen with cannon. Night had set in and our horses were exhausted: we halted. The 9th light arrived about ten o'clock.

We then advanced; the attack was resumed; village, artillery, caissons, all were taken. General Odonel endeavoured to keep his ground with his rear-guard; but he was observed by one of our quarter-masters, who wounded him and made him prisoner. It was midnight, our troops were overcome with fatigue, and we pursued our triumph no farther.

The enemy fled precipitately in the direction of Nordlingen, where we possessed artillery and depôts. It was important to prevent his reaching that point. Murat detached some parties, who, by harassing and impeding him in his march, forced him to take up a position, that is to say, to lose time. On the other hand, General Rivaud was to put the bridge of Donnavert in a state of security, and to proceed with the surplus of his force to the Wiesnitz. Every passage was intercepted. These arrangements being made, the Prince began his march and came up with the Archduke, who was deploying on Neresheim. We attacked him with the enthusiasm inspired by victory: the shock was irresistible; the cavalry fled, and the infantry laid down their arms. Guns, standards, troops, all were taken in a mass: the most terrible disorder prevailed. Klein, Fauconet, and Lanusses, continued the pursuit, intercepted the enemy on every side, and dispersed him in every direction. Werneck was summoned to surrender; he hesitated; but a combination of extraordinary circumstances at length induced him to do so. The officer appointed to escort the French flag of truce crossed several plains in quest of his chief. He met the Prince of Hohenzollern, to whom he communicated the object of his mission. The Prince accompanied him, not doubting that the Field-Marshal would accept the conditions. They directed their course to Nordlingen, which they found occupied, not by the Austrians, but by French troops. On the other hand, General Lasalle had advanced on Merking, and had taken a thousand men. The fugitives spread alarm in the enemy's head-quarters. These accounts staggered Werneck, and he shewed himself disposed to treat. He detained the French officer and sent as a hostage the Major of the regiment of Rannitz. He deferred the negotiation until next day; for he wished to try the chances of the night. As soon as it was dark, he proposed to combine his forces with those of the Archduke; but the French intercepted the road, and General Rivaud drove back Lichtenstein, and penetrated the great park, which our hussars attacked in the rear. Werneck dared not go farther; he thought himself surrounded, and he negotiated. Our troops occupied the heights in order to be prepared against a surprise: but night advanced; and Hohenzollern, who on the preceding day had regarded the capitulation as inevitable, now availed himself of darkness to elude it. General Miskiery followed his example: they escaped with the cavalry and a few infantry troops, which had formed a part of the corps that had laid down arms. It might have been supposed that they were bound by the engagements of their chief; but no such thing; at least they thought so, for they rejoined the wrecks of the Archduke's force, with which they threw themselves on the Prussian territory. We came up with them at Gunderhausen, and demanded the fulfilment of the convention. The Prince of Schwartzenberg referred to orders, wished to clear up doubts, to write, to explain; in a word, to gain time.

The Prussians insisted on their neutrality; they required that the city should not be attacked, and that the enemy's column should evacuate it. A person in magisterial robes came, escorted by a party of the Archduke's officers, to threaten us with the displeasure of King William. Klein was not the man to be intimidated by this kind of masquerade: he sent to the Grand Duke the magistrate in the Austrian interest, and gave the signal for the attack. The Prince of Schwartzenberg was quite disconcerted: he had not imagined that the General was so near at hand. He protested against the violation of the Prussian territory, and proposed that we should respect it and not occupy Gunderhausen. Klein told him to set a good example, and he would follow it. We continued to advance, and yet Schwartzenberg came to no decision. Murat, tired of being taken for a dupe, gave orders for terminating the discussions and marching forward. The enemy's rearguard then set off at full gallop, and left us in possession of the place. We pursued him for several leagues, without being able to come up with him. It was night, and we took a position. We resumed our march at daybreak; but the Archduke had fled so rapidly that we did not overtake the rear of his baggage until we reached Nuremberg. A piquet of our advance-guard charged him, and obliged the escort battalion to lay down their arms. The piquet then pressed forward, and entered a woody road, thronged with artillery and baggage, pursuing some hundreds of dragoons, who vainly endeavoured to rally themselves. The great body of the Austrian force was awaiting us in an advantageous position. Our chasseurs were obliged to fall back; but the hussars and carabiniers advanced, and the army was completely routed. The Archduke himself narrowly escaped being made prisoner. This was a finishing stroke to the corps who had escaped from Ulm. In the short space of five days, 7000 brave men marched over forty-five leagues, destroyed an army of 25,000 men, took their military chest and baggage, carried off 128 pieces of cannon, 11 standards, and made from 12 to 15,000 prisoners. Of all the Archduke's force nothing now remained but a few thousand unfortunate men scattered about in the woods.

Klein, however, persisted in his demands, and Werneck himself urged the fulfilment of the conditions that had been entered into. They required that the officers included in the capitulations should surrender themselves prisoners. The French General addressed his remonstrances to the Archduke, or, in his absence, to the General commanding the Austrian army; but such disorder prevailed, that the flag of truce was obliged to advance into the very heart of Bohemia before he could find an officer to receive his dispatches. The answer was long expected; but it at length arrived. It was a letter from General Kollowrard, who transmitted to us the following correspondence:

To Count Hohenzollern, Lieutenant-General in the service of his Imperial and Royal Majesty.

"You have submitted Lieutenant-general Werneck's letter to my consideration. I must inform you that, according to the rules of war and the law of nations, I regard the pretensions of the French General as very illegal.

"Consequently I declare that you, and the troops with whom you have returned, cannot be included in the capitulation. I therefore order you as well as them to continue to serve as before.

Signed,   Ferdinand.
Countersigned,   Morvahl.
      Major and Aide-de-Camp.

" Egra, Oct. 23, 1805."

By this document the capitulation was rendered no capitulation; and thus Hohenzollern had fled without any violation of honour. He seemed astonished at being required to surrender in a mass troops which he was losing no less effectually in detail. His letter was curious; it was as follows:

To Field Marshal Baron Werneck.

"Dear Comrade,

"I cannot conceal my astonishment at the proposition that has been made to me to surrender with the cavalry which formed part of your corps. When I left you, you in my presence refused to enter into any capitulation; and, for my part, I intended to bring back the cavalry to the army at all hazards, if you could not extricate yourself with the infantry. I endeavoured to do this, and I succeeded. I do not understand by what law I can be accounted a prisoner of war, not having been present at your arrangements, in which I should never have suffered myself to be included. Having been separated from you since yesterday, I no longer conceive myself bound to fulfil your orders: I receive the commands of his Royal Highness our General-in-chief.

"I have the honour to be your very humble and obedient servant,

Signed, Lieut.-Gen. Hohenzollern,
Privy Counsellor."

Napoleon was satisfied with himself, with the army and with every body. He expressed his approbation of our conduct by the following proclamation:

"Soldiers of the Great Army!

"In the space of fifteen days we have finished the campaign. All that we proposed to do has been accomplished. We have driven from Bavaria the troops of the House of Austria, and restored our ally to the sovereignty of his States.

"That army which, with equal presumption and imprudence, came to station itself on our frontiers, has been annihilated.

"But what does it signify to England? Her object is fulfilled. We are no longer at Boulogne, and her subsidy will be neither more nor less.

"Of the 100,000 men who composed that army, sixty thousand are prisoners: they will supply the place of our conscripts in agricultural labours.

"Two hundred pieces of cannon, the whole park, ninety standards, and all their Generals, are in our hands. Scarcely 15,000 men have escaped.

"Soldiers! I announced to you a great battle; but thanks to the ill concerted plans of the enemy, I have obtained all the success I anticipated without encountering any risk; and it is a circumstance unparelleled in the history of nations that so great a triumph should have diminished our force only by 1500 men rendered unfit for service.

"Soldiers! this success is due to the full confidence you reposed in your Emperor, to your patience under fatigue and privation of every kind, and to your singular intrepidity.

"But we shall not stop here. You are eager to commence a second campaign.

"The Russian army, which English gold has transported from the further extremity of Europe, will experience a similar fate.

"The present campaign is particularly connected with the glory of the French infantry; the question which has already been determined in Switzerland and Holland, will now be decided for the second time; namely, whether the French infantry be the first or the second in Europe.

"There are among the Russians no Generals over whom I can hope to obtain glory. All my care will be to gain the victory with the least possible effusion of blood: my soldiers are my children."

CHAPTER VIII.

We had now done with the Austrians, and we advanced to meet the Russians. Kutusoff affected resolution, and we thought him disposed to fight. We congratulated ourselves on this new opportunity of augmenting our glory. But all this was mere pretence on the part of Kutusoff; he abandoned the Inn, the Traun, and the Ems, and disappeared. We pressed forward on Vienna; we advanced with inconceivable speed: never was a movement executed with such rapidity. The Emperor became apprehensive; he feared lest by this precipitancy our rear might be endangered, and our flank exposed to the Russians. " Murat," said he to me, " runs on like a blind man ; he presses forward as though the only object were to enter Vienna. The enemy has nobody to oppose him ; he may dispose of all his forces and destroy Mortier. Direct Berthier to stop the columns." Berthier came ; Marshal Soult received orders to fall back as far as Mautern. Davoust took up his position at the junction of the roads of Lilienfeldt and Neustadt, and Bernadotte stationed himself at Mælck. But these arrangements did not prevent the engagement of which Napoleon feared the issue. Four thousand French were attacked by the whole of the enemy's force; but skill, courage, and the necessity of conquering, made amends for our inferiority of numbers: the Russians were driven back. The intelligence of this astonishing victory set our whole force in motion: the Emperor pursued his march with even more eagerness than he had before evinced in suspending it. He wished to come up with the Austrians, to take the passage of the Danube, to turn and cut off their allies, and beat them before they could receive reinforcements. He hastily dispatched orders: men and horses, all were immediately in motion. "The field is open," said Napoleon, "Murat may yield to his natural impetuosity; but he must take a wider range, he must surprise the bridge." He immediately wrote to him as follows:—" The grand object at the present moment is to pass the Danube, in order to drive the Russians from Krems by attacking their rear. The enemy will probably destroy the bridge of Vienna; and yet, if there should be any possibility of gaining it undamaged, that must be done. This consideration alone can induce the Emperor to enter Vienna; and in that case you must introduce into the city only a portion of your cavalry and the grenadiers. It is necessary that you should ascertain the force of the civic guard in Vienna. The Emperor presumes that you have planted some pieces of cannon to intercept the passage across the Danube between Krems and Vienna. Some parties of cavalry should be stationed on the right bank of the river; but you mention nothing of this to the Emperor. His Majesty thinks it necessary to know what he has to trust to; so that if it should be possible to intercept the Danube below Vienna, it may be done. General Suchet's division will remain with a portion of your cavalry on the great road leading from Vienna to Bukersdorf, at least if you be not master of the bridge across the Danube, and if it has not been burned. In that case, Suchet's division must repair thither, in order to be enabled to cross the river with your cavalry and grenadiers, and to march on as rapidly as possible to fall on the communications of the Russians. I think it probable that the Emperor will remain all the day at Saint-Polten.

" His Majesty recommends you, Prince, to transmit to him frequent accounts of your proceedings.

" When you arrive at Vienna, provide yourself

with the best maps that can be procured, of the environs of that city and of Lower Austria.

"Should General Count Giulay, or any other individual, wish to have an interview with the Emperor, send him hither with all speed.

"The civic guard on duty at Vienna must amount to upwards of five hundred men.

"When once you reach Vienna you may easily obtain intelligence of the arrival of the other Russian columns, as well as of the design of those who have established themselves at Krems.

"You will have your own cavalry, together with the corps of Marshals Lannes and Davoust, in the operation of turning the Russians and falling on their rear. As to the corps of Marshals Bernadotte and Soult, they cannot be disposed of until we shall definitively know what course the Russians may adopt.

"After ten o'clock in the morning, you may enter Vienna. Endeavour to surprise the bridge of the Danube, or, if it should be destroyed, adopt the most speedy means of crossing the river: that is the grand affair at present. But if, before ten o'clock, M. de Giulay should present himself with proposals for negotiating and inducing you to suspend your march, you may stop your movement on Vienna, but you must nevertheless direct your attention to the best means of crossing the Danube at Klosterburgh, or some other favourable point.

" The Emperor directs that between Seghartz-Kirchen and Vienna you shall station, at the distance of two French leagues from each other, posts of cavalry consisting of ten men each, whose horses will serve as relays to the officers whom you may send with accounts of your movements. The men forming these posts may bear despatches from Seghartz-Kirchen to Saint-Polten. Marshal Bessières will station posts of the Emperor's guard."

CHAPTER IX.

We were at Saint-Polten. Napoleon was riding on horseback on the Vienna road, when he perceived an open carriage advancing, in which were seated a priest and a lady bathed in tears. The Emperor was dressed as usual in the uniform of a colonel of the chasseurs of the guard. The lady did not know him. He enquired the cause of her affliction, and whither she was going." " Sir, she replied, "I have been robbed at about two leagues from hence by a party of soldiers, who have killed my gardener. I am going to request that your Emperor will grant me a guard. He once knew my family well, and lay under obligations to them." —" Your name?" enquired Napoleon—" De Brunny," answered the lady; "I am the daughter of M. de Marbœ'uf, formerly governor of Corsica."— " I am delighted to meet with you, Madam," exclaimed Napoleon, with the most charming frankness, " and to have an opportunity of serving you. I am the Emperor." The lady was amazed. Napoleon consoled her, and directed her to wait for him at head-quarters. He treated her with the utmost attention, granted her a piquet of chasseurs of his guard, and sent her away happy and contented.

Napoleon had received a report, which he was reading with an air of satisfaction. I entered his closet. " Well, Rapp," said he, " do you know that we have parties of our troops in the very heart of Bohemia?"—" Yes, Sire."—" Do you know what sort of cavalry has beat the Houlans, captured posts, and taken magazines?"—" No, Sire."—" Our infantry mounted on draught horses!"—" How?"— He handed me the report. Some of our detachments who had penetrated into Bohemia, suddenly found themselves in an open tract of country: they had but twenty dragoons; they would not fall back, and they dared not advance further. In this perplexing situation, the commander thought of an expedient. He collected together all the baggage horses, mounted his infantry, and thus equipped, led them through the thick forests in the neighbourhood of Egra. Some parties of the enemy's cavalry who advanced to oppose them were driven back; we took men, horses and provisions; the latter were committed to the flames. I returned the report to the Emperor. " Well," said he, "what think you of this new kind of cavalry?"— " Admirable, Sire."—" Men who have French blood in their veins," observed he, " always know how to deal death among the enemy's ranks."

We marched close upon the enemy's rear-guard. We might easily have taken it; but we avoided doing so. We wished to lull his vigilance: we did not press him closely, and we circulated reports of peace. We suffered both troops and baggage to escape us; but the loss of a few men was of little consequence. The preservation of the bridges was the important point: if they should be broken, it was determined that we should repair them; we took our measures accordingly. The troops, who were posted in *echelon* on the road, were warned to allow no demonstration to escape them that was likely to put the enemy on his guard. No one was permitted to enter Vienna; but every thing being examined, and every arrangement completed, the Grand Duke took possession of the capital, and directed Lanusses and Bertrand to make without delay a *reconnaissance* on the river. They found at the gates of the suburb a post of Austrian cavalry. There had been no fighting for upwards of three days. It appeared as though an armistice had been entered into. Lanusses and Bertrand accosted the Austrian commandant, commenced a conversation with him, followed him closely, and would not suffer him to quit them. On reaching the banks of the river, they still persisted in following him, in spite of his wish to get rid of them. The Austrian became impatient; the French generals asked leave to communicate with the general commanding the troops stationed on the left bank of the river. They obtained permission to do so; but the 10th hussars were not allowed to accompany them, and they were consequently obliged to halt and take a position. Meanwhile our troops were advancing, led by the Grand Duke and Marshal Lannes. The bridge still remained undamaged; but the trains were laid, and the gunners held their matches in readiness: the least sign that might have indicated the intention of passing by force would have ruined the enterprize. It was necessary to resort to artifice; and we succeeded in imposing on the simplicity of the Austrians. The two marshals dismounted, and only a small detachment entered upon the bridge. General Belliard advanced, walking with his hands behind his back, accompanied by two officers of the staff: Lannes joined him with some others; they walked about, talking together, and at length joined the Austrians. The officer commanding the post, at first directed them to stand back; but he at length permitted them to advance, and they entered into conversation together. They repeated what had already been affirmed by General Bertrand, namely, that the negotiations were advancing, that the war was at an end, and that there would be no more fighting and slaughter. "Why," said the Marshal, "do you keep your guns still pointed at us? Has there not been enough of bloodshed? Do you wish to attack us, and to prolong miseries which weigh more heavily on you than on us? Come, let us have no more provocation; turn your guns." Half persuaded and half convinced, the commanding officer yielded. The artillery was turned in the direction of the Austrians, and the troops laid down their arms in bundles. During this conference the platoon of our advance-guard came up slowly, and at length it arrived, masking sappers and gunners, who threw the combustible matters into the river, sprinkled water on the powder, and cut the trains. The Austrian commander, who was not sufficiently acquainted with the French language to take much interest in the conversation, perceived that the troop was gaining ground, and endeavoured to make us understand that he could not permit it. Marshal Lannes and General Belliard tried to satisfy him; they observed that the cold was severe, and that our men were only marching about to warm themselves. But the column still continued to advance, and it was already three quarters over the bridge. The commander lost all patience, and ordered his troops to fire: they instantly took up their arms, and the artillerymen prepared their guns. Our situation was terrible: a little less presence of mind on our part, and the bridge would have been blown up, our troops in the river, and the campaign at an end. But the Austrian had to deal with men who were not easily disconcerted. Marshal Lannes seized him by the one arm and General Belliard by the other. They threatened him, and drowned his voice when he attempted to call for help. Meanwhile the Prince of Hogsberg arrived accompanied by General Bertrand. An officer set off to render an account of the state of affairs to the Grand Duke; and on his way transmitted to the troop an order to quicken their march and arrive speedily. The Marshal advanced to meet the Prince, complained of the conduct of the commander of the post, requested that he might be punished and removed from the rearguard, where he might impede the negotiations. Hogsberg fell into the snare: he deliberated, approved, contradicted, and lost himself in a useless conversation. Our troops made the most of their time; they arrived, debouched, and the bridge was taken. Reconnaissances were immediately ordered in every direction; and General Belliard led our columns on the road leading to Stockrau, where they took a position. Hogsberg, mortified at his ill-timed loquacity, proceeded to the Grand Duke, who, after a short conversation, referred him to Napoleon, and also crossed the river.

The Austrian piquet still kept guard on the bridge. We bivouacked in confusion: the troops were mingled together at Stockrau as on the banks of the river. Napoleon found that this interspersion was not convenient, and he sent the Houlans to Vienna, where they were disarmed.

We arrived at Austerlitz. The Russians had a force superior to ours. They had repulsed our advance-guard; and they thought us already subdued. The attack commenced; but instead of that easy conquest which had been obtained merely by their guard, they every where experienced the most obstinate resistance. The battle had already lasted an hour, and it was still far from being decided in their favour. They resolved to make a last attempt on our centre. The Imperial guard deployed; infantry, cavalry, and artillery, advanced on the bridge, without the movement being perceived by Napoleon; for the nature of the ground screened it from his observation. A discharge of musketry was soon heard: a brigade, commanded by General Schinner, had been penetrated by the Russians. Napoleon ordered me to take the Mamelukes, two squadrons of chasseurs, and one of grenadiers of the guard, and to go forward to reconnoitre the state of things. I set off at full gallop, and it was not until I came within gun-shot of the scene of action, that I discovered the disaster. The enemy's cavalry was in the midst of our square, and was sabring our troops. A little further back we discerned masses of infantry and cavalry forming the reserve. The enemy relinquished the attack, and turned to meet me. Four pieces of artillery arrived and were placed in battery. I advanced in good order; I had the brave Colonel Morland on my left, and General

Dallemagne on my right. " Do you see," said I to my troop, " our friends and brothers trampled on by the enemy: avenge them, avenge our colours." We rushed on the artillery, which was taken. The cavalry, who awaited us, was repulsed by the same shock; they fled in disorder, and we, as well as the enemy, trampled over the bodies of our troops, whose squares had been penetrated. The men who had escaped being wounded were rallied. A squadron of horse grenadiers arrived to reinforce me; and I was enabled to receive the reserves, who came up in aid of the Russian guard. We resumed the attack, which was maintained with terrible fury. The infantry dared not venture to fire; all was confusion; we fought man to man. Finally, the intrepidity of our troops triumphed over every obstacle. The Russians fled and dispersed. Alexander and the Emperor of Austria witnessed the defeat. Stationed on a height, at a little distance from the field of battle, they saw the guard, which was expected to decide the victory, cut to pieces by a handful of brave men. Their guns and baggage had fallen into our hands, and Prince Repnin was our prisoner. Unfortunately we had a great number of men killed and wounded. Colonel Morland was no more, and I had myself received a sabre wound in the head.

I went to render an account of this affair to the Emperor. My broken sabre, my wound, the blood with which I was covered, the decided advantage we had gained with so small a force over the enemy's chosen troops, inspired Napoleon with the idea of the picture which was painted by Gerard.

The Russians, as I have already mentioned, hoped to defeat us with their guard alone. This presumption offended Napoleon, and it was long before he forgot it.

After the battle of Austerlitz, Napoleon made me a General of Division, and sent me to the Castle of Austerlitz until I should recover from my wound, which, however, was not dangerous. The Emperor visited me several times; once on the day on which he granted an interview to the Emperor of Austria. He put into my hands two letters which had been intercepted by our advanced posts; one was from Prince Charles, and the other from a Prince Lichtenstein. Their contents were rather important; and I got them translated. On his way back in the evening, Napoleon came and had these letters read to him. He talked to me a great deal about Francis II., his complaints and regrets; and told me many curious circumstances respecting him.

We set out for Shœnbrunn; and in about a

fortnight after our arrival thither, Napoleon sent for me: " Are you able to travel?" said he:— " Yes, Sire."—" Well, then, go and give an account of the battle of Austerlitz to Marmont, in order to vex him for not having come; and observe the effect that it will produce on the Italians." He then gave me the following instructions:

" Monsieur General Rapp, you will proceed to Gratz, where you will remain as long as may be necessary to communicate to General Marmont the details of the battle of Austerlitz. Inform him that the negotiations are open, but that nothing is concluded; and that he must therefore hold himself in readiness for any event that may occur. You must also make yourself acquainted with General Marmont's situation, and ascertain what number of the enemy's force is before him. Tell him, that I desire he will send spies into Hungary; and that he will communicate to me all the information he may collect. You must next repair to Laybach, where you will find Marshal Massena, who has the command of the eighth army corps; and transmit to me a correct report of his situation. You will inform Massena, that if the negociations are broken off, as it is possible they may be, he will be sent to Vienna.

Let me know what amount of the enemy's force Marshal Massena has before him ; and report to me the situation of his corps in every point of view. You will next proceed to Palmanova, after strongly urging Marshal Massena to arm and provision the fortress in an effectual way, and you will inform me of the state in which it is. Next proceed and examine the posts which we occupy before Venice, and ascertain the state of our troops. Thence you will repair to the army of General Saint-Cyr, who is about to march on Naples : you must ascertain the nature and the amount of his force. You will return by the way of Klagenfurth, where you will see Marshal Ney, and then rejoin me. Do not fail to write to me from every place at which you stop. Despatch estafettes to me from Gratz, Laybach, Palmanova, Venice, and the place where the army of Naples may be stationed. I pray God to take you into his holy keeping.

"NAPOLEON.

"Schœnbrunn,
" 25 Frimaire, year XIV."

I rejoined Napoleon at Munich, whither he had gone to be present at the marriage of Prince Eugène. The Prince came from Italy, and I accompanied him. During my absence, peace had been concluded at Vienna. The Emperor had an interview with Prince Charles: he intended to have presented him with a magnificent sword; but he was displeased with the Archduke, and the sword was not given.

We set out for Paris. Acclamations resounded on every side: Napoleon was never received with so much enthusiasm.

CHAPTER X.

During our stay at Ulm, the Prussians suddenly conceived the idea that they had an ancient inheritance of glory to defend. They were roused, and they took up arms. Haugwitz came to inform us of this sudden reminiscence. But the battle of Austerlitz had taken place in the interim. When the Minister arrived, nothing was thought of but alliance and devotion. Napoleon was not the dupe of these diplomatic protestations: he was aware of the intrigues and the chivalric scenes that had been resorted to for the purpose of exciting the multitude. Previous to the action he had said; "If I am beaten, they will march upon my rear; if I am victorious, they will say that they wished to have taken part with me." They knew not how to make choice either of peace or war; and they watched the progress of events. This indirect policy was not without its effect; it cost them Anspach, Bareuth, a part of the grand duchy of Berg, and their possessions in Westphalia. They became enraged. I was sent to Hanover, which we had abandoned to them. The ostensible motive of my journey was the delivering up of the fortress of Hameln; its real purpose was to learn the state of the public mind. I was directed to discover what was the general opinion with regard to the Prussians, whether war was spoken of, whether the army wished for it, and finally, to buy up at Hamburgh all the pamphlets against Napoleon and France which I could procure.

My mission was not difficult of execution. The Prussians were exasperated and insolent; the Hanoverians detested them. The north of Germany, however, relied on Prussia, whose power remained undiminished. The Count of Schulemburgh was governor of King William's new acquisition: he gave me rather a cold reception. Our success at Ulm and Austerlitz appeared to him but indifferent. The latter battle he affirmed was indecisive. He said it was like the battle of Zorndoff, which was fought by Frederick the Great against the Russians, and in which Count Schulemburgh had himself been engaged. "What sort of victories would he have?" said the Emperor, when I told him this anecdote.

I went from Hanover to Hamburgh, where I found Bourienne. Here I was well received, and I knew the reason why.

I returned to France, and on my way passed through Munster, where I saw General Blucher, whom I had known some years before. I paid him a visit. He was not well disposed towards the French; yet he received me with a great deal of civility.

I remained a week with Augereau at Frankfort, in order to see and hear all I could; for such were my instructions. Napoleon had just made a demand for contributions on that town, and the inhabitants were alarmed lest they should be obliged to pay them.

We occupied Darmstadt. Marshal *******, who had established his head-quarters in the capital of that principality, was neither a favourite with the Court nor with the people; and his staff was still less liked. The Grand Duchess sent me an invitation, through Augereau, who seemed to be partial to that country; I declined it, not having any instructions to that effect. She commissioned him to transmit to me her complaints. They were very severe.

I departed for Wesel. I was to examine the state of feeling in that quarter, which was already occupied by our troops.

On my return, I gave Napoleon an account of all that I had seen and heard. I concealed nothing from him. I spoke particularly in behalf of Darmstadt; but he was enraged against the Duchess. She had written a terrible letter to the King of Bavaria, relative to what she termed the ill-assorted union of her niece Augusta with Prince Eugène. Among other insulting expressions she made use of the words *horrible marriage*. The Emperor, who conceived that the glory of having achieved great deeds was well worth the advantage of having descended from those who probably had no glory to boast of, could not pardon the feudal prejudices of the Duchess. He was on the point of depriving her of her states; but Maximilian interceded for her, and she escaped with the punishment of a six months' occupation by our troops; that is to say, her people were obliged to atone for the offence which her vanity had led her to commit.

Scarcely a fortnight had elapsed since my return to France. The Court was at Saint-Cloud, and Napoleon was at the theatre. In the middle of the performance he received a despatch from the Grand Duchy of Berg. He opened it. It contained an account of an attack made on our troops by some Prussian detachments. " I see," said he, " they are determined to try us. Mount your horse and seek the Grand Duke at Neuilly." Murat was already acquainted with the affair; he came immediately. Napoleon conversed with him for an instant, and gave me orders next day to take the command of the military division at Strasburgh; to organise battalions and marching squadrons at that place; to direct them in succession upon Mentz, and to send to the latter place a large quantity of artillery. The infantry embarked on the Rhine in order to arrive earlier at the place of their destination.

I corresponded directly with Napoleon. I employed couriers, telegraphs, and all the most speedy modes of communication. I could not venture to put a hundred men in motion, to change the place of a gun, or to move a musquet, without informing him. I had been two months engaged in these preparations, when he arrived at Mentz, whence he wrote to me to join him at Wurtzburg. He sent me a letter for the Grand Duke of Baden, and directed me to deliver it to the Prince myself. The object of this letter was to request him to send his grandson, the present Grand Duke, to the army. I found the venerable old man in his ancient castle of Baden; he seemed at first much affected by the contents of the letter; but he soon made up his mind to send the young Prince, and he ordered preparations for his departure. He did me the honour to recommend his grandson to me in a very affectionate manner. The Prince set out on his journey two days afterwards, and joined us at Wurtzburg. The King of Wirtemberg was already there. He had just determined on his daughter's marriage with Jerome. Napoleon was in particularly good humour. The alliance pleased him. He was no less satisfied with the Grand Duke; for Murat had singularly prepossessed him in favour of that Prince. In a letter which Murat addressed to the Emperor some days before, he said;—" I waited on the Grand Duke of Wurtzburg, whom the letter, and the news which I communicated to him, that the treaty admitting him into the confederation had been signed at Paris, have relieved from the greatest anxiety; for he very much dreaded not being received into the Confederation. He seemed particularly affected by the sentiments of good will on the part of your Majesty which I expressed to him. He evinces the greatest readiness to contribute every thing in his power to the service of the army. To-day his admission into the Confederation of the Rhine was proclaimed. Every preparation has been made for receiving your Majesty at the Castle, where nothing seems to be neglected which may render your stay here convenient and agreeable."

We had yet received no positive information with regard to the Prussians; we knew not whether they were on the road to Magdeburg, in Saxony, or at Gotha; or even what was the amount of their force. We had, however, a sufficient number in the field. Gentlemen are not more scarce on the other side of the Rhine than elsewhere: but the reports were so contradictory, that it was impossible to form any distinct idea on the subject. At one time it was said that the enemy's advance-guard was at Hoff; that Coburg and Memmingen were occupied; that the Prussians avoided partial actions, and wished to try their fortune in a pitched battle. At another time it was affirmed that Hohenlohe was advancing on Schleitz; that Ruchel had formed his junction; that the Queen had gone to Erfurt; and that the head-quarters were removed from Hoff to Nauenburgh. This arrangement did not correspond with the nature of the places. It seemed inconceivable. We were as uncertain with respect to the extent of the enemy's forces as we were concerning their line of operations. Amidst all these various accounts we learnt that Cronach was occupied. The Grand Duke sent to inform us, that that citadel was under repair, and would soon be in a state of defence. Napoleon was astonished that the Prussians had not made themselves masters of it. " What could have prevented them," said he, " since they absolutely wanted war? Was it the difficulty of the attempt?—The place was destitute both of provisions and artillery. They had sufficient courage for the enterprize. Did they not consider the place of sufficient importance to try to secure it? That fort commands three great outlets; but these gentlemen care little about positions, they are reserving themselves for grand strokes; we will give them what they want."

Napoleon every moment received accounts of the Prussian army. Ruchel, Blucher, and the Duke of Brunswick, were impatient to commence the war, and Prince Louis was even more so. He urged and hastened hostilities, and feared to let the opportunity escape. He was, besides, a man of great courage and talent; all accounts agreed on this point. Napoleon, who did not dislike this petulant eagerness, was conersing with us one evening respecting the generals of the enemy's army. Some one present happened to mention Prince Louis. "As for him," said he, "I foretell that he will be killed this campaign." Who could have thought that the prediction would so soon have been fulfilled?

Prussia at length explained herself. She required us to abandon our conquests, and threatened us with her displeasure if we refused to evacuate Germany and recross the Rhine. The demand was modest, and worthy of those who urged it. Napoleon could not finish reading the document; he threw it away contemptuously. "Does he think himself in Champagne?" said he. "Does he want to give us a new edition of his manifesto? What! does he pretend to mark out a route for our march back. Really, I pity Prussia, I feel for William. He is not aware what rhapsodies he is made to write. This is too ridiculous. Berthier, they wish to give us a rendezvous of honour for the 8th; a beauteous Queen will be a witness to the combat. Come, let us march on; and shew our courtesy. We will not halt till we enter Saxony." Then turning immediately to his secretary, he hastily dictated the following proclamation:

GENERAL RAPP. 75

" Soldiers!

" The order for your return to France was issued. You were already within a few days' march of your homes: triumphal fêtes awaited you, and the preparations for your reception had commenced in the capital; but while we thus too confidently resigned ourselves to security, new plots were hatching under the mask of friendship and alliance. Cries of war have been raised at Berlin, and for two months we have been provoked with a degree of audacity which calls for vengeance.

" The same faction, the same headlong spirit, which, under favour of our internal dissensions, led the Prussians fourteen years ago to the plains of Champagne, still prevail in their Councils. If they no longer wish to burn and destroy Paris; they now boast their intention to plant their colours in the capital of our allies. They would oblige Saxony, by a disgraceful transaction, to renounce her independence, by ranking her in the list of their provinces. They seek, in fine, to tear your laurels from your brows. They expect us to evacuate Germany at the sight of their army. What madness! Let them learn that it would be a thousand times easier to destroy the great capital, than to sully the honour of the children of the great people and their allies. In their former attempt the plans of our enemies were frustrated. They found in the plains of Champagne only shame, defeat, and death; but the lessons of experience are forgotten, and there are men in whom the feelings of hatred and jealousy never become extinct.

" Soldiers, there is not one of you who would wish to return to France by any other path than that of honour. We ought not to return except by passing beneath triumphal arches.

" What! have we braved the inclemency of the seasons, the ocean and the desert, have we subdued Europe often united against us; have we extended our glory from East to West, only to return now, like deserters, after having abandoned our allies, and to be told that the French Eagle has fled in dismay before the Prussians.

" But they have already arrived at our advance posts. Let us, then, march upon them, since forbearance will not check their infatuation. Let the Prussian army experience the fate which it shared fourteen years ago. Let us teach them that if it is easy to obtain an increase of territory and power with the friendship of the great people, their enmity (which can only be provoked by the neglect of prudence and reason) is more terrible than the storms of the ocean."

Our soldiers only wished to fight. The Prussians occupied Saalfeld and Schleitz; we charged them, routed them, and made a thousand prisoners. These were the two first engagements which we had with them. I quitted Murat, whom I had been ordered to follow, and went to render an account of the affair of Schleitz to Napoleon, who had established his head-quarters some leagues in the rear, at the residence of a Princess of Reus-Lobenstein. On my arrival I found Napoleon engaged with Berthier. I informed him of the success of the Grand Duke, and of the defeat of Tauenzien. "Tauenzien!" exclaimed Napoleon, "one of the Prussian intriguers! It was well worth our while to urge on the war to such a length." He told me I might retire and take some rest, as I should be roused in a few hours to set out on a mission. I had no idea whither I was to go. I was called about 5 o'clock. The Emperor gave me a letter for King William, who at that time, I believe, held his head-quarters at Sondershausen. "You must go," said he, "as fast as you can after the King of Prussia, and deliver to him this letter from me. I ask him once more for peace, though hostilities have already commenced. You must endeavour to convince the King of the danger of his situation, and the fatal consequences which may result from it. You will return immediately and bring me his answer: I shall now march on Gera." Our baggage was still in the rear. I had no carriage; but I procured one from the coach-house of the Princess of Reus-Lobenstein, put four good horses to it, and started about six o'clock. Before I had proceeded a league on my journey, Napoleon sent after me. I returned and went to his study, where he had been occupied the whole of the night. He desired me to deliver the letter to Berthier. "Upon reflection," said he, "I will not have one of my aides-de-camp charged with such a message. You are persons of too great importance to be exposed to the chance of meeting with a bad reception." The letter was sent two days after by M. de Montesquiou: he started, I believe, from Gera. The treatment he experienced is well known: he was stopped by the Prince de Hohenlohe, at that time general-in-chief of the Prussian army, who obliged him to be present at the battle of Jena, and did not send the letter, as it is affirmed, until after the action.

Several persons in Napoleon's suite were of opinion, that if I had executed the commission with which I was at first charged, I should have come up with the King of Prussia, and the war perhaps would not have taken place. I do not think so. The gauntlet was thrown, there was no alternative but to take it up. I do not even think that Napoleon was more inclined for peace than King William.

CHAPTER XI.

We were now in possession of the whole course of the Saale, and in a fair way to turn the enemy's army. The calculations of the Duke of Brunswick were completely frustrated. He had formed the idea of coming up with us on the Maine, of occupying our wings by detached corps, and penetrating our centre before we could concentrate our forces. He still possessed all the threads of that vast spy system which had harassed France since the emigrations. He knew the force and the route marked out for several corps which were marching from Meudon, and he did not doubt of anticipating us. Napoleon took a pleasure in cherishing this illusion; he made preparations, and caused reconnaissances to be taken through the whole of that line. The Duke had no longer any doubt of having penetrated our intentions; we were to debouch by Kœnigshaften; he made certain of that; he felt perfectly convinced of it. Our movements on his centre were only a snare, a *ruse de guerre;* we wished to deceive him, in order to prevent him from debouching by the forests of Thuringen, whilst we proceeded towards Coburg and Memmingen, in woody and mountainous countries, where his cavalry would have no opportunity of acting, or at least would be deprived of its advantage. It was of the utmost importance to anticipate us, and he hurried to Kœnigshaften.

The enemy were engaged in the woods; Napoleon marched on Schleitz, sixty leagues from the presumed point of attack. The third corps quietly reposed on the 10th at Nauenburgh, in the rear of the Duke of Brunswick. Hostilities were of only two days' date, and that Prince, who was already uncovered on his left, was on the eve of being entirely cut to pieces. His communications with the Elbe were in danger; and he was nearly reduced to the same extremities as Mack, whom he had so violently censured. His advance-guard, on arriving on the Maine, found the field unoccupied. This circumstance seemed incomprehensible; but still it never led him to suspect the danger to which he was exposed. The rout of Saalfeld alone shook the confidence which he had placed in his own safety. He hastily retraced his course. Weimar and Hohenlohe were directed to come up speedily, and the army of reserve was ordered to make a forced march. But some parties mistook their route, and others did not use sufficient despatch, so that a portion of the troops were not engaged in the battle. The Duke, who was disconcerted at a system of movements so novel to him, knew not what determination to adopt. All these marches and arrangements, so rapidly succeeding each other, formed a mass of confusion, in which he could discern neither plan nor object. The occupation of Nauenburgh relieved him from this perplexity: he saw his left wing about to be turned, or at least exposed; he would not wait longer; he hastily rallied his army of reserve, which was advancing upon Halle, and left Hohenlohe at the camp of Capellendorf to mask the retrograde movement. His troops, who had not shared the disasters of Saalfeld and Schleitz, ridiculed the beaten corps; they shouted "The King for ever! the Queen for ever!" &c. They resolved to avenge the affront offered to the Prussian arms: there were not enough Frenchmen for them. The Duke himself had resumed his confidence. On the Auerstadt road be found not more than thirty chasseurs. His communications were free; it was impossible they could be intercepted: it was not easy to surprise a skilful manœuvrer like the Duke. Hohenlohe's Prussians were encamped behind the heights of Jena: their masses extended as far as the eye could reach; they were prolonged beyond Weimar. Napoleon reconnoitred them on the evening of the 13th, and fixed the attack for the following day. In the night he distributed orders for the movements of the different corps. "As to Davoust, he must march on Apolda, so as to fall on the rear of the enemy's army. He may take whatever route he may deem most expedient; I leave that to himself, provided he take part in the battle: if Bernadotte be at hand he may support him. Berthier, issue instructions accordingly." It was ten o'clock at night; all the arrangements were made, and yet the general commanding the enemy's force flattered himself with the hope that we could not debouch. But the axe of the pioneers removed every obstacle; the rock was cut, and trenches were opened: the action commenced on the right and the left; the conflict was terrible. Davoust, in particular, was placed in a situation in which a man of less firmness might have found his courage fail him. Bernadotte refused to support him; he even forbade two divisions of the reserve cavalry, which, however, were not under his command, from taking part in the action. He paraded round Apolda, while 26,000 French troops were engaged with 70,000 picked men, commanded by the Duke of Brunswick and the King of Prussia. But this circumstance only added to the glory of the commander, whom it might have ruined. Davoust's plans were so well laid, his generals and his troops deployed with such skill and courage, that Blucher, with his 12,000 cavalry, had not the satisfaction to cut a single company. The King, the guards, and the whole army, attacked our troops without obtaining better success. Amidst the deluge of fire that surrounded them on all sides, the French preserved all their national gaiety. A soldier, whom his comrades had nicknamed *the Emperor,* impatient at the obstinacy of the Prussians, exclaimed, " On with me, grenadiers!—Come, follow the Emperor!"—He rushed into the thickest of the battle, the troop followed him, and the Prussian guards were penetrated. He was made a corporal: his friends remarked that he only wanted the protectorate.

At Jena the victory had been no less brilliant: the rout was complete and general; the enemy fled in the utmost confusion.

In the evening I was directed, together with

the Grand Duke, to pursue the wrecks of the Prussian army. We took some Saxon battalions, and we entered *pêle-mêle* with them into Weimar. We stationed our posts before the town, despatched some parties of cavalry on Erfurt road, and presented ourselves at the castle. M. de Pappenheim, whom I recollected having seen in Paris, came out to meet us. He was quite alarmed; but we assured him he had no cause for apprehension. All the Court, with the exception of the Grand Duke and his family, were at Weimar. The Duchess received us with perfect politeness. I was acquainted with several ladies of her suite, one of whom has since become my sister-in-law. I endeavoured to calm their fears. They took courage. Some few disorders took place; but they were of little importance.

Murat took up his quarters at the castle. I set out to join Napoleon at Jena, in order to render him an account of the events of the evening. He did not think that they would go beyond Weimar. He was highly satisfied. The courage of the Duchess astonished him. He did not imagine that the Court would have waited for him. He did not like the family; this he often repeated. The night was far advanced, and Napoleon had just received despatches from the second corps. "Davoust," said he to me, " has had a terrible engagement: he had King William and the Duke of Brunswick opposed to him. The Prussians fought desperately: they suffered dreadful slaughter. The Duke has been dangerously wounded; and the whole army seems to be in terrible disorder. Bernadotte did not behave well. He would have been pleased had Davoust been defeated; but the affair reflects the highest honour on the conqueror, and the more so as Bernadotte rendered his situation a difficult one. That Gascon will never do better."

The battle was lost. The Russians were no longer eager to carry on the war; they wished for and invoked peace. They were anxious to terminate a contest in which they had had such ill success. By dint of wishing for an armistice, they at length persuaded themselves that one had been granted. Kalkreuth announced it: Blucher swore that it was concluded: how could it be discredited. Soult, however, was not to be caught in the snare. The imprudent generosity evinced at Austerlitz had rendered him distrustful. He refused to afford a passage to the troops whom he had cut off. " The convention you speak of is impossible!" said he to the Field Marshal. " Lay down your arms. I must receive the Emperor's orders. You shall retire if he permit it." Kalkreuth was unwilling to resort to this kind of expedient. It always has somewhat the appearance of a defeat: and he would rather have experienced one in good earnest. Some other columns were more fortunate. But it was only deferring the evil moment: they were obliged to surrender some leagues further on. It was not worth while to resort to the deception.

The King himself was disheartened by his misfortunes. Our hussars gave him neither truce nor respite. He recollected all that Napoleon had done to avoid hostilities; and he addressed a letter to him. It was rather late to reply to overtures which had been so ill received. " It would have been better," said Napoleon, " had he explained himself two days sooner; but no matter, I am willing to accede to any thing that is compatible with the dignity and interests of France. I will send Duroc to the King of Prussia. But there is something still more urgent yet. Duroc, set out immediately. Proceed to Nauenburgh, to Dessau, wherever we have wounded troops. See that they want for nothing: visit them for me, each man individually. Give them all the consolation their situation requires. Tell them—tell the Marshal, that he, his generals and his troops, have acquired everlasting claims on my gratitude."

He was not satisfied with this message. He wrote to assure him how much he was pleased with his conduct. His letter was inserted in the order of the day. The troops were transported with it: even the wounded men could not refrain from expressing their delight.

The Emperor established his head-quarters at Weimar. He shewed every possible mark of respect to the Duchess, whom he found to be an amiable and sensible woman, and of very dignified manners.

Meanwhile the enemy was rallying on Magdeburg. The wrecks of the army that had been engaged at Jena, the army of reserve, and the troops of Old and New Prussia, hastily repaired to that place. The Duke of Wirtemberg had already taken a position at Halle; and Bernadotte proceeded thither. His corps had not been engaged at Auerstadt; and he was eager for an opportunity to compensate the portion of glory he had lost. He attacked the Prussians with the bayonet; killing and routing all that opposed him. The carnage was dreadful. On the following day, Napoleon visited the field of battle. He was struck with the sight of the heaps of dead which surrounded the bodies of some of our soldiers. He approached; and, observing on their uniform the numbers of the 32d, " So many of that regiment," said he, " have been killed in Italy, in Egypt, and elsewhere, that I should think none can now remain."

He proceeded to Dessau, and shewed every consideration to the old Duke, who was there with his son. Some months before, a M. de Gussau, who was attached to the Court of Baden, had said to me in Paris, " You will probably go to war with the Prussians. Should that be the case, and should you advance in this campaign as far as Dessau, I charge you to respect its venerable sovereign, who is the father of his subjects." M. de Gussau must have been very much astonished to find, that the French, instead of going only to Dessau, advanced as far as the Niemen, and subsequently to twenty leagues beyond Moscow.

CHAPTER XII.

The Prussians fled at full speed; but the more rapidly they retreated, the more eagerly we maintained the pursuit. Being overtaken within sight of Magdeburg, they took refuge behind the entrenchments, where they were soon forced to lay down their arms. The garrison was invested; and William, who was there, thought himself happy in escaping. All around him had crouched beneath the storm. Prussia was no longer the valiant nation which entertained the idea of driving us back upon the Rhine. A reverse of fortune had overthrown her; a single blow had levelled her with the dust. She flew to meet defeat; she yielded, and delivered herself up. Never was a nation laid so low. Her fall was about to be completed: all our corps were preparing to march on Berlin, and to take possession of the city. Napoleon, however, reserved that honour for the corps which had most contributed to the victory; namely, that commanded by Davoust. The following are the instructions which he addressed to the Marshal:

"ORDER TO MARSHAL DAVOUST.

"Wittemberg, Oct. 23d, 1806.

"If the parties of light troops, which you have of course despatched on the roads leading to Dresden and the Spree, inform you that you have no enemies on your flanks, you will direct your march so as to be able to make your entry into Berlin on the 25th of the present month, at noon. You will cause the General of Brigade, Hullin, to be acknowledged as commander of the garrison of Berlin. You may leave whatever regiment you think fit to do duty in the city. You will despatch parties of light cavalry on the roads to Kustrin, Langsberg, and Frankfort on the Oder. You will station your army corps at the distance of a league or a league and a half from Berlin; the right supported on the Spree, and the left on the road to Langsberg. Fix your head-quarters on the road to Kustrin, at some country residence in the rear of your force. It is the Emperor's intention to afford his troops a few days' repose; and therefore you will construct for them huts of straw and wood. Generals, staff-officers, colonels, and others, must be lodged in the villages in the rear of their divisions, and no one in Berlin. The artillery must be stationed in positions which cover the camp; the artillery-horses at the piquets, and all in the best military order.

"You will cut, that is to say, intercept, as early as possible, the navigation of the Spree by a strong party, so as to stop all the boats that may attempt to proceed from Berlin to the Oder.

"To-morrow our head-quarters will be at Potsdam. Send one of your aides-de-camp to inform me where you may be on the nights of the 23d and 24th.

"If Prince Ferdinand should be in Berlin, present your compliments to him, and give him a guard, with entire freedom from quartering.

"Publish immediately the order for disarming the troops in Berlin, leaving only 600 militia for the police-duty of the city. The arms of the citizens must be conveyed to some place that may be determined on, to be at the disposal of our army.

"Make known to your corps that the Emperor, in directing it to be the first to enter Berlin, gives a proof of his satisfaction of the excellent conduct of the troops at the battle of Jena.

"Be careful to direct that all the baggage, and particularly that which is in bad condition, shall halt at the distance of two leagues from Berlin, and rejoin the camp, without passing through the capital, but by proceeding along another road on the right. Finally, make your entrance into Berlin in the best possible order, and by divisions, each division having its artillery, and marching at the interval of an hour after each other.

"The camp being formed, give orders that the troops proceed to the city only by thirds, so that there may be always two-thirds at the camp. As his Majesty expects to make his entrance into Berlin, you may provisionally receive the keys of the city, informing the magistrates that they must nevertheless deliver them up to the Emperor on his arrival. You must require the magistrates and persons of distinction to receive you at the gates of the city, in all due form; and direct your officers to make the best appearance that circumstances will permit. The Emperor proposes that you shall make your entrance by the high road of Dresden.

"The Emperor will probably take up his abode in the palace of Charlottemburgh. Give orders that every thing may be prepared for his reception.

"There is a little rivulet which falls into the Spree, at the distance of a league and a half or two leagues from Berlin, and which intersects the road leading to En."

CHAPTER XIII.

We set out for Potsdam; and we were overtaken by a storm: it was so violent and the rain fell in such torrents, that we took refuge in a neighbouring house. Napoleon was wrapped in his grey military great coat, and, on entering the house, he was much astonished to see a young female, who seemed to be much agitated by his presence. She proved to be a native of Egypt, and she evinced for Napoleon all the religious veneration which he had been accustomed to receive from the Arabs. She was the widow of an officer of the army of the East; and fate had conducted her to Saxony, and to the very house in which the Emperor was now received. Napoleon granted her a pension of 1200 francs, and undertook to provide for the education of her son, who was the only dowry her husband had left her. "This," said Napoleon, "is the first time I ever took shelter against a storm. I felt a presentiment that a good action awaited me."

We found Potsdam uninjured. The Court had even fled so precipitately that nothing had been removed. Frederick the Great's sword and belt, and the cordon of his orders, all were left. Napoleon took possession of them. "I prefer these trophies," said he with enthusiasm, "to all the King of Prussia's treasures. I will send them to my veterans who served in the campaign of Hanover. I will present them to the governor of the Hospital of Invalids, by whom they will be preserved as a testimony of the victories of the great army, and the revenge it has taken for the disasters of Rosbach."

No sooner had we entered Potsdam than we were besieged by deputations; they came from Saxony, from Weimar, and from all quarters. Napoleon received them with the utmost affability. The envoy of the Duke of Brunswick, who recommended his subjects to the generosity of the French, was, however, received less courteously than the rest. "If," said Napoleon to the person who presented the deputation, "I were to demolish the city of Brunswick, if I were to leave not a stone of the walls standing, what would your Prince think of me? And yet would not the law of retaliation authorize me to do in Brunswick what the Duke would have done in my capital? To announce the design of destroying cities may be the act of a madman; but to attempt to sully the honour of a whole army of brave troops, to wish to mark out a course for us to quit Germany merely on the summons of the Prussian army, is a fact which posterity will with difficulty credit. The Duke ought not to have attempted such an outrage. When a general has grown grey in the career of arms, he should know how to respect military honour. It was not, certainly, in the plains of Champagne that the Duke acquired the right of insulting the French standard. Such a proposition can reflect dishonour only on him who made it. The disgrace does not attach itself to the King of Prussia; but to the general to whom, in the present difficult circumstances, he resigned the care of his affairs; in short, to the Duke of Brunswick, whom France and Prussia will blame for the calamities of the war. The violent example set by the old General served as an authority for impetuous youth, and led the King to act in opposition to his own opinion and positive conviction. However, Sir, you may assure the inhabitants of Brunswick, that the French will prove themselves generous enemies; that it is my desire, as far as regards them, to alleviate the miseries of war; and that the evils which may arise from the passage of the troops through their territory, is contrary to my wish. Tell the Duke of Brunswick that he shall be treated with all the consideration due to an enemy's officer; but that I cannot acknowledge one of the King of Prussia's generals as a sovereign. If the House of Brunswick should forfeit the sovereignty of its ancestors, the blame must rest with the author of the two wars; who, in the one, wished to sap the very foundation of the great French capital; and, in the other, attempted to cast disgrace on 200,000 brave troops, who, though they may perhaps be defeated, will never be found to depart from the path of glory and honour. Much blood has been shed within a few days. Prussia is the victim of great disasters; and she may justly blame the man who, with a word, might have averted them, if, like Nestor, raising his voice in the Council, he had said:—

"Inconsiderate youths, be silent! Women, return to your domestic duties. And you, Sire, listen to the companion of the most illustrious of your predecessors. Since the Emperor Napoleon does not wish to maintain hostilities, do not oblige him to chose between war and dishonour. Do not engage in a dangerous conflict with an army, which prides itself in fifteen years of glorious achievements, and whom victory has accustomed to subdue every thing.

" Instead of holding this language, which would have been so well suited to the prudence of his age and the experience of his long career, he was the first to raise the cry of war. He had even violated the ties of blood, by arming a son (Prince Eugène of Wirtemberg) against his father. He threatened to plant his standard on the palace of Stuttgard; and accompanying all these acts by imprecations against France, he declared himself the author of that wild manifesto, the production of which he had disavowed for the space of fourteen years, though it was out of his power to deny having affixed his signature to it."

Spandau had been surrendered to Marshal Lannes. Napoleon visited the fortress, and inspected it minutely. He sent me to Berlin, which had been entered by Davoust, and directed me to present his compliments to old Ferdinand and his wife. I found the Prince very melancholy and dejected: he had just lost his son. The Princess appeared more calm and resigned. I also went to pay compliments to the Prince Henry and the Princess of Hesse, sister to the King of Prussia. The former appeared very sensible to the attention evinced by Napoleon; the latter had retired to a wing of the castle, where she lived tranquilly in the society of her grand-children. The situation of this Princess inspired me with interest and veneration. She appeared to take courage, and she begged me to recommend her to Napoleon, who paid her a visit immediately on his arrival. She inspired him with the same favourable sentiments which I had conceived for her.

The Emperor fixed his head-quarters at Charlottemburgh. On the following day, he made his entrance into the capital, and addressed the following proclamation to the army:—

"Soldiers!

"You have fulfilled my expectations, and fully justified the confidence of the French people. You have endured privation and fatigue with courage, equal to the intrepidity and presence of mind which you evinced on the field of battle. You are the worthy defenders of the honour of my crown, and the glory of the great French people. So long as you continue to be animated by the spirit which you now display, nothing can oppose you. I know not how to distinguish any particular corps. . . . . You have all proved yourselves good soldiers. The following is the result of our exertions in this campaign.

"One of the first powers in Europe, which lately proposed to us a dishonourable capitulation, has been overthrown. The forests and defiles of Franconia, the Saale, and the Elbe, which our fathers would not have crossed in seven years, we have traversed in seven days; and in that short interval we have had four engagements, and one great battle. Our entrance into Potsdam and Berlin has preceded the fame of our victories. We have made 60,000 prisoners, taken sixty-five standards, (among which are the colours of the King of Prussia's guards), six hundred pieces of cannon, and three fortresses. Among the prisoners, there are upwards of twenty generals. But notwithstanding all this, more than half our troops regret not having fired a single musket. All the provinces of the Prussian monarchy, as far as the Oder, are in our power.

"Soldiers! the Russians boast of coming to meet us, but we will advance to meet them; we will save them half their march: they will meet with another Austerlitz in the midst of Prussia. A nation which can so soon forget our generous treatment of her, after that battle, in which the Emperor, his court, and the wrecks of his army, owed their safety only to the capitulation we granted them, is a nation that cannot successfully contend with us.

"While we march to meet the Russians, new corps, formed in the interior of our empire, will repair hither, to occupy our present stations, and protect our conquests. My people all rose indignantly on hearing the disgraceful capitulation which the Prussian ministers, in their madness, proposed to us. Our frontier roads and towns are filled with conscripts, who are burning with eagerness to march in your footsteps. We will not again be the dupes of a treacherous peace. We will not lay down our arms until we compel the English, those eternal enemies of France, to renounce their plan of disturbing the Continent, and to relinquish the tyranny which they maintain on the seas.

"Soldiers! I cannot better express the sentiments I entertain for you, than by assuring you that I bear in my heart the love which you daily evince for me."

CHAPTER XIV.

Napoleon next proceeded to the camp, and reviewed the third corps; and every individual who had particularly distinguished himself was rewarded, either by promotion or by a decoration. The generals, officers, and subalterns, were assembled round the Emperor. " I wished to call you together," said he " in order to express my satisfaction of your brilliant conduct in the battle of the 14th. I lost many brave men, whom I looked upon as my sons; I deeply regret them; but, after all, they fell on the field of glory—they perished like true soldiers! You have rendered me a signal service on this memorable occasion. We are, in particular, indebted to the excellent conduct of the third corps, for the great results we have obtained. Tell your men that I am satisfied with the courage they have displayed. Generals, officers, subaltern officers, and privates, you possess eternal claims on my gratitude and kindness." The Marshal replied, that the third corps would always prove itself worthy of the Emperor's confidence; that it would constantly be to him what the 10th legion was to Cæsar.

M. Denon was present at this interesting scene, which his pencil will, perhaps, commemorate: but, whatever be the talent of the artist, he can never convey an idea of the satisfaction and kindness which beamed in the features of the sovereign; or the devotedness and gratitude expressed in the countenances of all present, from the Marshal down to the meanest soldier.

The proclamation which Napoleon had addressed to the troops inspired them with new ardour. They rushed forward to pursue the wrecks of the forces, which had been engaged at Halle and Jena. The Prince of Hohenlohe had rallied a considerable mass, with which he might have escaped us; but he was not sufficiently speedy, he lost time, and these delays afforded us the hope of seeing him cut off. Napoleon impatiently looked for this event. "Bernadotte," said he to me, as we were entering the palace, " must by this time be at Cremen. He will surely have come up with the Prussians; Murat will attack them with his usual impetuosity; both together must have a greater force than is necessary to beat them. In a few days hence the Prince of Hohenlohe, with all his corps, will be in my hands; and

I shall soon after have all their artillery and baggage. But we must act together; for it is not probable that they will suffer themselves to be taken without coming to an engagement."

Every thing happened as Napoleon had foretold. The Prussians, who were thrown into disorder by the attack of our cavalry, and the showers of grape shot, were summoned to surrender by General Belliard, and they laid down their arms. Twenty-five thousand picked troops, forty-five standards, seventy-four pieces of artillery, defiled before us: it was another conquest of Ulm. The Emperor was transported with his success: " This is well," said he; " but we have not yet got Blucher, who is so clever at making extempore armistices. We must have him also." He immediately addressed the following lines to Murat: " Nothing is done, so long as any thing remains undone. You have turned General Blucher's cavalry; let me soon hear that his force has experienced the fate of Hohenlohe's." Berthier also wrote to him as follows, to call his attention to the Duke of Weimar: " Independently of the little detached columns, there are three principal ones: 1st. That commanded by Prince Hohenlohe, which you have taken at Prentzlow; 2d. Blucher's column, which at daybreak on the 28th quitted

Wissemberg, and which you must certainly have fallen in with to-day at Passelwalch; and 3d. The Duke of Weimar's column, which escaped Marshal Soult, and effected the passage of the Elbe, as it would appear, near Saudon and Havelsberg, on the 26th, whence it proceeded in the direction of Wursterhausen, Newrupin, Grausee, or Furstemberg. From Havelsberg to Furstemberg is a distance of twenty-five leagues; consequently the Duke of Weimar cannot reach Furstemberg on the 28th. But from Furstemberg to Passelwalch is only twenty leagues distance; and if the enemy's column should take that route, you will certainly fall in with it at Passelwalch on the 30th or 31st. Thus it may be presumed that nothing can escape between you and Marshals Lannes and Bernadotte. Such is the information which I am enabled to communicate to you from the accounts that have reached the Emperor."

But the Duke was tired of sharing the disasters of the Prussian army. He negotiated and transferred the command of his troops to Blucher, who, intent on his retreat, fled without caring or even knowing where he went. His route disconcerted Napoleon. "What does he intend?" said he; "whither is he going? I cannot imagine that he will throw himself into Holstein; for when once there, he will find no means of retreat. He cannot recross the Elbe; he will be driven up, and his troops will be drowned. He will never think of making such an attempt. We shall soon have him here." Blucher laid down arms some days after. He had passed through the whole of Prussia, and had violated the Danish territory, with no other object than to defer for a few days the surrender of between 20 and 25,000 men, the standards, and last artillery of the Prussians. With a little more skill, Blucher might have turned his obstinacy to better account. " Well," said Napoleon, on learning this news, " they are now advancing with the Austrians. They will be more reserved in future; they will say nothing more about Ulm. In three weeks they have four times renewed it. Blucher must be sent to France, to Dijon; there he may amuse himself in forging armistices. Write to General Belliard." The following despatch was sent off:

"Berlin, Oct. 13, 1806.

" To GENERAL BELLIARD, CHIEF OF THE GENERAL STAFF OF THE RESERVE OF CAVALRY.

" It is the Emperor's intention that the greatest care be taken that all the prisoners belonging to the column of General Blucher and the Duke of Weimar, should be sent to France. His Majesty wishes that all the generals and officers should also proceed to France. General Blucher will be conducted by an officer to Dijon. The young Prince of Brunswick must also be escorted by an officer to Chalons-sur-Marne. All the other officers must be conveyed to the different quarters of France fixed upon by the minister Dejean for the prisoners of war."

We did not venture to interrupt the Emperor until he had finished dictating the despatch; but when he had concluded it we interceded in favour of General Blucher. We represented that he had laid down arms, that he was no longer dangerous, and that it was necessary to make some allowance for his hussar habits. Napoleon acknowledged the justice of our suggestions, and Blucher retired to Hamburgh.

CHAPTER XV.

Prince Hatzfeld had come to Potsdam as a deputy from the city of Berlin, and had been well received. He rendered an account of his mission, as well as I can recollect, to Count Hohenlohe, and reported to him the state of the troops, artillery, and ammunition, that were in the capital or which he had met on the road: his letter was intercepted. Napoleon delivered it to me, with orders immediately to arrest the Prince, and send him to the head-quarters of Marshal Davoust, which were two leagues distant. Berthier, Duroc, Caulincourt, and I, vainly endeavoured to appease the anger of Napoleon. He refused to listen to our representations. M. de Hatzfeld had transmitted reports relative to military affairs which were quite unconnected with his mission: he had evidently been acting the part of a spy. Savary, who, in his quality of commander of the military gendarmerie, usually took cognizance of affairs of this kind, was then on a mission. I was obliged to assume his functions during his absence. I gave orders for the arrest of the Prince; but instead of having him conducted to the head-quarters of Davoust, I placed him in the chamber of the officer commanding the palace guard, whom I directed to treat him with every mark of respect.

Caulincourt and Duroc withdrew from the Emperor's apartment. Napoleon was left alone with Berthier, and he directed him to sit down and write the order by which M. de Hatzfeld was to be arraigned before a military commission. The Major-general made some representations in his favour. "Your Majesty will not, for so trivial an offence, shoot a man who is connected with the first families in Berlin. The thing is impossible, you will not think of it." The Emperor grew more angry. Neufchatel persisted in his intercession; Napoleon lost all patience, and Berthier quitted the room. I was called in. I had overheard the scene that had just taken place. I was afraid to hazard the least reflection: I was in a state of agony. Besides the repugnance I felt in being instrumental to so harsh a measure, it was necessary to write as rapidly as the Emperor spoke; and I must confess I never possessed that talent. He dictated to me the following order:—

"Our cousin Marshal Davoust will appoint a

military commission, consisting of seven colonels of his staff, of which he will be the president, to try the Prince of Hatzfeld on a charge of treason and espionnage.

"The sentence must be pronounced and executed before six o'clock in the evening."

It was about noon. Napoleon directed me to despatch the order immediately, and to send with it the Prince of Hatzfeld's letter. The latter part of the instruction I did not however obey. My mind was racked by the most painful emotions. I trembled for the Prince, and I trembled for myself; since, instead of sending him to Davoust's head-quarters, I had lodged him in the palace.

Napoleon wished to have his horse saddled, as he intended to visit Prince and Princess Ferdinand. As I was going out to give the necessary orders I was informed that the Princess of Hatzfeld had fainted in the antichamber, and that she had previously expressed a wish to speak to me. I went to her. I did not conceal from her the displeasure of Napoleon. I told her that we were going to ride out on horseback, and I directed her to repair to Prince Ferdinand, and to interest him in favour of her husband. I know not whether she did so; but on our arrival at the palace we found her in one of the corridors, and she threw herself in tears at the feet of the Emperor, to whom I announced her name.

The Princess was in a state of pregnancy. Napoleon was moved by her situation, and directed her to proceed to the castle. He, at the same time, desired me to write to Davoust, to order the trial to be suspended:—he thought M. de Hatzfeld had departed.

Napoleon returned to the palace, where Madame de Hatzfeld was waiting for him. He desired her to enter the saloon: I was present. "Your husband, Madam," said he, "has brought himself into an unfortunate scrape. According to our laws he deserves to be sentenced to death. General Rapp, give me his letter. Here, Madam, read this." The lady trembled exceedingly. Napoleon immediately took the letter from her hand, tore it, and threw the fragments into the fire. "I have no other proof against the Prince of Hatzfeld, Madam; therefore he is at liberty." He ordered me immediately to release him from his confinement at head-quarters. I acknowledged that I had not sent him there; but he did not reproach me; he even seemed pleased at what I had done.

In this affair, Berthier, Duroc, and Caulincourt, behaved as they did on all occasions, that is to say, like gallant men: Berthier's conduct was particularly praiseworthy.

No sooner had the Prince of Hatzfeld returned to his family, than he was made acquainted with all that had passed. He wrote me a letter expressive of his gratitude and the emotions by which he was agitated. It was as follows:—

" My dear General,

" Amidst the sensations of every kind which I experienced yesterday, I was not unmindful of the marks of your sensibility, and the interest you evinced for me. Yesterday evening I devoted wholly to the society of my family; and therefore I could not until to-day discharge the debt I owe to you.

" There are moments in life, the recollection of which can never be effaced; and if you attach any value to the profound gratitude and esteem of an honest man, you will be rewarded for the interest you have shewn for me.

" Accept the assurance of my high consideration, and of those sentiments which render it impossible I can ever forget you.

" I have the honour to be,
" My dear General,
" Your very humble and very obedient servant,
" PRINCE DE HATZFELD."

" Berlin, Sept. 30, 1806."

Envoys soon arrived at Berlin from all the courts of Germany, petitioning Napoleon to shew favour to their respective Princes. The Duchess of Weimar deputed to us a M. de Müller, who prayed for a reduction of imposts, and for the return of the Duke, who was, I believe, at Hamburgh. The Emperor did not like the formality of the diplomatist. He found him troublesome, and he sent him to me. " I have," said he to me, " directed Talleyrand to refer this gentleman to you; as I wish you to settle the affairs of the Court of Weimar." He would not hear the name of the Duke mentioned; he was as indignant against him as he was favourably disposed towards the Duchess. However, his anger became a little appeased, and he styled the Duchess his cousin;—a distinction which was then of some importance. The Duke received permission to return to his states. On his way thither he requested to be presented to Napoleon; but that very day we set out for Poland. He did me the honour to write me a letter, thanking me for what I had done for his family; to whom, I believe, I had indeed rendered some service. At a subsequent period, I again proved useful to the Duke of Weimar, as I shall hereafter have occasion to mention. The following is the letter he addressed to me. I quote documents of this kind, because they describe the events of the period to which they refer, and also because they are honourable to him to whom they are addressed.

"Sir,

"Inspired with the warmest gratitude for the many favours you have shewn to my family, and for the feelings of kind interest which you have evinced for us, I was anxious for an opportunity to assure you by word of mouth how much I am sensible of your goodness; and at the same time to express to you, by the particular desire of the Duchess, the high esteem she entertains for you. Unfortunately, the precipitate departure of his Majesty the Emperor and King prevented me from personally presenting my respects to you this day. But I flatter myself that the period is not far distant, when I shall enjoy the happiness of giving you a verbal assurance that the high consideration I bear to you is unalterable, and that I shall never cease to be,

"Sir,

"Your very humble and very obedient servant,

"The DUKE OF WEIMAR."

"Berlin, Nov. 24, 1806."

CHAPTER XVI.

The Elector of Hesse, also, wished to treat; but the Emperor was so much offended with that Prince, that he would not receive his envoy. "As to him," said he, "his reign is ended."

The gates of Magdeburgh were opened to Marshal Ney. Along with the keys, there was brought to the Marshal a little box, containing some valuables belonging, as it was said, to the Elector. They were found in the fortress.

Colbert, Custrin, and Stettin, were capitulating. The Grand Duke had detached the light cavalry from Prentzlow, and they unexpectedly appeared before the garrison. Evening was advancing. General Lasalle announced that troops were following him. He summoned, threatened, and intimidated the Governor, and induced him to come to overtures; but General Belliard arrived, broke off the negotiation, and declared, that if the fortress were not surrendered in the space of an hour, he would overwhelm it with cannon-balls. The Prussians took the alarm: they imagined that the army, the park, all was ready to destroy them, and they surrendered to our hussars. Custrin was managed still better. Our troops made a movement to cross the Oder. In course of their march they fell in with some hundreds of Prussian troops, whom they dispersed. The garrison fired upon them, and balls were flying among our ranks. General Gudin intimated, that if the useless firing were not discontinued the garrison should be immediately blown up. The governor, becoming alarmed, proposed arrangements; but they were rejected: he was told that none could be made. He persisted; but the General continued his march, and there was no one to receive his propositions. A despatch was sent off to General Petit, who was a considerable distance off. The flag of truce still persisted in coming to arrangements. "What arrangement would you have me listen to?" said the General, gravely. "My instructions are positive. If the garrison be not surrendered in two hours, I am ordered to destroy it. We are preparing our batteries; forty mortars or howitzers will immediately vomit a deluge of fire on your ramparts. There is the colonel of the artillery;" (it happened, however, to be the colonel of the eighty-fifth regiment of the line who at that moment came forward;) "you shall see whether I am exaggerating. Colonel, are your guns mounted, are your preparations completed?"— " All is ready, General; I only await your orders." —" But stay for one moment, Sir; we will offer terms of peace. You see," said he to the Prussian officer, " your town is about to be destroyed. You may as well avert misfortunes which cannot change the state of affairs. Whether we be defeated or victorious, we will nevertheless make the most of our present advantages. A capitulation or a siege, we care not which. Choose, but choose quickly; and observe, that I will treat with none but the Governor." The latter soon appeared upon the Oder.

General Gauthier went to receive the Governor, and conducted him to a neighbouring house. General Petit joined them, and the capitulation was signed. Four thousand Prussians, with stores of provisions and ammunition, surrendered to a regiment of infantry who had not even summoned them, and who could not go forward to attack them. These men were justifiable in asking us to cross the Rhine: they found us dangerous neighbours.

Napoleon sent Duroc to the King of Prussia; but nobody believed there would be peace.

As Caulincourt and I were walking about in

the court-yard of the Castle, a tall young man, with fair hair, came up to us and saluted us. This was Prince Paul of Wurtemberg. He had just quitted the Prussian army, in which he had served contrary to the wish of his father, with whom, as well as with the Emperor, he was much out of favour. " What is your Highness's errand here?" enquired Caulincourt. The Prince replied, that he wished to be restored to the good graces of the Emperor, and he requested the General to announce him. The Duke de Vicenza agreed to do so; but Napoleon would not receive the Prince. He ordered him to be arrested, and escorted by an officer of gendarmerie to the States of the King his father, where he was detained for several years. Caulincourt exerted every effort to soften the rigours of his captivity.

Our head-quarters were transferred to Posen. The spirit of insurrection which had manifested itself on the first appearance of our troops, burst forth with new violence. Kalisch had disarmed the Prussian garrison, and the example was followed in many other fortresses. Nothing was heard but imprecations upon the authors of the division. Villages, towns, and even the city of Warsaw, though occupied by the Russians, sent deputations, and demanded the proclamation of the independence of Poland. " I would willingly consent to it," said Napoleon; " but, if the match were once kindled, who knows where the conflagration might end? My first duty is to attend to the interests of France: I must not sacrifice her for Poland. We must leave the fate of the latter to time, the sovereign who rules all; he alone can shew us what we ought to do."

Duroc rejoined us at Posen. We set out for Warsaw. On the way the Grand Marshal's carriage was overturned, and his clavicle was broken by the fall. Napoleon was very much concerned for the accident: Duroc was a man whose services were almost indispensable to the Emperor. He always enjoyed the highest favour and the greatest confidence, which he in every respect deserved. Few men were so distinguished for tact, spirit of business, and skill, as Duroc; and at the same time few were so remarkable for modesty. His devotion to the Emperor was without bounds. He had a good heart, and he was an honest man: his only fault was his fear of displeasing, and his excessive timidity.

At length we entered the Polish capital; the King of Naples had preceded us, and had driven the Russians from the city. Napoleon was received with enthusiasm. The Poles thought the moment of their resuscitation had arrived, and that their wishes were fulfilled. It would be difficult to describe the joy they evinced, and the respect with which they treated us. The French troops, however, were not quite so well pleased; they manifested the greatest repugnance to crossing the Vistula. The idea of want and bad weather inspired them with the greatest aversion to Poland: they were inexhaustible in their jokes and epigrams on the country. They nevertheless beat the Russians in the marshes of Nasielsk, at Golymin, at Pultusk, and subsequently at Eylau.

At a review, during which the Poles were pressing upon our troops, a soldier, in a loud tone of voice, vented imprecations on the country and the bad weather. A young female who was standing by said:—" You are very ungrateful to dislike our country; for we like you very much."—"You are very kind," replied the soldier; "but if you wish me to believe you, you must give a good dinner to me and my comrade here." The friends of the young woman took the two soldiers home and regaled them.

The French soldiers were particularly fond of passing their jokes at the theatre. One evening, when the curtain was very late of rising, a grenadier, who was among the spectators, became impatient at the delay. " Begin!" he called out, from the further end of the pit; " begin directly, or I will not cross the Vistula."

M. de Talleyrand, who was driving in his carriage at a short distance from Warsaw, stuck in the mud, and twelve hours elapsed before he could be extricated. The soldiers who were much out of humour, enquired who he was. The minister for foreign affairs replied an individual of his suite. " Why does he come to a country like this with his diplomacy?" said one of the soldiers.

The French troops used to say that the four following words constituted the whole language of the Poles:—*Kleba? niema; vota? sara:* (some bread? there is none; some water? we will go and fetch it.) This was all that was to be heard in Poland.

Napoleon one day passed by a column of infantry in the neighbourhood of Nasielsk, where the troops were suffering the greatest privations, on account of the mud, which prevented the arrival of provisions. " Papa, kleba?" exclaimed a soldier. " Niema," replied the Emperor. The whole column burst into a fit of laughter: they asked for nothing more.

I relate these anecdotes, because they shew the kind of spirit which animated our troops. These brave veterans deserved more gratitude than they obtained.

Napoleon was amused with these jokes, and he smiled whenever allusion was made to the reluctance of the army to cross the Vistula. Some Generals augured unfavourably of the disposition of the troops, and expressed their regret to find that disgust had succeeded enthusiasm. "Have you spoken to them of the enemy?" said the Emperor; "are they without enthusiasm when they face him?" Those men, said he to me afterwards, know not how to appreciate my troops. They do not know that they burn with ardour whenever the Russians and victory are spoken of: I will rouse them. He called one of his secretaries, and dictated to him the following proclamation.

"Soldiers!

"This day twelvemonth, at this very hour, you were on the memorable field of Austerlitz: the Russian battalions were dismayed, and fled in disorder, or were surrounded and compelled to lay down their arms to the conquerors. On the following day they circulated reports of peace; but these were false. No sooner had they, through generosity that was perhaps reprehensible, escaped the disasters of the third coalition, than they plotted a fourth. But the ally, on whose tactics they founded their principal hope, is no longer what he was: his citadels, his capitals, his magazines, his arsenals, 280 standards, 700 pieces of cannon, five great garrisons, are in our power. The Oder, the Warta, the deserts of Poland, the severity of the weather, have not for a moment impeded your advance: you have braved every danger, and surmounted every obstacle; your enemies every where fled at your approach. In vain did the Russians attempt to defend the capital of ancient and illustrious Poland. The French eagle hovers over the Vistula. At your approach the brave and unfortunate Poles fancied they again beheld the legions of Sobieski returning from their memorable expedition.

" Soldiers! we will not lay down our arms until a general peace shall have established and secured the power of our allies, and restored to France her freedom of trade and the possession of her colonies. On the banks of the Elbe and the Oder we have conquered Pondicherry, our establishments in India, the Cape of Good Hope, and the Spanish Colonies. What should give the Russians the right of deciding the fate of Europe? What should give them the right of defeating our just designs? Are not they, as well as we, the men who fought at Austerlitz?"

The troops were assembled in the square of Saxony. It was the anniversary of the coronation, and the Russians occupied the suburb of Prague. These circumstances, these recollections, this perspective of glory, were hailed by loud acclamations. Our troops were inspired by the prospect of victory, and all their prejudices vanished. The enemy covered the left bank of the river. All the vessels had been towed away; but one of our quartermasters, in defiance of the Cossack lances, succeeded in getting possession of a boat. This was enough: the enemy raised his camp during the night, and we passed without any impediment. The Bug presented greater difficulties; its left bank is flat and marshy, and well calculated for defence; but Benigsen knew not how to avail himself of his advantages. We threatened his flanks, and we succeeded in floating the boats that had been sunk. The enemy hesitated, and the river was crossed. The Russians returned to the charge: they endeavoured to carry the head of the bridge, which we had raised at Okuniew; but all had been foreseen; Davoust had adopted every necessary precaution, and the enemy was routed, beaten, and compelled to repass the Wkra.

CHAPTER XVII.

Meanwhile old Kaminski had taken the command of the Russian army, and had fixed his head-quarters at Pultusk. His Generals concentrated their forces, and every thing denoted the design of removing to this side of the river. Napoleon hastened forward with the view of driving them from their position. He visited the entrenched camp of Okuniew, reconnoitred the river, the position of the Russians, and the plain which it was necessary to cross in order to come up with them. This plain, which was covered with trees, cut down wood, and marshes, was almost as difficult to carry as the redoubts, behind which the Cossacks had sheltered themselves. The Emperor examined it for a considerable time. Some clumps of trees intercepted his view; but he called for a ladder, and mounting on the roof of a hut, he was enabled to observe the nature of the position occupied by the Russians, and the movements that were taking place on the opposite bank of the river. "We will pass," said he; "send an officer hither." The second chief of the staff of the 3d corps presented himself, and wrote down to the Emperor's dictation the following arrangements.

"The first division is to proceed to the island, and to form itself at as great a distance as possible from the enemy.

"All the troops of the 3d division must remain at the head of the bridge; and are to take no share in the attack: they are to remain in reserve.

"Battalions are to be formed with the eight companies of voltigeurs, which, with the battalions of the 13th light, will form three columns. These three columns are to proceed as secretly as possible to the three extremities of the canal, and will halt in the centre of the island, so as to be beyond reach of the fusillade. Each of these columns will have three pieces of cannon in its rear.

"Each company will detach its cannon, escorted by a company of voltigeurs. These companies will commence the fusillade, covering themselves with the hedges. Meanwhile the artillery officers will plant their batteries, and fire grape-shot on the battalions and troops with which the enemy will not fail to oppose our passage.

"Bridges may be constructed under the protection of this artillery.

"The three columns are to cross the river; and

as soon as they shall be stationed on the opposite side, three piquets of horse chasseurs, each consisting of sixty men, will cross to charge the enemy, pursue him speedily, and make prisoners.

" The 17th regiment will cross immediately after, and range itself in the order of battle, leaving between each battalion a space of twenty-five toises; in the rear of which will be stationed three squadrons of light cavalry. The remainder of the division will afterwards cross, and form itself in the rear."

We advanced towards the heights occupied by the enemy, whom we attacked on the right and the left: he was unable to resist the shock, and was repulsed. Our troops evinced unexampled valour: Napoleon applauded their courage; and he called Generals Morand and Petit, on whom he bestowed the most flattering compliments. He wished to afford some repose to the corps, who had just been engaged; and he detached Friant's division in pursuit of the Russians. Our voltigeurs came up with them at Nasielsk, attacked their left wing, routed, cut them up, and took three pieces of cannon: they pursued them into the woods; the fusillade commenced on both sides, and we experienced obstinate resistance. We had no artillery, and we could not drive from their position, columns which were protected by the nature of the ground, and the grape-shot; but the courage of our troops made amends for their deficiency of artillery. The signal for the attack was given: the 48th, led on by the intrepid Barbanegre, rushed headlong upon the enemy's masses, and routed them. Night approached, and the darkness enabled them to escape from the thrusts of our bayonets. We collected several pieces of cannon, which had stuck in the mud on the road.

Some formidable masses of the enemy's force were before us; but they did not venture to wait until we came up with them: they fled, some towards Golymin and others towards Pultusk. I pursued those who fled in the former direction, with the division of dragoons which the Emperor had entrusted to my command. The Marshal detached Daultane to cover the rear of the 5th corps, which he knew had proceeded to Pultusk. There had been a complete thaw for the space of two days;—a circumstance which was uncommon in Poland at that season of the year. The ground over which we passed was a clayey soil, intersected with marshes: the roads were excessively bad: cavalry, infantry, and artillery stuck in the bogs; and it cost them the utmost difficulty to extricate themselves. We advanced only a short league in the space of two hours. Many of our officers stuck in the mud and remained there during the whole of the battle of Pultusk. They served as marks for the enemy to shoot at.

The third division had no sooner debouched from the village than it was informed by its pioneers that a considerable mass of cavalry covered, at some distance a column of artillery and baggage. General Friant ordered them to be watched by detachments of cavalry, as he was well convinced that the cloud of Cossacks would disperse on the appearance of the infantry. They fled, and we took artillery, ammunition, carriages and cassoons of every kind. The General, pleased with these advantages, went to take up a position for the night, when a heavy cannonade was heard; it proceeded from Marshal Lannes' forces, who were driven by the Russians from Pultusk. We had our turn on the following day: they occupied a wood whence we wished to dislodge them; our columns advanced, the voltigeurs were in front, and the infantry were disposed *en echelon* behind them. We experienced obstinate resistance on the part of the enemy. He attacked us: we charged with the bayonet; and our battalions drove him back on his own masses. We remained masters of the field : it was covered with the bodies of the dead, and with bags which the Russians had thrown down in order to fly with the greater speed. The infantry was dislodged, and the cavalry now advanced. I went forward to meet them and drove them back. But the voltigeurs, who were dispersed about in the marshes, overwhelmed us with their balls: I had my left arm broken.

I had been four times wounded in the first campaigns of the army of the Rhine, under Custine, Pichegru, Moreau, and Desaix; twice before the ruins of Memphis, and in Upper Egypt before the ruins of Thebes; at the battle of Austerlitz and at Golymin. I also received four other wounds at Moscow, as I shall hereafter have occasion to mention.

From Golymin I was removed to Warsaw. Napoleon arrived there on the 1st January, and he did me the honour to come and see me. "Well, Rapp," said he, " you are wounded again; and on your unlucky arm too." It was the ninth wound which I had received on my left arm, and the Emperor therefore called it my unlucky arm.—" No wonder," Sire, said I, " we are always amidst battles." " We shall perhaps have done fighting," he replied, " when we are eighty years old."

MM. Boyer and Yvan dressed my wound in his presence. When Napoleon saw that the bone was really broken, he said, " His arm must be amputated. He is now very ill; and this wound may be his death." M. Boyer smiled and said, " Your Majesty would go too hastily to work: the General is young and vigorous; we shall cure him."—" I hope," said I, " this is not the last time you will have occasion to make me suffer martyrdom."

Napoleon soon left Warsaw for the battle of Eylau, and established his head quarters at Osterode. Here I was appointed to the government of Thorn, whither I was directed to proceed to complete the restoration of my health. I forwarded provisions, artillery, and ammunition, to carry on the siege of Dantzic.

I was now the Providence of the Prussian Generals. They wrote to me intreating my intercession in their behalf. Blucher himself did not disdain to solicit the *grace* of his Majesty the Emperor and King of Italy. He was at first to have been conducted to Dijon, as has been already mentioned; but he had laid down arms, and therefore it signified little whether he was at Dijon or elsewhere. He was permitted to retire to Hamburgh; but he soon grew tired of that city, and begged to be allowed to go to the neighbourhood of Berlin. The following is the letter which he addressed to me on this subject :—

"Monsieur General,

"Your Excellency will probably remember that I had the honour of becoming acquainted with you some years ago, on your journey to Munster; and the marks of attention you then condescended to show me induce me to hope, that the unfortunate situation in which I am now placed will not be absolutely indifferent to you. I take the liberty of addressing your Excellency, to intreat your intercession with his Majesty the Emperor of France and King of Italy, that he may graciously order passports to be granted for myself, the two officers my sons, and the rest of my family, to enable us to retire to the environs of Berlin, or into Pomerania, to one of my estates. Having lost my all by the chances of war, I find it impossible to support the expenses attending a residence in a city where every thing is so enormously dear as in Hamburgh. Moreover I am in ill health, and I feel that it is only by living in the bosom of my family, and leading a very retired life, that I shall be able to recover myself.

"These reasons, and the generosity of his Majesty the Emperor, induce me to hope that he will deign to relieve my painful situation by permitting me to make choice of a place of residence; and the protection which your Excellency may condescend to grant me in this affair will add feelings of the deepest gratitude to the sentiments of high consideration, with which I have the honour to be,

"Your Excellency's
"Very humble and very obedient Servant,
"BLUCHER, Lieut.-Gen.

"Hamburgh, November 15, 1806."

The Emperor refused to grant the request, but the General cannot have forgotten the manner in which I treated him. It is in his power to say whether the French know how to respect misfortune.

On the surrender of Dantzic, I was appointed Governor of the city, with the rank of General-in-chief.

Napoleon arrived at Dantzic on the 29th of May, and he spent two days there. He expected that this new acquisition would afford immense resources, particularly in specie. I received the strictest orders to collect the contributions, which amounted to twenty millions, and which were extended to thirty in provisions by the treaty which I sometime after entered into with the town. I was furnished with a *carte blanche,* and was authorized to adopt any means I chose for effecting the collection; but I found the thing impossible. It occasioned me the greatest annoyance. Sometimes one measure of severity was resorted to, and sometimes another. The common people, as well as the richest and most considerable of the citizens, were all threatened in their turns. I constantly used my utmost endeavour to elude these violent orders; I spared the inhabitants of Dantzic many causes of discontent. At the peace, they still owed 17,000,000 of contributions.

Napoleon was present at the battles of Heilsberg, and Friedland. Eight days after his departure he wrote to me as follows:—

"M. de Talleyrand will proceed to Dantzic, and will stay with you some time. You will receive and treat him like a prince. You are aware of the esteem and attachment I entertain for that Minister," &c. He might have escaped many misfortunes had he never quarrelled with Talleyrand.

After the treaty of Tilsit, Napoleon sent me private instructions. He informed me of the probability of peace, and ordered me to keep a vigilant eye over Prussia and the Royal family. He was still incensed against William and his subjects. I could not guess the reason. Berthier explained it to me; and I did not think it a just one. Berthier came to Dantzic to deliver me fresh instructions, and to remind me of the directions I had received, to be on my guard against the plots which might be hatching around me. I was to remain at Dantzic until the cessation of hostilities. The Russians were for us. We had fine sport with the English; in less than two years those islanders were to be obliged to sue for peace.

In fine, I remained at Dantzic. I corresponded directly with Napoleon: most of his letters evinced an extraordinary degree of dissatisfaction, in which I must confess I myself participated for a considerable time.

The language and conduct of some Prussian officers contributed to keep up the prejudice against them. I treated them with great severity; the least fault was punished to the utmost; but at the same time I always rendered them justice, and never allowed them to be molested. Tranquillity, however, was restored. Each party mutually laid aside their animosity, and confidence was re-established. I saw and received the Prussians; and I may say, that from the first year after I obtained the command, all the reports which I forwarded to Paris were distinguished by moderation and truth. I represented to Napoleon that it was difficult for the Prussians so soon to forget their former greatness; that the public mind was becoming tranquil, and that the King, the ministers, and the Royal family never ceased to recommend to the people that resignation which misfortune renders indispensable.

I always wrote to this purport. I had no cause to complain of any one; for my own part, I was on very good terms with the civil and military authorities. I saw them frequently; and all of them, I may say, placed the greatest confidence in me. They were sensible of the justice of my proceedings.

All the commandants, however, did not act in the same way: their reports, and the disasters of Baylen, excited fresh doubts in Napoleon's mind with regard to the conduct of Prussia. He charged me to double my vigilance: "Overlook nothing in the Prussians," he said to me in one of his letters; "they must not be allowed to raise their heads."

The news of the disasters which we had experienced in the peninsula at length spread over Germany, and awakened new hopes; the public mind was violently agitated. I informed Napoleon of this; but he disliked the revival of painful recollections, and was still more averse to unpleasing anticipations of the future. He replied to me: "Germans are not Spaniards; the character of the German bears no resemblance to that of the fierce Catalonian."

CHAPTER XVIII.

The interview of Erfurt took place. Napoleon set out for Spain; he attacked and dispersed all that were opposed to him; and the English army would have been destroyed had he been enabled to pursue it himself; but the fourth Austrian war broke out, and he was obliged to hurry to the assistance of Bavaria. Prince Berthier sent me orders to rejoin the army. The Emperor was already with it; I found him at Landshut, just after he had gained the battle of Ratisbonne; I was not well pleased with my reception: he asked me drily, " How do your Prussians and Dantzickers get on? You ought to have made the latter pay me what they owe me. You see we have not all been killed in Spain; I still have men enough left to beat the Austrians." I felt the allusion.

We marched on Vienna. The Emperor became more good-humoured, and treated me more kindly. The battle of Esslingen took place. Thousands of brave men lost their lives; Marshal Lannes was disabled; the cavalry and artillery were destroyed; and the village of Esslingen, the most important point that remained for us to defend, was inundated by twenty battalions of Hungarian grenadiers. We could no longer maintain our station: the enemy had already penetrated into the square-work which Napoleon had directed to be fortified the day before. Count Lobau advanced to meet them, and checked their progress; but they immediately received reinforcements. The Emperor perceived this, and I was directed to take two battalions of the young guard, and to hasten to the assistance of our troops: I was to disengage them, to effect a retreat with them, and to take a position between the village and the remainder of the guard, on the banks of the Danube, near the bridge which had been broken. The Austrian columns advanced from all quarters on this point: our position became most hazardous. On our left, Massena still occupied Gros Aspern; he had lost great numbers of his force, but he still maintained his ground. I placed myself at the head of my two battalions and entered the village. I drew up my troops in the rear of General Mouton, and went to deliver to him the Emperor's orders; but the whole of the enemy's reserve, under the command of the Archduke Charles, deployed at some distance. " You have," said I to Count Lobau, "astonished those masses by your resistance; let us charge them with the bayonet, and drive them back upon the columns that are advancing: if we succeed, the Emperor and the army will give us credit for our success; if we fail, the responsibility will rest with me."— " With both of us," replied the General. Our five battalions moved forward, charged, repulsed, and dispersed the enemy at the point of the bayonet. We were masters of the village. The Archduke endeavoured in vain to recover it: five times he led his troops to the charge, and five times he was defeated. He experienced immense loss: ours was also considerable. Generals Mouton and Grosse were wounded; several other officers were killed. Napoleon was delighted with this affair; he complimented me very highly, and added, " If ever you did well in not executing my orders, you have done so to-day; for the safety of the army depended on the taking of Esslingen."

Napoleon thought that the people of Vienna were more unfavourable to us than in our preceding campaigns; he made the remark to me. I replied that despair had contributed greatly to produce the feeling; that the people were every where tired of us and of our victories. He did not like this sort of reflections.

Schill was then traversing Saxony: Napoleon was informed of the circumstance, and was vexed at it. This was a mode of sounding the public opinion. Prussia was making a prelude to that insurrectionary war, which she afterwards maintained against us. I confess, I did not believe the fact when I heard of it; I entertained too high an opinion of the national loyalty. I endeavoured to subdue the Emperor's prejudices; but his suspicions were stronger than any thing I could say to remove them. Another circumstance contributed to render him distrustful;—the conduct of the Russians was not more frank than that of the Prussians; they were shuffling. This want of good faith rendered him furious: he resolved to be revenged on them; but he required time for it.

The battle of Wagram took place: I was not engaged in it. Three days before the battle, I had accompanied Napoleon to the island of Lobau: I was in one of the Emperor's carriages with General Lauriston. We were overturned, and I had one of my shoulders dislocated, and three ribs broken.

The Emperor pursued the enemy as far as Znaim, and returned to establish himself at Schoenbrunn; where he afterwards learnt the defeat and death of Schill. This news gave him satisfaction, though he would have been better pleased had that partisan been taken prisoner.

During the negotiations there were several conspiracies at Vienna. Some persons, who were convicted of having been engaged in them, were condemned to death; two citizens and a Jew were to be executed; I was fortunate enough to obtain their pardon.

Napoleon was pretty generally in good humour; but the reports forwarded to him by the police occasionally interrupted his gaiety. His enemies had spread a ridiculous report of his insanity, which vexed him. "It is the fauxbourg St. Germain," said he, "which invents these fine stories; they will provoke me at last to send the whole tribe of them to *la Champagne pouilleuse.*"

One day I was soliciting him for the promotion of two officers: "I will not make so many promotions," said he; "Berthier has already made me do too much in that way." Then, turning to Lauriston; "Lauriston," said he, "we did not get on so fast in our time; did we? I continued for many years in the rank of Lieutenant!"— "That may be, Sire, but you have since made up famously for your lost time."—He laughed at my repartee, and my request was granted.

CHAPTER XIX.

MEANWHILE the negotiations for peace were proceeding very slowly, and Germany was still suffering. A young man, instigated by a blind feeling of patriotism, formed the design of delivering his country from him whom he regarded as the cause of its misfortunes. He presented himself at Schoenbrunn on the 23d October, while the troops were defiling: I was on duty; Napoleon was standing between the Prince de Neufchatel and me. The young man, who was named St. * * *, advanced to the Emperor. Berthier, conceiving that he was about to present a petition, stepped forward and told him to deliver it to me. He replied that he wished to speak to Napoleon; but he was again told, that if he had any communication to make, he must apply to the aide-de-camp on duty. He withdrew to a short distance, repeating that he would speak with Napoleon only. He came forward again, and approached very near the person of the Emperor. I drew him back and told him in German that he must withdraw: that if he had any thing to solicit, he would be heard after the parade. His right hand was thrust into a side-pocket under his great-coat, and he held a paper, one end of which was visible. I was struck with the expression of his eyes when he looked at me: his decided manner roused my suspicions. I called to an officer of gendarmerie who was on the spot, and ordered him to be put under arrest and conducted to the Castle. The attention of every one present was so occupied with the parade, that nobody noticed what was going forward. I was soon after informed that a large carving knife had been found on St. * * *. I told Duroc what I had learnt, and we went together to the place to which he had been conducted. We found him sitting on a bed, on which were laid the portrait of a young female, a portfolio, and a purse containing a few old louis-d'or. I asked his name. —" I can tell it only to Napoleon," was his reply. —" What did you intend to do with the knife that was found upon you?"—" That I can tell only to Napoleon."—" Did you propose to assassinate him?"—" Yes, Sir."—" Why?"—" That I can tell only to him."

I went to communicate this singular circumstance to the Emperor. He desired that the young man might be conducted to his closet. I went out to give this order; and on my return I found Bernadotte, Berthier, Savary, and Duroc, with the Emperor. St. * * * was brought in by two gendarmes, with his hands tied behind him. He appeared perfectly composed. The presence of Napoleon made not the least impression on him, but he saluted him respectfully. The Emperor asked him whether he could speak French, and he replied in a firm tone: " Very little." Napoleon then directed me to ask him, in his name, the following questions:—

" Where were you born?"—" In Naumburgh."—" What is your father?"—" A protestant minister."—" How old are you?"—" I am eighteen years of age."—" What did you intend to do with the knife?"—" To kill you."—" You are mad, young man ; you are an *illuminato*."—" I am not mad; and I know not what is meant by an *illuminato*."—" You are sick, then."—" I am not sick; on the contrary, I am in good health."—" Why did you wish to assassinate me?"—" Because you have caused the misfortunes of my country."—" Have I done you any harm?"—" You have done harm to me as well as to all Germans. "—" By whom were you sent? Who instigated you to this crime?"—" Nobody. I determined to take your life, from the conviction that I should thereby render the highest service to my country and to Europe."—" Is this the first time you ever saw me?" —" I saw you at Erfurt at the time of the interview."—"Did you then intend to assassinate me?" —" No; I thought that you would no longer wage war in Germany; I was then one of your most ardent admirers."—" How long have you been in Vienna?"—" Ten days."—"Why did you so long defer the execution of your design?"—" I came to Schoenbrunn a week ago; but the parade was over when I arrived, and I postponed the execution of my design until this day."—" I tell you, you are either mad or sick."—" Neither the one nor the other."—" Desire Corvisart to come here."— " Who is Corvisart?"—" He is a physician," I replied. " I have no need of him." We remained silent until the doctor arrived. St. * * * evinced the utmost indifference. At length Corvisart made his appearance. Napoleon directed him to feel the young man's pulse. " Am I not quite well, Sir?"—" He is in very good health," said the doctor, addressing himself to the Emperor.—" I told you so," said St.* * *, with an air of satisfaction.

Napoleon was embarrassed by the unconcerned manner of the offender.

"You are a wild enthusiast," said he; "you will ruin your family. I am willing to grant your life, if you ask pardon for the crime which you intended to commit, and for which you ought to be sorry."—" I want no pardon," replied St. * * *, " I feel the deepest regret for not having executed my design."—" You seem to think very lightly of the commission of a crime!"—" To kill you would not have been a crime, but a duty."—" Whose portrait is that that was found upon you?"—" It is the portrait of a young lady to whom I am attached."—" She will be very much distressed to hear of the unhappy situation in which you are placed!"—" She will regret to hear that I have not succeeded. She detests you no less than I do."—" Would you not be grateful were I to pardon you?"—" I would notwithstanding seize the first opportunity of taking your life."

Napoleon was confounded. He ordered the prisoner to be led away; and then entered into conversation with us, and said a great deal on the subject of the *illuminati*. In the evening he sent for me, and said: "The circumstance that occurred to-day is very extraordinary. The plots of Berlin and Weimar are at the bottom of this affair."—I repelled these suspicions. "Women are capable of any thing," resumed Napoleon.—

"Neither man nor woman connected with those two courts," I replied, "would ever conceive the idea of so atrocious a crime."—"Recollect the affair of Schill."—"It bears no resemblance to a crime like this."—"You may say what you please, General, but I know I am no favourite either at Berlin or Weimar."—"That's very true: you cannot reasonably expect to be a favourite at either of those courts. But because they dislike you, does it follow that they would assassinate you?" He communicated the same suspicions to * * * * *.

Napoleon ordered me to write to General Lauer, directing him to interrogate St. * * *, with the view of obtaining some confession from him. But he made none. He persisted in asserting that he had acted entirely from the impulse of his own mind, and not from the instigation of any one.

The departure from Schoenbrunn was fixed for the 27th of October. Napoleon rose at five in the morning and sent for me. We walked out to the great road to see the Imperial Guard pass along on its departure for France. We were alone. Napoleon again spoke to me of St. * * *. "That a young man of his age," said he, "a German, a protestant, and well educated, should attempt the commission of such a crime, is a thing unparalleled. Enquire how he died."

CHAPTER XX.

A HEAVY fall of rain obliged us to return from our walk. I wrote to General Lauer, requesting that he would give us an account of the last moments of St. * * *. He informed me that the prisoner had been executed at seven in the morning of the 27th; that he had taken no sustenance since the 24th; that food had been offered to him, but that he had constantly refused it, because, as he said, he had sufficient strength to walk to the place of execution. He was informed that peace was concluded; and this intelligence seemed to agitate him. His last words were:—*Liberty for ever! Germany for ever! Death to the Tyrant!* I delivered the report to Napoleon. He desired me to keep the knife that had been found upon the criminal: it is still in my possession.

Napoleon informed me that the preliminaries of the peace were not yet signed, but that the articles of the treaty were all drawn up, and that it would be ratified at Munich, where we were to stop.

We arrived at Nymphenburgh: the Court of Bavaria was residing there at the time. I had not had the honour of seeing the King since the campaign of Austerlitz. He lodged me in his palace, and gave me many proofs of his confidence and kindness. He described to me the unhappy situation of his subjects; and added, that if another state of things were not speedily established, he should be obliged to put the key under the door and set off. These were the expressions he used.

I bore this last conversation in mind; for I was determined to report it, not with the view of injuring the King, but for the sake of proving to Napoleon that all the indemnities which he granted to his allies were far from satisfying them and compensating for the burthens imposed on them by the war.

Peace was ratified. We left Nymphenburgh and arrived at Stuttgard. Napoleon was received in a style of magnificence, and was lodged in the palace, together with all his suite. The King was laying out a spacious garden, and men who had been condemned to the galleys were employed to labour in it. The Emperor asked the King who the men were who worked in chains: he replied that they were for the most part rebels who had been taken in his new possessions. We set out on the following day. On the way Napoleon alluded to the unfortunate wretches whom he had seen at Stuttgard. " The King of Wurtemberg," said he, " is a very harsh man; but he is very faithful: of all the sovereigns in Europe he possesses the greatest share of understanding." We stopped for an hour at Rastadt, where the Princes of Baden and Princess Stephanie had arrived for the purpose of paying their respects to the Emperor. The Grand Duke and Duchess accompanied him as far as Strasburgh. On his arrival in that city he received despatches which again excited his displeasure against the Faubourg St. Germain. We proceeded to Fontainbleau: no preparations had been made for the Emperor's reception; there was not even a guard on duty: but shortly after, the whole court arrived, as well as the different members of Napoleon's family.

The Emperor had several long conferences with the Minister of Police. He complained of the Faubourg St. Germain. The contrast of humility and boldness alternately displayed by the old nobility, in the anti-chambers and saloons, disconcerted him: he could scarcely conceive that these men were so base and perfidious as to destroy with the one hand while they solicited favours with the other. He appeared inclined to severity; but Fouché dissuaded him from that course. "It is a traditionary remark," said he, " that the Seine flows, the Faubourg intrigues, solicits, devours, and calumniates. This is in the order of nature; every thing has its attributes." Napoleon yielded; he avenged himself only on men. It was proposed that he should make a solemn entry into the capital; but this he declined: the conqueror of the world was superior to the triumphs which transported the Romans. On the following day the court left Fontainbleau. The Emperor rode to Paris without stirrups: he outstripped all his escort; none but a chasseur of the guard was able to keep up with him. In this manner he arrived at the Tuileries.

Napoleon was now approaching one of the most important epochs of his life.

CHAPTER XXI.

The Imperial divorce was publicly spoken of in Paris, but opinions varied with regard to the choice of the future Empress. The Princesses of Russia and Saxony, and the Archduchess of Austria, were talked of. The Russian alliance first became the subject of consideration. M. de Metternich learnt this and made overtures which were accepted. All the members of the Imperial family were, however, averse to the Austrian alliance. They dreaded the subtlety of the Vienna court, and foresaw that it would consent and lend itself to any thing the Emperor might require, until a favourable opportunity should occur, when the mask would be thrown off, and Austria would be foremost in bringing about his ruin; but the marriage was determined on, and remonstrances were useless. I was appointed to be present at the ceremony: this was no trifling favour, for a great part of the court was obliged to mingle with the crowd. I must confess, however, that I had no right to expect it, as I had indulged in some reflections on the divorce, which had been reported to the Emperor. I felt for Josephine, who had always proved herself amiable, simple, and unassuming. She was banished to Malmaison: I frequently visited her, and she made me the confidant of her sorrows. I have seen her weep for hours together; she spoke of her attachment for Bonaparte, for so she used to call him in our presence. She regretted the close of her splendid career: this was very natural.

The day after the marriage we received orders to attend and make the three bows to the Imperial couple, who were seated on the throne. I could not obey the summons, being confined by a headache, which attacks me pretty regularly every week; I sent to inform the Grand Marshal of this circumstance. Napoleon did not believe I was unwell; he thought I was unwilling to submit to the etiquette, and he was therefore displeased with me. He gave orders that I should return to Dantzic. The Duke de Feltre met me on the Boulevards, and communicated to me the Emperor's intentions. I applied for instructions: Napoleon answered drily, that I had only to keep watch over Prussia, to treat the Russians with respect, and to give an account of what was going on in the ports of the Baltic; adding that I might dispense with passing through Berlin. I stayed a few days at Strasburg, and Frankfort, and arrived on the 10th of June at Dantzic.

I was very well received by the troops and the inhabitants. They complained very much of General Grabowski: the Dantzickers did not like him, but they were in the wrong, he was an excellent man.

The garrison was soon increased. It received an augmentation of Saxon, Baden, Wurtemburgh, Westphalian, and Hessian troops: they formed a complete army. This increase of force displeased me, because it imposed a heavy burthen on the citizens: for my own part, I had no reason to complain. The sentiments of the troops were by no means equivocal, and their respective sovereigns, with but few exceptions, seized that opportunity of assuring me of their good will. I shall content myself with the insertion of the King of Bavaria's letter.

"Munich, April 15, 1811.

"My dear Rapp,

"You are about to have my 14th regiment of infantry under your command: I recommend it to your kindness and attention. The Colonel is a brave man, who will fulfil his duty. The Lieutenant-colonel and the two Majors are valuable men, as are all the officers of the regiment. The troops are excellent, and in good condition: they are very well pleased, my dear General, to be placed under the command of an officer like you; *und noch dazu ein Elsasser,* (and moreover a native of Alsace.)

" Address yourself directly to me whenever you may have any thing to communicate relative to the welfare of my troop, if you have any complaint to make, or if it fails in the discharge of its duty—a circumstance which I hope will not occur. I eagerly seize this opportunity, my dear Rapp, to repeat to you the assurance of my constant friendship.

" MAXIMILIAN JOSEPH."

I received instructions to close the port of the town, and to watch those of Prussia. Davoust came to take the command of Hamburgh: I was not under his orders, but I was to correspond with him, and with M. de St. Marsan. Though I was not acquainted with the latter gentleman, yet I esteemed him greatly; his letters proved him to be a worthy man, who was desirous of seeing harmony restored between the two nations. This was also my wish.

Our opinions perfectly agreed. * * * * * * * frequently wrote to advise me not to place confidence in that diplomatist, whom he described as a traitor sold to King William and his ministers. He doubtless wrote to the same effect to Napoleon; but fortunately, when that prince had once formed his opinion with respect to any individual, he paid little attention to the reports that were addressed to him. Nothing short of finding him, as Napoleon himself expressed it, with his hand in his pocket, could induce him to withdraw his confidence.

My situation, however, became disagreeable. On the one side, the Dantzickers complained of the maintenance of the troops, of the burthens that were imposed upon them, and of being deprived of their trade. On the other, the ministers urged me to collect the contributions in order to meet the expenses of a secret expedition and the extension of the fortifications. The contractors threatened to stop the supplies. I knew not what to do. I derived some funds from the taxes raised on Prussia; but these were insufficient. However, by dint of perseverance and representations, I succeeded in obtaining the sums necessary for paying the supplies, and by degrees the town was relieved from that burthen.

Funds were assigned to me for completing the fortifications, and making the necessary preparations for the secret expedition, which however was no longer a secret.

The French ministers once proposed to Napoleon to have the garrison maintained by the Prussian government. A letter was written to me for my advice on this subject, and I replied, that if ever such a determination should be entered into, I would immediately quit Dantzic, in spite of every consideration. I must do justice to Marshal Davoust, who was likewise consulted in this business. He showed that the measure was dangerous and impracticable. The idea was abandoned.

I cannot pass over in silence a strange misunderstanding in which I became involved at Dantzic.

I gave a dinner to which I invited the Prussian and Russian residents. I placed the former on my right hand and the latter on my left. The Russian resident took offence at this arrangement. He imagined I intended to affront him, the Russian court, and all the Russians in the world. He complained of my conduct; and his complaint was transmitted from St. Petersburgh to M. de Champagny, who communicated it to Napoleon. I was blamed; I was said to have been wanting in the respect due to the resident of a great nation, in assigning the post of honour to the resident of Prussia, and I was called upon to make reparation for the error I had committed. I confess I felt hurt at this. My reply to the minister was that I did not give diplomatic dinners; that the foreign Consuls were not accredited with the Governor but with the Senate; that I might place beside me at my own table whomsoever I pleased; that I conceived the complaints of the resident to be ridiculous, and that 1 would not receive him again. I kept my word, and here the affair ended. I consider it proper to relate this anecdote, because it proves the attempts which were making even at that period to conciliate the good graces of Russia.

CHAPTER XXII.

Nothing could have been more repugnant to the wishes of the Dantzickers than having among them French custom-house officers, whom for some time there had been an idea of establishing at Dantzic. I repelled the proposition as strenuously as I possibly could. The presence of these officers would have destroyed the small portion of trade which I still tolerated, notwithstanding the outcries of Napoleon.

This measure would have been felt as no less a grievance along the whole coast of the Baltic, which, I frankly confess, I did not watch with the vigilance that was prescribed to me. Complaints were in consequence poured out against me; but I knew from whence they proceeded, and I did not concern myself much about them. Napoleon was, however, enraged at my indulgence; he reproached me for it. " To allow the Prussians and Dantzickers to carry on trade," said he, " is to betray me." * * * * * wrote to the same effect, and sent spies in every direction. Napoleon became tired of reports and complaints. He directed Bertrand to inform me how much he was dissatisfied with me. That General wrote to me, " The Emperor knows, my dear Rapp, that you permit contraband trade in Prussia and at Dantzic; I must inform you that he is displeased with you," &c. Outcries were raised, but I paid no regard to them, and continued to exercise my power with moderation. The Custom-house establishment was set on foot. It is well known how severely it was felt, particularly in the conquered countries. The individuals connected with this department in Dantzic aped independence, and refused to obey any orders save those of the Minister Sucy. In support of these pretensions reference was made to the example of the Custom establishment of Hamburgh. I cut the matter short, by sending the Director of the Customs to Weichselmunde, where he underwent six days' imprisonment. Such an act of severity was unexampled; it was accounted as great a crime as high treason. The minister complained of it; but, to his great surprise, Napoleon replied, that if I had inflicted punishment I had reasons for doing so. " Besides," said he, " Dantzic is in a state of siege, and in that case a Governor is omnipotent." The officers of the Customs learnt that they had presumed too much on their credit; they became more circumspect, and behaved themselves better to the Dantzickers. Trade recovered a certain degree of security, which was augmented by my releasing several ships that had been captured by our pirates. Fresh remonstrances were made, but with no better success than before.

I received orders to commit all articles of English merchandize to the flames. This measure would have been most disastrous: I evaded it, and notwithstanding the presence of the officers of the Customs, Dantzic lost no more than what amounted to two hundred francs, and Kœnigsberg still less. I do not speak of the merchandize procured by captures.

The continental system, and the rigorous measures employed by Napoleon in the North of Germany, excited more and more dissatisfaction. The people were exasperated. I was frequently applied to for reports on their situation: I described them such as they really were—oppressed, ruined, and driven to the last extremity. I pointed out those secret societies, in which the whole nation was enrolled, where hatred brooded on vengeance, and despair collected and combined her plans. But Napoleon looked upon those societies with contempt. He little knew the character of the Germans. He thought they possessed neither vigour nor energy; he compared them and their pamphlets to " those little dogs who bark but dare not bite." At a later period we learned, by experience, what they were capable of.

I was also frequently called upon for reports respecting the affairs of Russia and the army which was assembling at Wilna. I was applied to for my opinion as to what course France or Germany would adopt, in case of an expedition to the other side of the Niemen turning out unfortunate, or failing altogether. My answer was literally as follows. It will be difficult to give credit to a prediction which has unfortunately been so fully realised: —

" If your Majesty should experience reverses, you may be assured that the Russians and Germans would all rise in a mass to throw off the yoke. A crusade would be set on foot. All your allies would abandon you: even the King of Bavaria, on whom you place so much reliance, would join the coalition. I make an exception only in favour of the King of Saxony; he, perhaps, would remain faithful to you; but his subjects would compel him to make common cause with your enemies."

Napoleon, as may be supposed, was not well

pleased with this communication. He sent it to Marshal Davoust, directing him to peruse it, and to write to inform me that the Emperor was greatly astonished that one of his aides-de-camp could have presumed to address such a letter to him,— that my reports resembled the pamphlets published on the other side of the Rhine, which I appeared to find pleasure in reading,—that, finally, the Germans should never be treated as Spaniards. The Marshal executed his commission, and I was for a long time out of favour with Napoleon. Experience has proved whether or not my judgment was correct; and I took the liberty to make that remark to the Emperor, as I shall state hereafter.

When he obliged the King of Prussia to send to Magdeburgh all the prohibited merchandize which had been confiscated at Konigsberg, I addressed him in the most urgent tone: I represented to him how much that measure was calculated to excite discontent, and to exasperate the nation. M. de Clerambaut, who was then Consul General, wrote to him in the same strain; but our representations were not attended to.

The war with Russia was on the eve of breaking out; Napoleon deliberated as to the course he should pursue with regard to Prussia. To enter into an alliance with King William would not have been the means of subduing the doubts and prejudices of that monarch. To dethrone him would have been a violent measure; but it was one, however, which was advised by many persons whom I will not name. The Emperor was urged to deprive the Prussian monarch of his States, and to keep possession of them himself. Perhaps William has never yet been made fully acquainted with the danger which threatened him; I knew its full extent: I pitied the King of Prussia and his subjects, and I opposed the design to the utmost of my power.

Instructions had already been sent to ****. That general expected to commence his march immediately. What was his astonishment when, instead of an order for invading Prussia, he received information of a treaty of alliance with that country? The intelligence of that event afterwards reached me, and it afforded me great satisfaction.

CHAPTER XXIII.

The grand army was already on the Vistula. Napoleon quitted Paris, repaired to the capital of Saxony, and thence to Dantzic. He had been preceded by the King of Naples, who had solicited permission to go to Dresden, but without success. The refusal had mortified him exceedingly: he told me that the Emperor caused him great vexation and unhappiness; such, at least, was his own account. We were the first persons whom the Emperor received. He began the conversation with me by a rather odd question—" What do these Dantzickers do with their money; they gain a good deal, and I spend a good deal among them?" I replied that their situation was far from being prosperous—that they were suffering greatly; in short, that they were at their last gasp. "There will be a change soon," he replied, " that is agreed upon; but I will keep them to myself."

He was fatigued, and in consequence the King of Naples and I withdrew. I was recalled in a moment, and I remained with the Emperor while he dressed. He asked me several questions respecting the duty of the fortress. When he was dressed, and his valet-de-chambre had left the room, he said, " Well, General Rapp, the Prussians have become our allies, and the Austrians will shortly be so too." " Unfortunately, Sire," replied I, " we do a great deal of mischief as allies; I receive complaints against our troops from all quarters." " That is merely a passing cloud," said he: " I shall see whether Alexander really intends to go to war; I will avoid it if I can." Then, changing the conversation all at once, he said, " Did you observe how queer Murat looked? he seems ill." I replied, " No, Sire, he is not ill, but out of humour.'—"Why out of humour?" said he; " is he not satisfied with being a King?"— " He says, he is not a King."—" Why, then, does he act so like a fool? He ought to be a Frenchman, and not a Neapolitan."

In the evening I had the honour to sup with Napoleon, the King of Naples, and the Prince de Neufchatel. Before we sat down to table we conversed on the subject of the war with Russia: we were in the saloon. The Emperor suddenly perceiving a marble bust on a bracket, said, " Whose head is that?" " Sire," I replied, " it is the Queen of Prussia's." " So, General Rapp, you keep the bust of the fair Queen in your house: She did not like me." "Sire," I replied, "I presume I may be allowed to possess the bust of a pretty woman: besides she is the wife of a King who is now your ally."

Next morning we went out on horseback; Napoleon visited the fortress, and did not appear satisfied with the works. When he perceived that I was not aware what object displeased him, he flew into a passion and said, before a number of persons, "That he did not understand why his governors took upon themselves to act the part of sovereigns, and that he wished his orders to be executed." There had, indeed, been a little deviation from the strict letter of his commands; but it was trifling, and was not worth the words that were made about it. The King of Naples said to me, in a low tone of voice, "Do not vex yourself about these reproaches; the Emperor is out of temper. He received letters this morning which put him in an ill humour." We afterwards returned home. Napoleon received the generals and officers under my command, as well as the civil authorities. To the latter he put many questions respecting trade and finances. They deplored the state of their affairs. "It will change soon," said he, "I will keep you to myself; it is a thing determined upon: none but the great families prosper." Then perceiving M. de Franzins the elder, he said, "You do not complain, M. de Franzins; your affairs are in a thriving condition; you have amassed a fortune of at least ten millions."

In the evening I had again the honour of supping with Napoleon, the King of Naples, and the Prince de Neufchatel. Napoleon maintained silence for a long time: at length he suddenly asked how far it was from Dantzic to Cadiz. "Too far, Sire," I replied. "Ah! I understand you, General," said he; "but we shall be further off a few months hence."—"So much the worse," I added. The King of Naples and the Prince de Neufchatel did not speak a word. "I see, Gentlemen," said Napoleon, "that you do not wish for war. The King of Naples does not like to leave his beautiful kingdom, Berthier wishes to hunt at Gros Bois, and General Rapp longs to be back to his superb hotel in Paris." "I must confess," I observed, "Sire, that your Majesty has not spoiled me; I know very little of the pleasures of the capital."

Murat and Berthier continued to observe profound silence: they seemed to be piqued at something. After dinner they told me that I had done right to speak as I did to Napoleon. "But," replied I, "you should not have allowed me to speak alone."

CHAPTER XXIV.

Napoleon quitted Dantzic, and proceeded to Konigsberg. Murat accompanied him, and General Belliard was also there. He spoke to them a great deal about Spain, and his brother, with whom he was dissatisfied. General Flahaut returned from a mission on which he had been sent to Prince Schwartzenberg. He rendered an account of the devotedness of the Prince, and of his impatience to attack the Russians. The Emperor did not appear to place perfect reliance on the sincerity of the Prince; however, he allowed himself to be persuaded that, at length, his protestations might become sincere, and that benefits might inspire sentiments of gratitude. He explained his plan and intentions as follows:—" If Alexander," said he, " persists in his refusal to execute the conventions which we have mutually entered into, if he will not accede to the last proposals I made him, I will pass the Niemen, defeat his army, and possess myself of Russian Poland. This last territory I will unite to the Grand Duchy: I will convert it into a kingdom; where I will leave 50,000 men, whom the country must support. The inhabitants wish to form themselves again into a national corps. They are a warlike people, and will soon possess a numerous and disciplined force. Poland wants arms: I will supply them: she will be a check upon the Russians; a barrier against the irruptions of the Cossacks. But I am embarrassed on one point; I know not what course to adopt with regard to Galicia. The Emperor of Austria, or rather his Council, is reluctant to part with it: I have offered ample compensation for it, but it has been refused. I must await the course of events, which alone can show us what ought to be done. Poland, if well organized, may furnish 50,000 cavalry,—what say you, General Belliard?" "I think so, Sire," replied the General; "if your Majesty would mount the infantry of the Vistula on horseback, it would make excellent light cavalry, and might thus be successfully opposed to the cloud of Cossacks which precede the Russian forces."—The Emperor said, "We shall see what can be done. You will return with Murat and leave your Swiss: by the by, what do you think of the Swiss?"—"They will march, Sire; they will fight. They have improved greatly; they would not be known for the same troops that they were six weeks ago. I will go and see them to-morrow."—"Well," observed the Emperor, "rejoin Murat and inspect all the cavalry in company with him."

The proposals which the Emperor had spoken of were not accepted. The Russians complained of our forces and our commercial measures, and they required that we should evacuate Germany. We marched forward and arrived on the banks of the Niemen, which five years before had been the scene of our victories. The troops raised shouts of joy. Napoleon proceeded to the advanced posts, disguised as a chasseur, and reconnoitred the banks of the river, in company with General Axo. He afterwards spoke for a few moments with the King of Naples; pointing out to him the points at which it would be proper to throw bridges over the river, and directing him to concentrate his troops, in order that the passage might be rapidly effected. The cavalry was mounted; the infantry was under arms; never was there a grander spectacle. Eblé set to work; the pontoons were laid at midnight: at one o'clock we were on the right bank of the Niemen, and General Pajol was at Kowsno, which had been evacuated by Bagawouth, and we took possession of it without striking a blow. We continued to press on; we marched incessantly, but we perceived only a few Pulks of Cossacks blending with the line of the horizon. We arrived at Wilna, and found its immense magazines in flames. We extinguished the fire, and the greater part of the provisions were saved.

CHAPTER XXV.

The conflagration, the sight of the ground which had been so often trodden by the Polish legions on their return from their glorious expeditions, excited fresh ardour; the troops were inspired by the force of their recollections. We dashed on in pursuit of the enemy; but the rain fell in torrents and the cold had become severe. We were now in the bogs and quagmires of Pultusk, and we were destitute both of shelter and clothing. All this, however, would have been nothing, had the Russians ventured to let us come up with them; but they reached the Borysthenes and crossed the Dwina, flying and ravaging the country which they passed through: we were maintaining a racing contest, rather than carrying on a war. They had now lost all unity and connexion, and we abandoned the hope of coming to an engagement. The enemy, however, having gained ground by dint of speed, succeeded in rallying his forces, and he took refuge in the works which he had constructed at Drissa. But he was soon in danger of being attacked in his intrenchments and of having his retreat cut off. He did not venture to incur this double risk, and therefore fled. He would have been lost, had he delayed for a few hours: all the necessary arrangements were made for attacking his flank and intercepting him. He owed his safety to a *coup de main*. Some of our advanced corps, not being sufficiently vigilant, were surprised by Wittgenstein. Napoleon concluded that the Russians were marching upon us, and halted his columns. This delay saved them: when we arrived at Beszenkownzi they had effected their retreat. The King of Naples followed them. He came up with them, and attacked them at Ostrowno. He charged them some leagues further on and routed all their rear-guard. The following is his report, which I insert because it is characteristic of the manner of this prince, who deserved to die only on the field of battle:—

" I ordered the first corps of the reserve of cavalry

and two battalions of light infantry to advance. They were followed by Delzons' division. We came up with the enemy's rear-guard about two leagues from Ostrowno. It was advantageously posted behind a deep ravine, with a great mass of artillery, and having its front and flanks covered by thick woods. A little firing took place on both sides; I sent the battalions to check the enemy's infantry who were repulsing our hussars. Delzons' division arrived and the cavalry had nothing farther to do. The Viceroy made his arrangements, and we marched upon the enemy and crossed the ravine. The foreign cavalry which lined the bank of the Dwina protected our left, and debouched in the plain. The rest of the light troops advanced along the high road in proportion as the enemy's infantry retrograded. The cuirassiers were left in reserve behind the ravine, and the batteries were mounted. My right was covered by immense woods, and I had numerous parties of pioneers. The enemy was driven to the second position in the rear of the ravine, where the reserve was stationed. He brought us back into the ravine, and he was again repulsed : he drove us back a second time, and was on the point of taking our guns, which had got entangled in a defile, through which they were passing in order to take a position on the heights. Our left was repulsed, and the enemy made a bold movement on our right: the foreign brigade was on the point of being dispersed. In this state of things nothing but a charge of cavalry could enable us to recover ourselves; I attempted it. We advanced to meet the enemy's infantry, which was marching boldly along the plain. The brave Poles rushed on the Russian battalions: not a man escaped, not a single prisoner was made; all were killed, not even the wood protected them from the sabres of our cavalry. At the same time the squares were broken by the charge. General Girardin, who was leading the battalions on the left, made a movement on the right, and advanced along the high road on the enemy's rear; the troops on the right performed the same manœuvre. General Piré supported them; he charged at the head of the eighth hussars. The enemy was routed, and owed his safety only to the ravines which retarded our advance. The whole division followed the movement: the infantry advanced along the high road and the cavalry debouched on the heights. I gave orders for firing on five or six cavalry regiments that were before us. In this situation your Majesty came up with me; you ordered me to pursue the enemy, and I drove him to a league and a half beyond Witepsk.

Such, Sire, is the narrative of our late engagement with the Russians. The enemy has had about three thousand killed and a great number wounded; we have scarcely lost a man. This result was, in a great measure, the work of Count Belliard, who on this occasion gave new proofs of his devotedness and courage. To him we are indebted for the preservation of the artillery of Delzons' division."

Fatigue and even lassitude have, in the long run, the effect of inspiring courage. Barclay experienced this. He several times entertained the design of risking the fate of a battle; but a foreboding of defeat constantly possessed him at the sight of our troops. Whenever he found them within sight, he hurried his retreat; he beheld without concern his magazines, his guns, and his works fall into our hands. He had but one object in view, which was to keep constantly a few leagues in advance of us. Bagration imitated this example, but he occasionally evinced resolution. He had several engagements with our advance-guard. Marshal Davoust pursued him vigorously; but the King of Westphalia advanced but slowly. A dispute arose between this sovereign and Vandamme; and, in consequence, the orders were not executed. This circumstance saved the Russian Prince. He gained ground, reached Mohiloff, and was beaten: he certainly would have fared worse but for the dispute between Vandamme and the King of Westphalia, which Napoleon of course could not foresee. The Russians, who were dispersed along the banks of the Niemen, combined their forces on the shores of the Borysthenes. They were preparing for the defence, and we for the attack of Smolensko.

CHAPTER XXVI.

I had left Dantzick, and I traversed Lithuania; the country was dreary, it was made up of woods and steeps—an unlimited picture of poverty and desolation. It was at that season of the year when Nature displays her riches, yet vegetation was weak and drooping, every thing in those fatal countries depicted wretchedness, every thing foretold the disasters which were to overwhelm us.

The rain still continued, the roads were broken up, and impassable, the men were losing themselves in the mud, and perishing from fatigue and hunger: ten thousand horses lay lifeless on the ground that we had gone over within these two days; never had such a frightful mortality before signalized the commencement of a campaign; our soldiers, continually sliding on the clayey ground, were exhausted in fruitless exertions: most of them were unable to keep up, they lagged behind; the allied troops especially had a prodigious number in arrear. It was easy to foresee that the issue of the war would be disastrous: we had in our favour force and courage, but Nature took part with them;—we were to fall. However, I arrived at Wilna; I found there the Duke de Bassano, whose prognostics were less gloomy, General Hogendorp, Napoleon's aide-de-camp, with whom I was yet unacquainted, and General Jomini, who afterwards deserted our colours. All augured better than myself of the struggle in which we were engaged. It presented itself, indeed, under specious auspices: all Poland was in motion; men, women, peasants, citizens, gentlemen, all were animated with the most noble enthusiasm; troops were organising, administrations were forming, resources were collecting, and the people were preparing themselves to drive oppression beyond the Borysthenes. The Diet of Warsaw had opened;

the Polish nation, which had so long been beaten by the tempest, thought that it had at last reached a port; no sacrifice seemed too much for it. The speech of the President had excited general acclamations, every where it had been received with joy. I was curious to read it; M. de Bassano gave it me. "It might have been better," he observed, "but still it is tolerable." The Emperor would have wished it stronger in facts, and its expressions less tinged with the affectation of learning. It was the energy of the patriot, and not the measured movements of the orator, that was necessary in so serious a juncture; nevertheless it produced its effect.

"For a long time there had existed in the centre of Europe a celebrated nation, mistress of an extensive and fruitful country, brilliant with the double glory of war and arts, protecting for ages, with an unwearied arm, the barriers of Europe against the barbarians who raged around its frontiers. A numerous people prospered in this land. Nature repaid their labours with liberality. Often had her kings taken a place in history by the side of those who had most honoured the supreme rank.

"This country is Poland; you are that people: but what are you become? How has the dilaceration of our country been effected? How has this family, which even when it was divided did not separate, which had remained united through ages of divisions, how has this powerful family seen itself dismembered? What have been its crimes, who its judges? By what right has it been attacked, invaded, effaced from the list of states and nations? Whence have the oppressors come, whence the chains? The indignant universe would answer us—every state, every people would tell us that it thought that it saw its tomb open by the side of that of Poland; and that in the audacious profanation of the laws on which all societies alike repose, in the insulting contempt which was manifested for them to accomplish our ruin, the world might think itself put in subjection to the temporary purposes of monarchs, and that now it would have no other law. Europe, alarmed and threatened, would point out to our just resentment the empire which, while it caressed us, was particularly preparing to press upon her with an increased force. It is Russia that is the author of all our evils. Within a century she advances with gigantic stride towards a people who before were ignorant of her name.

"Poland perceived immediately the first effects of this increase of the Russian power. Placed in her immediate vicinity, she received her first, as her last blows. Who could enumerate them from the time when, in 1717, Russia tried her influence by the disbanding of the Polish army? Since that epoch, what moment has been exempt from her influence or her outrages? If this crafty power joined herself to Poland, it is to impose on her, as in 1764, that fatal guarantee which made the integrity of our frontiers dependent on the perpetuation of anarchy; to make that anarchy the means of accomplishing her ambitious designs. The world knows what they have been since that unlucky epoch. It is since then that, by partition after partition, Poland has been seen completely to disappear, without crime and without vengeance; it is since that time that the Poles have heard with indignation the insulting language of the Repnins, of the Sivers; it is since then that the Russian soldier bathed himself in the blood of their fellow-citizens, as a prelude to that for ever execrable day, must we recall it, in which, in the midst of the shouts of a savage conqueror, Warsaw heard the cries of the population of Prague, which was destroyed by fire and murder. Pole, for it is time to make that name which we should never lose resound in your ears, these are the hateful means by which Russia has succeeded in appropriating to herself our fine provinces; these are the claim, the only claim, she possesses on us. Force alone could enchain us, force may also break the fetters which she alone has forged. These fetters shall be broken. Poland, then, shall exist,—what do we say? She exists already, or rather she has never ceased to exist. How can the perfidy, the plots, the violence, under which she has fallen—how can they have affected her right? Yes, we are still Poland; we are so by the title that we hold from nature, from society, from our ancestors, from those sacred titles which the universe recognizes, and which form the safeguard of mankind."

I was carried away by enthusiasm. I had so often seen the brave Polish legions in Italy, in Egypt, and elsewhere! They were right indeed, they were still Poland. "In point of courage," I said to the Duke, "nothing will surprise me on the part of this brave people; but I own I did not suspect it of this sort of talent." "You are right," replied M. de Bassano, "they have plenty of other things to do than to make harangues!" "Who, then, is the writer?" "The Abbé." "What Abbé? Do you think the Emperor has a predilection for churchmen?" "No; but in fine, at the present time, it is not without powerful considerations that an embassy is confided to a priest." "Is it the

Archbishop?" "The very man; we have sent him to Warsaw to intoxicate the Poles by his eloquence. I do not think him very skilful in business, but he is entirely devoted to the Emperor;—that is the main affair. His enemies accuse him of being ambitious and restless, without steadiness in his affections, or in his ideas of praising white and black; of being the mere creature of circumstance. I believe this picture a caricature. I myself am persuaded that, if events compromise the glory of our arms, he will not be seen among the ranks of our detractors." " I firmly believe it; he has abused the Cossacks too much ever to become their patriarch."

The deputation of the Diet was still at Wilna. I was acquainted with a few of the members. I saw them; they talked to me of their hopes, of their means, of their rights. These ideas struck me, I gave an account of them to the Duke.— " You are admirable!" said he in reply. " What! do you not recognize the Archbishop? Do you not see with what art he betrays himself? and these biblical reminiscences, to whom would you have them occur but to a priest. Besides I will give you the document."

" Sire, the Diet of the Grand Duchy of Warsaw, assembled at the approach of the powerful armies of your Majesty, recognized at the outset that it had rights to reclaim and duties to fulfil; with an unanimous voice, it has constituted itself a general confederation of Poland; it has declared the kingdom of Poland re-established in its rights; and, at the same time, that the acts of usurpation and arbitrary power, by which its existence had been destroyed, were null and of no effect.

"Sire, your Majesty labours for posterity and for history. If Europe cannot mistake our rights, she can still much less mistake our duties. A free and independent nation, since the remotest times, we have not lost our territory and our independence, either by treaties or by conquest, but by perfidy and treachery. Treachery has never constituted rights. We have seen our last king dragged away to St. Petersburgh, where he perished; and our nation torn to shreds by princes with whom we were not at war, and by whom we have not been conquered.

" Our rights appear thus evident to the eyes of God and men. We, Poles, we have the right to re-establish the throne of the Jagellons and Sobieskis, to re-assert our national independence, to re-assemble our divided members, to arm ourselves in defence of our native country, and to prove, by fighting in its defence, that we are the worthy descendants of our ancestors.

"Can your Majesty disown us or blame us, for having done that which our duty, as Poles, demanded of us; and for having resumed our rights? Yes, Sire. Poland is proclaimed from this day; she exists by the laws of equity, but she ought to exist in fact; right and justice proclaim our resolution to be legitimate; but it ought to be supported on our part. Has not God punished Poland enough for its divisions? will he perpetuate our misfortunes? and must the Poles, after having cherished the love of their country, go down to the tomb wretched and without hope? No, Sire. You have been sent by Providence, power is placed in the hands of your Majesty, and the existence of the Grand Duchy is due to the power of your arms.

"Say, Sire, Let the kingdom of Poland exist! and the decree will be to the world equivalent to the reality. We are sixteen millions of Poles, among whom there is not one whose blood, arms, and fortune, are not devoted to your Majesty: every sacrifice will appear to us light, if it has for its object the re-establishment of our native country. From the Dwina to the Dniester, from the Borysthenes to the Oder, one word only from your Majesty will command every arm, every effort, every heart. This unexampled war which Russia has dared to declare, notwithstanding the recollections of Austerlitz, Pultusk, Eylau, Friedland; in spite of the oaths taken at Tilsit and at Erfurth, is, we have no doubt, an effect of Providence, which, moved by the misfortunes of our nation, has determined to bring them to a termination. The second Polish war has only just begun, and already we pay our homage to your Majesty in the capital of the Jagellons. Already are the eagles of your Majesty on the Dwina, and the armies of Russia, separated, divided, cut up, wander in uncertainty, and seek in vain to unite and to form themselves, &c."

"It is well.—Yes, undoubtedly; but he is so enchanted with the *chef-d'œuvre*, that he would think himself wanting to his glory if he did not publish to the world that his genius protects Poland. Twenty times a-day I am obliged to moderate these excesses of self-love. This very morning I have been remonstrating with him on the impropriety of his freaks of vanity. He *Ossianizes;* do you recollect the word? It describes him admirably. But now, if his style goes well, his embassy scarcely moves. But for Duroc, who covers him with his wing, I would have already sent him to his flocks. What the devil has the almonership in common with embassies? Why should he put himself to the trouble of so much exertion, to do nothing of any possible use?"

CHAPTER XXVII.

I RESUMED my route: it was through forests, steeps, every thing that is most wild in nature; but I met at every step officers who were going on missions; they gave me news of my friends, of the army. I forgot the scenes that I was passing through; I discussed the probable chances of the war; they talked to me of the valour of the troops, of the prodigious activity of the Emperor. It was indeed inconceivable, the movements, the administrations, the measures of security and precaution; he embraced every thing, he was equal to every thing. The instructions that were given to M. d'Hautpoult are an example of it. They merit preservation.

" The orderly officer d'Hautpoult will go to Ostrowno, and from thence to Beszenkowiczi. He will see at Ostrowno whether the village is inhabited, and whether it has an engineer to reorganize it; he will see at Beszenkowiczi whether the bridges are erected, and if a bridge of rafts has been substituted for the fixed one, which would not stand the first swelling of the river; he will see whether the *tête-du-pont* is in progress; he will see also the hospital, the workhouse, the magazines, and in fine, if the country begins to be re-organized. He will give me an account of the troops that he may meet, whether cavalry, artillery, or military equipages. He will see at Beszenkowiczi the fourth regiment of the chasseurs of the guard, and the battalion of Hesse Darmstadt, which I have commanded to remain there till farther orders. There should also be there several pieces of artillery; he must take care that every thing be in its proper position, and that the works at the *tête-du-pont* be proceeded with in order to finish it. He will inform himself if there are any news of the Cossacks, and, if it is necessary, he will remain one day at Beszenkowiczi in order to see every thing, and draw up his despatch. He will write to me from that quarter, taking care to send his letter by the first estafette that may pass through Beszenkowiczi. He will continue his road to Polozk, from whence he will send me his second despatch; he will see the functionaries of the town, hospital, and workhouse. He will inform me how many prisoners the Duke de Reggio has taken in the different affairs which have just taken place; how many wounded; all that he can learn on this matter, and on the situation of the Duke de Reggio's corps. The Duke de Tarentum having taken Dünabourg, the orderly officer d'Hautpoult will learn whether the communication between the two corps has been effected. He will get every information which can make me acquainted with the nature of the forces opposed to the Duke de Reggio; he will remain with this Marshal (to whom he will send the inclosed letter) till he shall have attacked the enemy, cleared the right bank of the river, and effected his communication with Dünabourg.

"NAPOLEON."

But all this vigilance did not remedy the evil. The soldiers who were unable to keep up with their corps increased visibly; they encumbered our rear. I gave an account to the Emperor, whom I joined at the *bivouac* three leagues on this side of Smolensko, of the melancholy picture that I had had incessantly before my eyes during the whole of my journey. "It is the effect of long marches; I will strike a great blow, and every one will rally. You come from Wilna. What is Hogendorp doing?

he is wallowing in indolence. Has he not his wife with him?" I knew nothing about it; I could not answer. Napoleon replied, " If he had his wife, she must go back to France, or at least that he must send her to Germany on the rear. Berthier is going to write to him." Some papers were brought in that had just been translated; some were the accounts of the victories in which some handfuls of Cossacks had beaten us all; others were proclamations and addresses, in which we were designated as a troop of missionaries. " See," said Napoleon to me, " you had no suspicion that we were apostles; but here it is proved that we are coming with damnation for the Russians. These poor Cossacks are going to become idolators. But here is another of a different kind; here, read, it is pure Russian. Poor Platoff! All are of equal strength in these dreary climates!" I read it; it was a long rhapsody with which the patriarch seasoned a relic of St. Sergius that he offered to the Emperor Alexander. He ended it with this paragraph: "The city of Moscow, the first capital of the empire, the new Jerusalem, receives its Christ, as a mother, in the arms of her zealous sons; and through the mist which is rising foreseeing the brilliant glory of his power, it sings in transports, Hosanna, blessed be he who cometh!

Let the arrogant, the brazen Goliath carry from the borders of France mortal terror to the confines of Russia; pacific religion, this sling of the Russian David shall suddenly bow the head of his sanguinary pride. This image of St. Sergius, the ancient defender of the happiness of our country, is offered to your Imperial Majesty."

CHAPTER XXVIII.

The affair of Smolensko took place. The battle was obstinate, the cannonade violent. The Russians, taken in flank and enfiladed, were defeated. They could not defend those walls which so many times had witnessed their victories; they evacuated them; but the bridges and public buildings were a prey to the flames. The churches in particular poured out torrents of fire and smoke. The domes, the spires, and the multitude of small towers which arose above the conflagration, added to the effect of the picture, and produced those ill-defined emotions which are only to be found on the field of battle. We entered the place. It was half consumed, of a barbarous appearance, encumbered with the bodies of the dead and wounded, which the flames had already reached. The spectacle was frightful. What a train is that of glory!

We were obliged to turn our views from these scenes of slaughter. The Russians were flying; our cavalry rushed to the pursuit, and soon came up with the rear-guard. Korff attempted to make a stand; he was overwhelmed. Barclay came forward with his masses. We, on our side, received reinforcements; the action became terrible: Ney attacked in front, Junot on the flank: the enemy's army would have been cut off if the Duke had pressed forward. Wearied with not seeing him appear, Murat ran to him, "What are you about? Why do you not come on?" "My Westphalians are wavering." "I will give them an impetus." The King of Naples put himself at the head of a few squadrons, charged, and overthrew every thing that opposed him. "There is thy Marshal's staff half gained; complete the work, the Russians are lost." Junot did not complete it; whether from fatigue or distrust, the brave of the brave slumbered amidst the sound of the cannon, and the enemy, who were coming up to support their rear, again fell back on their line. The engagement became terrible; the brave Gudin lost his life, and the Russian army escaped us. Napoleon visited the places where the battle had been fought. " It was not at the bridge—it is there—at the village, where the eighth corps ought to have debouched—that the battle hinged. What was Junot doing?" The King of Naples endeavoured to extenuate his fault: the troops, the obstacles, all the customary commonplaces were employed. Berthier, who had always loved the Duke, interested himself for him; Caulincourt did the same. Every one pleaded to the utmost in favour of a brave man who could be reproached with nothing but a moment of forgetfulness. But the advantages we had lost were too great. Napoleon sent for me. "Junot has just lost for ever his Marshal's staff. I give you the command of the Westphalian corps: you speak their language, you will show them an example, you will make them fight." I was flattered with this mark of confidence, and expressed my sense of it; but Junot was covered with wounds, he had signalized himself in Syria, in Egypt, every where; I begged the Emperor to forget a moment's absence of mind on account of twenty years' courage and devotion. "He is the cause of the Russian army not having laid down its arms. This affair will, perhaps, hinder me from going to Moscow. Put yourself at the head of the Westphalians." The tone with which he pronounced these last words was already much softened. The services of the old aide-de-camp extenuated the inactivity of the 8th corps. I resumed: "Your Majesty has just talked to me of Moscow. The army is not in expectation of such an expedition." "The glass is full, I must drink it off. I have just received good news: Schwartzenberg is in Wolhinia, Poland is organizing, I shall have every kind of assistance."

I left Napoleon to make known to the Prince of Neuchâtel and the Duke de Vicenze the disgrace with which Junot was threatened. "I am afflicted," said the Prince to me, "to see his troops taken from him; but I cannot but own that he has caused the failure of one of the finest operations of the campaign. See on what the success of war depends; on the forgetfulness, on the absence of a moment: you do not seize the occasion in its flight, it disappears, and returns no more. No one has more courage or more ability. He adds to the qualities of the soldier the most extensive knowledge; he is intrepid, clever, agreeable, and good-natured. He forgot himself for an hour; he has made himself many enemies. However, I and Caulincourt will see what is to be done." They managed so well that Junot kept his post. I was very glad of it; first, because it saved him from disgrace, and next because I did not much like his troops. Unfortunately, lassitude had succeeded the impetuosity of his youth. He did not show at the battle of Moscowa that elasticity, that energy, of which he had so many times given an example; and the affair of Vereia raised to its height the dissatisfaction of the Emperor.

We learnt, some days after, the irruption of Tormasoff. We were uneasy; we discussed these long points, on the dangers to which one is exposed in advancing to an excessive distance beyond the line of one's operations. Without doubt Napoleon heard us. He came to us, talked a good deal of the manner in which he had secured the rear, of the corps which formed our wings, and of that chain of posts which extended from the Niemen to our actual position. "Tormasoff," he said to us, "has put all the children at Warsaw in alarm. They saw him already officiating at Prague; but see, he is sent back quicker than he came." He went into his closet, and began to dictate with indifference, but loud enough to prevent us losing a word, instructions for the Duke de Belluno.

Napoleon to the Major-General.

"Dorogobuj, August 26, 1812.

"My cousin, write to the Duke de Belluno to go in person to Wilna, in order that he may see there the Duke de Bassano, and inform himself of affairs and the state of things; that I shall be the day after to-morrow at Wjaczma, that is, five days' march from Moscow; that it is possible that, in that situation, communications will be intercepted; that some one then must take the command, and act according to circumstances; that I have ordered the 129th regiment, the Illyrian regiment, the Westphalian regiment which was at Kœnigsberg, and the two Saxon regiments, to march for Minsk; and that, moreover, I have placed between Minsk and Mohilow the Dombrowski division, twelve battalions strong, with a brigade of light cavalry; that it is important for his corps to approach Wilna, and that he must guide himself according to circumtances, in order to be in a condition to support Smolensko, Witepsk, Mohilow, and Minsk; that the Dombrowski division ought to be sufficient to keep up the communications from Minsk by Orza as far as Smolensko, since it has only to watch the Russian division of General Hetzel which is at

Mozyr, from 6 to 8000 men strong, most of them recruits, and against which, moreover, General Schwartzenberg can act; that the new reinforcements which I shall send to Minsk will also be able to assist against all accidents; and at all events the movement of the Duke de Belluno to Minsk and Orza, and from thence to Smolensko, appears to me calculated to support our rear; that I have four towns and men in garrison at Witepsk, and as many at Smolensko; that the Duke de Belluno taking position thus, between the Dnieper and Dwina, can easily communicate with me, will be able quickly to receive my orders, and will find himself in condition to protect the communications from Minsk and from Witepsk, as well as those from Smolensko to Moscow; that I suppose that General Gouvion Saint-Cyr has sufficient of the second and sixth corps to keep in check Witgenstein, and to have nothing to fear from him; that the Duke de Tarentum can march on Riga and invest the fortress; in fine, that I order the four demi-brigades, making 9000 men, who formed part of the Lagrange division, to march for Kowno; that also it should only be in case General Gouvion Saint-Cyr should be beaten by General Witgenstein, and obliged to pass the Dwina, that the Duke de Belluno is to march to his support in

the first instance; that, this case excepted, he is to follow his course for Smolensko. On this, &c.
   (Signed)   " NAPOLEON."

CHAPTER XXIX.

THE army continued its movements, always driving before it the troops it had defeated at Valontina. *Te Deums* were often sung in Russia; they are sung for every thing in that happy country: but the victories after Tolly's fashion did not calm the anxiety of the nation; she perceived that this mode of conquering would soon drive her into Siberia; she resolved to put her destinies into other hands. Kutusow drew from the feet of images his military inspirations; he fasted, he prayed, he flattered the priests and the nobility; Heaven could not refuse him its assistance: he was appointed. Admirable in courts, pasquinades are not sufficient on the field of battle; all religious mummeries are of no avail against a good manœuvre : he experienced it. The King of Naples, who had a soldier's contempt for amulets, attacks him and cuts his troops to pieces. He wished to make a stand at Chevarino, but the cavalry is put in motion, the charge is sounded, he is overturned, and thrown back on his intrenchments; courage overpowers the saints of Russia. This beginning did not augur well; Heaven answered coldly to the zeal of the Cossacks. Supplications were redoubled; Kutusow displayed his images; the army defiled before the virgin of Smolensko, of which we wished to dispossess the devout nation: prayers, vows and offerings were made, and the orators of the Calmucks uttered the following homily:—

" Brethren!

" You see before you, in this image, the object of your piety, an appeal addressed to Heaven that it may unite with men against the tyrant who disturbs the universe. Not content with destroying millions of creatures, images of God, this arch-rebel against all laws, both divine and human, penetrates into our sanctuaries with an armed hand, defiles them with blood, overturns your altars, and exposes the very ark of the Lord consecrated in this holy image of our church to the profanations of fortune, of the elements, and of sacrilegious hands. Fear not, then, but that God, whose altars have been thus insulted by this worm which his almighty power has drawn from the dust, will be with us; fear not that he will refuse to extend his buckler over your ranks, and to fight his enemy with the sword of Saint Michael."

"It is in this belief that I wish to fight, conquer, and die, certain that my dying eyes will see victory. Soldiers, do your duty : think on the sacrifice of your cities in flames, and on your children, who implore your protection ; think on your Emperor, your lord, who considers you as the nerve of his power, and to-morrow, before the sun shall have gone down, you will have traced your faith and your fidelity on your country's soil with the blood of the aggressor and his warriors."

The sword of Saint Michael is undoubtedly a formidable sword, but active soldiers are of still more consequence; Kutusow did not therefore spare libations ; he proportionably increased the fervour of the Cossacks. As for us, we had no inspired men, no preachers, not even subsistence ; but we bore the inheritance of a long glory; we were going to decide whether the Tartars or ourselves were to give laws to the world ; we were on the confines of Asia, farther than any European army had ever gone. Success was not doubtful: thus Napoleon saw, with the most lively joy, the processions of Kutusow. "Good," he observed to me, "they are now busy with pasquinades, they shall not escape us again." He reconnoitred, despatched orders for moving, and prepared himself for the battle of the morrow. The King of Naples thought these preparations superfluous ; he had made himself master of the principal redoubt; the left of this position was turned: he did not believe that the Russians would accept battle; he thought that they would withdraw during the night. This was not their project; they dug, they threw up the earth, they strengthened their position. The next day we perceived them all at work· It was eleven o'clock ; Napoleon sent me to reconnoitre ; I was charged to approach as near as possible to the enemy's line. I rid myself of my white feathers, I put on a soldier's cloak, and examined every thing with the greatest care possible ; I was only accompanied by one chasseur of the guard. In several places I passed by Russian sentinels: the village of Borodino was only separated from our posts by a narrow but a deep ravine : I advanced too far; they fired at me two discharges of grape-shot. I withdrew, and returned about two o'clock ; I came and gave an account of every thing I had seen. Napoleon was discoursing with the King of Naples and the Prince of Neuchâtel; Murat had entirely changed his opinion; surprised to see at day-break the enemy's line unmoved, he had thought action approaching, and had prepared for it. Other generals still maintained that the Russians would not dare to run the risk: as for me, I asserted the contrary. I observed that they had plenty of men, in a very good position; I was convinced that they would attack us, if we did not prevent them. Napoleon did me the honour to be of my opinion, which was also that of Berthier: he called for his horses, and made the same reconnoissance in person. He was received as I had been before Borodino; the grape-shot obliged him to withdraw. What he saw effectually convinced him that he had not been deceived: on his return he gave orders in consequence.

Night came on. I was in attendance; I slept in Napoleon's tent. The part where he slept was generally separated by a partition of cloth from that which was reserved for the aide-de-camp in attendance. The Emperor slept very little: I waked him several times to give him in reports and accounts from the advanced posts, which all proved to him that the Russians expected to be attacked. At three in the morning he called a valet de chambre, and made him bring some punch; I had the honour of taking some with him. He asked me if I had slept well; I answered, that the nights were already cold, that I had often been awaked. He said, "We shall have an affair to day with this famous Kutusow. You recollect, no doubt, that it was he who commanded at Braunau, in the campaign of Austerlitz. He remained three weeks in that place, without leaving his chamber once. He did not even get on horseback to see the fortifications. General Benigsen, though as old, is a more vigorous fellow than he. I do not know why Alexander has not sent this Hanoverian to replace Barclay." He took a glass of punch, read some reports, and added, "Well, Rapp, do you think that we shall manage our concerns properly to-day?"—"There is not the least doubt of it, Sire; we have exhausted all our resources, we are obliged to conquer." Napoleon continued his discourse, and replied: "Fortune is a liberal mistress; I have often said so, and begin to experience it."—"Your Majesty recollects that you did me the honour to tell me at Smolensko, that the glass was full, that it must be drunk off."—"It is at present the case more than ever: there is no time to lose. The army moreover knows its situation: it knows that it can only find provisions at Moscow, and that it has not more than thirty leagues to go. This poor army is much reduced, but what remains of it is good; my guard besides is untouched." He sent for Prince Berthier, and transacted business till half past five. We mounted on horseback: the trumpets sounded, the drums were beaten; and as soon as the troops knew it, there was nothing but acclamations. "It is the enthusiasm of Austerlitz. Let the proclamation be read."

" Soldiers!

"This is the battle that you have so long wished for! Henceforth victory depends on you; we want her; she will give us abundance of good winter-quarters, and a quiet return to our country. Behave yourselves as at Austerlitz, at Friedland, at Witepsk, at Smolensko; and let the remotest posterity quote your conduct on this day, and let it be said of you, ' he was at that great battle under the walls of Moscow.' "

The acclamations redoubled, the troops were incessantly demanding to fight, the action soon began.

CHAPTER XXX.

The wings were composed of Italians and Poles; Napoleon acted on the left of the enemy's masses. Beyond this we had no precise information; women, children, old people, cattle, all had disappeared; there was not a person left who could give us the least information. Ney marched towards the enemy, and broke through them with that force, that impetuosity, of which he had given so many proofs. We carried the three redoubts which supported the enemy. He came up with fresh troops; confusion began in our ranks; we gave up two of these works; the last even was in danger. The Russians already crowned the crest of the ditches. The King of Naples sees the danger, flies to the spot, alights from his horse, enters, mounts the parapet; he calls and animates the soldiers. The redoubt is strengthened, the fire becomes terrible, the assailants dare not try the assault. Some squadrons appear; Murat mounts his horse, charges, routs the columns scattered over the plain. We retake the retrenchments, and finally establish ourselves in them. This trait of boldness decided the fate of the day.

General Compans had just been wounded; I went to take the command of his division. It made a part of the corps d'armée of Marshal Davoust. It had already taken one of the intrenched positions of the enemy; it had also suffered much. I consulted, on my arrival, with Marshal Ney, whose right I supported. Our troops were in confusion, we rallied them, we rushed headlong on the Russians, we made them expiate their success. Neither discharges of cannon nor musquetry could stop us. The infantry, the cavalry, charged with fury from one extremity of the line to the other. I had never before seen such carnage. We had inclined too much towards the right; the King of Naples remained alone, exposed to the havoc of the batteries of Seminskoe. He had nothing but cavalry; a deep ravine separated him from the village: it was not easy to take it, but it was necessary to do so under pain of being swept away by the grape-shot. General Belliard, who only perceives a screen of light cavalry, conceives the design of driving it off and moving by the left on the redoubt. " Run to Latour Maubourg," Murat said to him; " tell him to take a brigade of

French and Saxon cuirassiers, to pass the ravine, to put all to the sword, to arrive at full gallop at the back of the redoubt, and to spike all the cannon. If he should fail, let him return in the same direction. You shall place a battery of forty pieces of cannon and a part of the reserve to protect the retreat." Latour Maubourg put himself in movement, routed, dispersed the Russians, and made himself master of the works. Friant came up to occupy them. All the reserve passed, and established itself on the left of the village. There remained a last retrenchment, which took us in flank and commanded our position. The reserve had taken one; it thought that it could take another. Caulincourt advanced, and spread far and wide confusion and death. He falls suddenly on the redoubt, and gets possession of it. A soldier hidden in an embrasure stretched him dead. He slept the sleep of the brave; he was not a witness of our disasters.

Every thing was in flight; the fire had ceased, the carnage had paused. General Belliard went to reconnoitre a wood situated at some distance. He perceived the road which converged on us; it was covered with troops and convoys, which were retreating. If they had been intercepted, all the right of the enemy's army had been taken in the segment in which it was placed. He came and informed Murat of it. " Run and give an account of it to the Emperor," said the Prince. He went, but Napoleon did not think the moment come. "I do not see sufficiently clear on my chess-board; I expect news from Poniatowski. Return, examine, come back." The General returned, indeed, but it was too late. The Russian guard was advancing; infantry, cavalry, all were coming up to renew the attack. The General had only time to collect a few pieces of cannon. " Grape-shot, grape shot, and nothing but grape shot," he said to the artillerymen. The firing began; its effect was terrible; in one instant the ground was covered with dead. The shattered column was dissipated like a shadow. It did not fire one shot. Its artillery arrived a few moments after; we got possession of it. The battle was gained, but the firing was still terrible. The balls and shots were pouring down by my side. In the space of one hour I was struck four times, first with two shots rather slightly, then with a bullet on the left arm, which carried away the sleeve of my coat and shirt close to the skin. I was then at the head of the sixty-first regiment, which I had known in Upper Egypt. There were a few officers present who were there; it was rather singular to meet here. I soon received a fourth wound; a ball struck me on my left hip and threw me headlong from my horse:—it was the twenty-second. I was obliged to quit the field of battle; I informed Marshal Ney of it, his troops were mixed with mine.

General Dessaix, the only general of that division who was not wounded, succeeded me; a moment after he had his arm broken; Friant was not wounded till afterwards.

I was dressed by the surgeon of Napoleon, who also came himself to visit me. "Is it, then, always your turn? How are things going on?" "Sire, I believe that you will be obliged to make your guard charge." "I shall take good care not to do so. I do not wish to see it destroyed. I am sure to gain the battle without its taking a part." It did not charge in effect, with the exception of thirty pieces of cannon, which did wonders.

The day ended; fifty thousand men lay on the field of battle. A multitude of generals were killed and wounded: we had forty disabled. We made some prisoners, took some pieces of cannon: this result did not compensate for the losses which it had cost us.

CHAPTER XXXI.

The Russian army retreated towards the capital: it made some resistance at Mojaisk, and arrived at Moscow. We took this city without striking a blow. Murat entered it in the train of the Cossacks, discoursed with their chiefs, and even gave a watch to one of them. They were expressing the admiration which his courage excited in them, and the dejection that a series of misfortunes produces, when some discharges of musquetry were heard: it was from a few hundred citizens who had taken arms. They themselves put an end to this useless firing, and continued their retreat.

Napoleon entered the next day. He fixed his quarters in the Kremlin, with a part of his guard, and the persons of his household; but we were so badly accommodated that I was obliged to take another lodging. I settled myself at some distance, in a house which belonged to a member of the Nareschkin family. I arrived at four o'clock in the afternoon. The town was still complete: the custom-house alone was a prey to the flames, which devoured it before any Frenchman appeared; but night came on—it was the signal for the fire. Left and right, every where there was a blaze; public buildings, temples, private property, all were in flames. The conflagration was general—nothing was to escape. The wind blew with violence; the fire made rapid progress. At midnight the blaze was so terrific, that my aides-de-camp waked me; they supported me; I reached a window from which I beheld the spectacle, which was becoming frightful. The fire was advancing towards us: at four o'clock I was informed that I must remove from my quarters. I left them; a few moments after, the house was reduced to ashes. I ordered them to conduct me in the direction of the Kremlin; every thing was in confusion. I returned back and went to the quarters of the Germans. A house belonging to a Russian General had been appointed for me; I hoped to be able to stay there to recover from my wounds; but when I arrived, volumes of fire and smoke were already issuing from it. I did not go in; I returned once more to the Kremlin. On the road I perceived some Russian artisans and soldiers, who were dispersed about in the houses, and were employed in setting fire to them: our patroles killed some of them in my presence, and arrested a considerable number. I met Marshal Mortier. "Where are you going?" said he to me. "The fire drives me out from wherever I fix my quarters: I am now determined to go to the Kremlin."—"Every thing there is in confusion, the fire is increasing in every direction; rather go from it."—"Where can one retreat?"—"To my hotel; my aide-de-camp will conduct you." I followed him; the house was close to the foundling hospital. We got there with difficulty; it was already in flames. I determined again to go to the Kremlin. I passed the Moskowa to fix myself opposite to the palace, which was yet untouched. I met in my road General Laribossière, accompanied by his son, who was ill; Talbouet joined us: we all quartered ourselves in the houses placed on the banks of the river. My landlord was an honest hatter, who felt for my situation, and bestowed all possible care on me. I was just settled with this worthy artisan, when the fire shewed itself on every side. I quitted in haste: the quays are narrow; if I had delayed, I could not have escaped with my carriage. We crossed the water, and established ourselves in the open air behind the walls of the Kremlin; this was the only means of getting any rest. The wind was still blowing with increasing violence, and it fed the flames. I removed once more, for the last time: I withdrew to the neighbourhood of one of the barriers; the houses were detached and scattered, the fire could not reach them. The one that I occupied was small, convenient, and belonged to a Prince Gallitzin. I supported while I remained there, during fifteen days, at the least a hundred and fifty refugee inhabitants.

Napoleon was, in his turn, obliged to retreat before the flames. He quitted the Kremlin, and fixed his head-quarters out of the town, in a palace where he took up his residence. He did not stay there long; he returned to the palace of the Czars as soon as the fire was extinguished. He sent, almost every morning, General Narbonne to inquire after me. This General, like many others of our army, was very uneasy. He often said to me, that the Emperor was wrong in calculating on peace; that we were not in a condition to dictate conditions; that the Russians had not sacrificed their capital to accept of disadvantageous terms. "They are amusing us, in order to take their revenge, and to have fairer sport."

CHAPTER XXXII.

Moscow was destroyed: the occupation of its ruins was neither safe nor advantageous: we were too far removed from our wings; we could not procure subsistence, and we had no interest in guarding the ruins. Every one was of opinion that we must not remain there, but it was not agreed what it was best to do. The King of Naples proposed to march towards Kaluga, to destroy there the only establishments which Russia possessed, and to return and go into cantonments on the Boristhenes. The Cossacks could not be followed to the extremity of the world; the longest flight must have its end; we were ready for fighting, but we did not wish to persevere longer in a chase. Such was the purport of the proclamation that he recommended before putting the army in motion. The Viceroy thought, on the contrary, that we should march towards the Russians, give them battle, and push them on Petersburg, and then march for Riga: we could thus have rejoined Macdonald, and afterwards established ourselves on the Dwina. Others presented other plans; all were good—all were practicable; but the Emperor had some particular information; he would have judged correctly, if the Russians had not received inspirations from England. Much fault has been found with this delay: it is an error, since events have condemned it; but those who exclaim against it were not in the secret of our affairs or negotiations; they may, without too much modesty, believe that the sagacity of that great man was not below that which Nature has given to them. He was deceived; we have felt the consequences; perhaps one day it will be known what combinations misled him. However that may be, we delayed, we negotiated, we gave battle; we decided nothing. The army of Moldavia was continuing its movement; it was advancing, but it was not yet known in what line it was to act. Some pretended that it would unite with Kutusow, others feared that it would march upon our rear. We were uncertain of what was preparing; the Emperor himself was not free from uneasiness, but he knew to a man what troops he had in *echelon* from the Rhine to Moscow; he thought his calculations safe; he confined himself to the despatching of instructions: those that he addressed to the Duke de Belluno are worth citing. They prove what kind of *slumber* it was that he has been reproached with.

NAPOLEON TO THE MAJOR-GENERAL.

"My cousin, inform the Duke de Belluno that I have not yet given orders for his movement, because that depends on the movement of the enemy: that the Russian army from Moldavia, consisting of three divisions, or twenty thousand men strong, infantry, cavalry, and artillery included, passed the Dnieper in the beginning of September; that it may march towards Moscow to reinforce the army under the command of General Kutusow, or towards Volhinia to reinforce that of Tormasoff; that General Kutusow's army, beaten at the battle of Moskowa, is at present on the Kaluga, which would lead us to believe that it expects reinforcements which might come from Moldavia, by the road of Kiow; that, in this case, the Duke de Belluno would receive orders to join the great army, either by the road of Jelnia and Kaluga, or any other; that if, on the contrary, the twenty thousand men from Moldavia relieve Tormasoff, this reinforcement will raise Tormasoff's force to forty thousand men; but that our right, under the command of Prince Schwartzenberg, would be still of equal force—as that Prince, with the Austrians,

Poles, and Saxons, has about forty thousand men; that moreover I have demanded of the Emperor of Austria, that the corps which the Austrian General Reuss commands at Leinberg should move; and that Prince Schwartzenberg should receive a reinforcement of ten thousand men; that, on the other side, the Emperor Alexander reinforces as much as he can the garrison of Riga, and the corps of Wittgenstein, in order to dislodge Marshal Saint-Cyr from Polozk, and the Duke of Tarentum from Riga and Dünaburg; that letters which came from Prince Schwartzenberg, dated the 24th, would tend to prove that the army of Moldavia, instead of coming towards Moscow, has reached the army of Tormasoff and reinforced it; that it is necessary then to know what will be done; that, in this state of things, I desire that the Duke de Belluno will canton his corps from Smolensko to Orsza; that he will keep up an exact correspondence by all the estafettes with the Duke de Bassano, in order that that Minister may write to him and give him all the news that he shall have from different parts; that he will send a steady, discreet, and intelligent officer to General Schwartzenberg and General Regnier; that this officer shall learn from General Schwartzenberg what is passing, and from General Regnier the true state of affairs; that he will regularly correspond with the Governor of Minsk ; and lastly, that he will send agents in different directions to know what is passing; that the division of Gerard shall be placed on the side of Orsza, where it will be four or five days' march from Minsk, three from Witepsk, four or five from Polozk; that the other division, which shall be between Orsza and Smolensko, shall be in a condition to give it speedy assistance; and that lastly, the third division shall be near Smolensko. That, by this means, his corps d'armée will rest itself, and be able easily to find subsistence; that it will be necessary to station it above the route, in order to leave the great communications free for the troops which arrive ; that in this position he will be equally able to march upon Minsk, or upon Wilna, if the centre of our communications and of our depôts be threatened; or if Marshal Saint-Cyr should be driven from Polozk, or to execute the order that he might receive to return to Moscow by the road of Jelnia and of Kaluga—if the taking of Moscow and the new state of things should determine the enemy to reinforce himself with a portion of the troops from Moldavia; that the Duke de Belluno will thus form the chief reserve, to go either to the relief of Schwartzenberg and cover Minsk, or to the assistance of Marshal Saint-Cyr and cover Wilna, or to Moscow to reinforce the main army. That General Dombrowski, who has a division of 8000 infantry, and 12,000 Polish horse, is under his orders, which will increase his corps d'armée to four divisions; that the brigade of reserve from Wilna, composed of four Westphalian regiments, of two battalions from Hesse-Darmstadt, which towards the end of the month will arrive from Swedish Pomerania, and of eight pieces of cannon, will also be under his orders; that, in fine, in the course of November, two new divisions will assemble;—the one at Warsaw, that is, the thirty-second division, which will be augmented by three battalions from Wurtsburg, and will remain under the command of General Durutte; the other at Konigsberg, that is, the thirty-fourth, which was in Pomerania under the orders of General Morand, and which, also increased by some battalions, will be commanded by General Loison. Thus, whether it be necessary to march to the assistance of Prince Schwartzenberg, or to the assistance of Marshal Saint-Cyr, the Duke de Belluno will always assemble a mass of forty thousand men; that, as the correspondence by estafette is quick, I always give my orders; and that it would only be in the event of Minsk or Wilna being threatened or menaced, that the Duke de Belluno should march of his own authority to protect these two grand depôts of the army; that the Duke de Belluno, having the general command over all Lithuania and the governments of Smolensko and of Witepsk, should every where accelerate the progress of the administration, and especially take efficacious measures that the requisitions for corn and forage be carried into effect; that there are ovens at Mohilow, at Orsza, at Rasasna, and at Dubrowna; that he must get a great deal of biscuit ready, and put himself in a situation to have thirty days' provisions secured for his corps, without taking any thing from the military transports, or from the convoys which may be passing for the army. The Duke de Belluno will take care to keep up a correspondence at Witepsk: he is at liberty to send troops to support that point, and to maintain himself there; he can then go in person to Mohilow, to Witepsk, or Smolensko, to know the ground, and to expedite the administration. If, by any accident, the communication with Moscow should be intercepted, he would take care to send cavalry and infantry to open it again."

We had no longer either food or forage; men and horses were alike exhausted; retreat became indispensable. A question arose as to the means of carrying away our wounded. I began to be able to walk; on the 18th I went to the palace: Napoleon asked with kindness in what state my wounds were, how I was going on. He showed me the portrait of the King of Rome, which he had received at the moment we were going to begin the battle of the Moskowa. He had shown it to most of the Generals. I had to carry orders; the battle began; we had other things to attend to. He wished now to make me amends; he looked for the medallion, and observed, with a satisfaction which betrayed itself in his eyes:—" My son is the finest child in France."

A moment after, a memorial was brought from the Intendant general, who required forty-five days to remove the wounded. " Forty-five days! he is deceived. If nothing were done, part would get well and part would die; there would only be the remainder to remove; and experience proves, that three months after a battle there remains but the sixth part of the wounded. I wish to remove them; I will not let them remain here exposed to the brutality of the Russians." We perceived from the saloon the workmen who were busy in taking away the cross of the great Ivan. " Do you see what a flock of ravens hover around that lump of old iron? Do they think to hinder us from taking it away? I will send that cross to Paris, I will have it placed on the dome of the Invalids."

It was the 18th of October; the departure was fixed for the 19th. My wound was not quite closed up. I mounted on horseback to see if I could bear the motion.

CHAPTER XXXIII.

The next day I went early to the Kremlin. Scarcely had I reached the palace, when Napoleon came out of it to leave Moscow for ever; he perceived me. " I hope that you will not follow me on horseback, you are not in a fit state to do it; you can get into one of my carriages." I thanked him, and replied that I thought I should be in a condition to accompany him. We quitted this capital, and we took the road of Kaluga; when we were about three leagues distance, the Emperor stopped to wait for news from Mortier, who had orders to destroy the Kremlin on leaving the place.

He was walking in a field with M. Daru; this gentleman left him; I was called. "Well, Rapp, we are going to retreat to the frontiers of Poland by the road of Kaluga: I shall take up good winter-quarters. I hope that Alexander will make peace."—"You have waited a long time, Sire; the inhabitants foretel that it will be a severe winter."—"Poh! poh! with your inhabitants. It is the 19th of October to-day, you see how fine it is. Do you not recognise my star? Besides, I could not leave without sending on all the sick and wounded. I was not to give them up to the rage of the Russians."—"I believe, Sire, that you would have done better to have left them at Moscow; the Russians would not have hurt them; whilst they are exposed for want of aid to die on the road." Napoleon was not of that opinion; but all that he said to me in the way of encouragement did not deceive even himself: his countenance bore the marks of uneasiness.

At last an officer despatched from the Marshal arrived: it was my aide de-camp Turkheim, who informed us that Moscow was tranquil; that some pulks of Cossacks had appeared in the environs, but they took care not to approach the Kremlin, or any of the quarters still occupied by the French troops. We proceeded on our march. In the evening we arrived at Krasno Pachra. The look of the country was not encouraging to Napoleon. The hideous aspect, the wild air of the slaves, was revolting to eyes accustomed to other climates. " I would not leave a man there; I would give all the treasures of Russia not to leave a single wounded man behind. We must take horses, waggons, carriages—every thing to carry them on. Send me a secretary." The secretary came; it was to write to Mortier what he had just been telling me. It is of use to copy the despatch: these instructions are not unworthy to be known. Those who have so often declaimed against his indifference should study them.

"To the Major-General.

" Acquaint the Duke de Treviso, that as soon as his business in Moscow is finished, that is, on the 23d at three o'clock in the morning, he is to begin to march, and that he must come on the 24th to Kubinskoe; and from that place, instead of going to Mojaisk, he is to proceed to Vereia, where he will arrive on the 25th. He will serve as an intermediate force between Mojaisk, where the Duke d'Abrantes is, and Borowsk, where the army will be. It will be right for him to send officers to Fominskoe to inform us of his march; he will take with him the Adjutant-commandant Bourmont, the Bavarians, and the Spaniards who are at the palace of Gallitzin. All the Westphalians of the first and second posts, and all the Westphalians that he can find, he must assemble and direct towards Mojaisk: if they are not in sufficient number, he will protect their passage with the cavalry. The Duke de Treviso will inform the Duke d'Abrantes of every thing relative to the surrender of Moscow. It is necessary that he write to us to-morrow the 22d, not by the road of Desma, but by that of Karapowo and Fominskoe. On the 23d he will send us a letter by the road of Mojaisk: his officer will leave the road at Kubinskoe to come to Fominskoe, as the head-quarters on the 23d are likely to be at Borowsk or at Fominskoe. Whether the Duke de Treviso perform his operation at three o'clock in the morning of to-morrow the 22d, or on the 23d at the same hour, as I have since ordered him, he is in either case to follow these same directions; by these means the Duke de Treviso may be considered as the rear-guard of the army. I cannot too strongly recommend to place on the waggons belonging to the young guard, or those belonging to the dismounted cavalry, in short, on all that can be found, the men who remain still in the hospitals. The Romans gave civic crowns to those who saved citizens; the Duke will deserve as many as he may save soldiers. He must mount them on his horses, and on those of all his people.

"This is what the Emperor did at the siege of Saint-Jean d'Acre. He ought the rather to take this step, because as soon as the convoy shall have joined the army, it will have waggons and horses, which the consumption of provisions will have rendered useless. The Emperor hopes that he shall have the pleasure of thanking the Duke de Treviso, for having saved five hundred men. He ought, as is but just, to begin with the officers, then the sub-officers, and to give the French the preference. He must assemble all the generals and officers, under his command, to make them sensible of the importance of this measure, and how much they will gain the Emperor's esteem, by saving for him five hundred men."

We marched on towards Borusk, where we arrived on the fourth day: the town was completely abandoned. In the mean time, Kutusow was peaceably engaged in issuing his proclamations: he was quite at ease in his camp at Tarentino; he kept up no watch, either on his front or wings; he had no idea at all of the movement we were making. He learned at last, that we were marching towards Kaluga; he soon broke up his cantonments, and appeared at Malojaroslawitz at the same time as our columns. The action began: we heard from Borusk a distant cannonade. I was suffering greatly from my wound, but I would not leave Napoleon: we mounted horse. We arrived towards evening in sight of the field of battle: they were still fighting; but the firing soon ceased. Prince Eugene had forced a position, which must have been defended to extremity. Our troops had covered themselves with glory. It is a day that the army of Italy ought to inscribe in its calendar. Napoleon bivouacked at a league and a half from the scene. The next day we took horse at half-past seven in the morning, to visit the ground on which the battle had been fought; the Emperor was placed between the Duke de Vicenza, Prince de Neuchâtel, and myself. We had scarcely quitted the huts where we had passed the night, when we perceived a cloud of Cossacks; they proceeded from a wood in advance on our right. They were drawn up in pretty regular files: we took them for French cavalry.

The Duke de Vicenza was the first who

recognised them. " Sire, these are Cossacks."—
" That is impossible," replied Napoleon. They
rushed upon us shouting with all their might. I
seized the Emperor's horse by the bridle; I
turned it round myself. " But these are our
troops?"—" They are the Cossacks; make
speed."—" They are Cossacks, indeed," said
Berthier.—" Without doubt," added Mouton.
Napoleon gave some orders and withdrew. I
advanced at the head of the squadron on duty:
we were overthrown; my horse received a wound
six inches deep, from a lance, and fell, with me
under him: we were trampled under foot by
these barbarians. Fortunately they perceived at
some distance a troop of artillery; they ran towards the spot. Marshal Bessieres had time to
come up, with the horse grenadiers of the guard:
he charged them, and retook from them the
covered waggons and the pieces of cannon, which
they were carrying away. I raised myself again
on my legs; I was replaced in my saddle, and proceeded as far as the bivouac. When Napoleon
saw my horse covered with blood, he feared that
I had again been wounded: he asked me whether
I was. I replied that I had got off with a few
contusions. He then began to laugh at our adventure, which, nevertheless, I did not find very
amusing.

I was well repaid by the account which he published of this affair; he loaded me with eulogiums: I never before experienced pleasure compared to that which I felt on reading the flattering things which he said of me. "General Rapp," says the bulletin, "had one horse killed under him in this charge. The intrepidity of which this general officer has given so many proofs, is manifested on all occasions." I repeat with pride the praises of this great man: I shall never forget them.

We returned to the field of battle: Napoleon wished to visit the place which had been the theatre of Prince Eugene's glory. He found that the position of the Russians had been excellent; he was astonished that they had allowed it to be forced. He perceived, from the appearance of the dead bodies, that the militia had been confounded with the troops of the line, and that if they had not fought with skill, they had gone to it at least with courage. The enemy's army retired some leagues, on the road to Kaluga, and encamped.

The retreat was intercepted: we threw ourselves to the right on Vereia; we arrived there early the next day, and slept there: it was in that town that Napoleon learned that the Kremlin had been blown up. General Winzengerode' had not sufficiently restrained his impatience; he had ventured into this capital before our troops had evacuated it. They cut up his retreat; he tried to make them believe that he came to treat with them. He was born on the territory of the Confederation; he had no inclination to be made a prisoner; he was taken nevertheless, in spite of the white handkerchief that he was waving. Napoleon sent for him, and fell into a violent passion, treated him with contempt, branded him with the name of traitor, and threatened to punish him; he even told me that a commission must be named to proceed with the trial of the gentleman immediately; he had him escorted by chosen gendarmes, and ordered him to be confined *au secret*. Winzengerode sought several times to exculpate himself; but Napoleon would not hear him. It has been pretended in the Russian army that this general spoke with courage, and said very strong things to the Emperor. It is not the fact:—anxiety was marked on his countenance, every thing expressed the disorder of mind into which the Emperor's anger had thrown him. Each of us endeavoured to appease the Emperor; the King of Naples, the Duke de Vicenza particularly, suggested to him how much, in the present situation of things, any violence towards a man who hid his origin under the quality of a Russian general, would be to be lamented: there was no council of war, and the affair rested there. As for us, Winzengerode ought not to complain of our treatment: his situation inspired us all with interest. His aide-de-camp was treated with much kindness. Napoleon asked him his name. "Nareschkin," replied the young officer.—"Nareschkin! one of that name is not made to be the aide-de-camp of a deserter." We were hurt at this want of consideration; we sought every means imaginable to make the general forget it.

CHAPTER XXXIV.

We set off the next day; and reached the great road from Moscow by Mojaisk.

The cold, the privations, were extreme; the hour of disasters had come on us! We found our wounded lying dead on the road, and the Russians waiting for us at Viasma. At the sight of these columns the soldiers collected a remnant of energy, fell upon them, and defeated them. But

GENERAL RAPP. 231

we were harassed by troops animated by abundance, and by hope of plunder. At every step we were obliged to halt, and fight; we slackened our march over a wasted country, which we should have gone over with the greatest rapidity. Cold, hunger, the Cossacks,—every scourge was let loose upon us. The army was sinking under the weight of its misfortunes; the road was strewed with the dead: our sufferings exceeded imagination. How many sick and wounded generals did I meet in this terrible retreat, whom I believed that I should never again see! Of this number was General Friant, whose wounds were still open; General Durosnel, who travelled with a nervous fever, almost continually delirious; and the brave General Belliard, who was wounded by a gun-shot, in the battle of the Moskowa. He had formerly penetrated nearly into Ethiopia; he had carried our colours farther than ever the Roman eagles had flown; he must have found a difference between the two climates.

We marched for Smolensko: it was to have been the end of our miseries; we were to have found there food and clothing, wherewith to defend ourselves from the pests which were consuming us: we were not more than eighteen leagues from it. Napoleon lodged in one of those little block-houses that had been constructed to receive detachments from fifty to sixty men, employed to protect the correspondence and communications. I was on duty: some time had elapsed since any despatches had arrived; at last one came. I delivered it to the Emperor. He opened the parcel with haste; a *Moniteur* was uppermost. He ran it over ; the first article which caught his eye was the enterprise of Mallet; he had not read the despatches, he did not know what it was. " What is this! what! plots! conspiracies!" He opened his letters, they contained the detail of the attempt: he was thunderstruck. That police which knew every thing, which guessed at every thing, had suffered itself to be taken by surprise. Napoleon could not recover himself. " Savary in *La Force!* The minister of the police arrested, carried to a prison, and there shut up!" I went to transmit some orders. The event had already transpired. Surprise, astonishment were depicted on every countenance; and some reflections were made which till then had been withheld. The carelessness of the agents of the police was manifest. They are only alert because there is a general belief in their vigilance. Napoleon was not astonished that these wretches who frequent saloons and taverns, who obstruct every thing, who insinuate themselves every where, should not have found out the plot; but he could not conceive the weakness of Rovigo. "Why did he not rather let them kill him, than be arrested! Doucet and Hullin showed much more courage."

We proceeded on our journey; we crossed the Borysthenes. The Emperor fixed his headquarters in a country-house that had been laid waste, twelve leagues from Smolensko, and one and a half behind the river. The banks, on the water-side, are very step in this part; they were covered with hoar frost. Napoleon was afraid that the artillery would not be able to get over them; he charged me to join Ney, who commanded the rear-guard, to remain with him till every thing was out of danger. I found the Marshal engaged in giving chase to the Cossacks: I communicated to him the orders that I had to transmit to him, and we retired to a block-house which was to support the passage, and where the headquarters were fixed.

A part of the infantry crossed over, the remainder bivouacked in a little wood, on the bank where we were. We were engaged all night in getting the cannon across. The last was on the ascent, when the enemy appeared.

They attacked immediately, with considerable masses; we received their charges without being shaken; but our end was attained: we had no object in fighting; we retreated. We left behind a few hundreds of men, whom wounds and exhaustion had put out of a condition to follow. Poor creatures! they complained, they groaned, and called for death; it was a heart-rending sight; but what could we do. Every one was bending under the burthen of life, and supported it with difficulty; no one had sufficient strength to share it with others. The Russians pursued us, they wished to pass by main force. Ney received them with that vigour, that impetuosity, which he always displayed in his attacks: they were repulsed, and the bridge became a prey to the flames. The firing ceased, we withdrew during the night. I joined Napoleon at Smolensko the day after the next in the evening. He knew that a ball had grazed my head, and that another had killed my horse; he observed to me: "You may be at ease now, you will not be killed this campaign."—"I hope that your Majesty may not be deceived; but you often gave the same assurance to poor Lannes, who nevertheless was killed."— "No! no! you will not be killed."—"I believe it; but I may be still frozen to death." The

Emperor bestowed eulogiums on Marshal Ney. " What a man ! what a soldier ! what a vigorous fellow !" He only talked thus by exclamations ; he could not find words to express the admiration which this intrepid Marshal inspired him with. The Prince de Neuchatel entered; the conversation again turned on Mallet and Savary. Napoleon was merry at the expense of the Duke; his surprise, his arrest, were the subject of a thousand pleasantries ; of which the burthen always was, that he should rather have been killed, than have allowed himself to be taken.

CHAPTER. XXXV.

THE retreat had been disastrous. Every scourge that Nature has in store we had experienced ; but every day brought us nearer to Smolensko: we were to find in that town repose and abundance. We were marching, hope sustained us ; she too was going to abandon us ; our misfortunes were to be as unheard-of as our victories. The fourth corps lost its cannon ; Augercau's brigade was destroyed, and Witepsk taken; we had no more ammunition, or means of subsistence; we were in a frightful situation: it was necessary to be resigned. We put ourselves in motion; we arrived the following day at Krasnoi. Kutusow, who was bearing on us with all his forces, had already an advanced-guard there; it retired at the sight of our soldiers, and took post a league farther on, halting on the left on the borders of a forest, which it covered with fires. Napoleon sent for me, and said—" We have the Russian infantry quite close to us; it is the first time that they have shown so much boldness. I command you to charge them with the bayonet about midnight, surprise them, teach them not to be so desirous to approach so near to my head-quarters. I place at your disposal all that remains of the young guard." I had made all the preparations, I was waiting near the fire of a Polish bivouac till the hour should arrive, when General Narbonne came and said, " Give up your troops to the Duke de Treviso; his Majesty does not wish you to be killed in this affair; he reserves for you another destiny." I received this counter-order with pleasure, I did not conceal it. I was weakened by fatigue, by sufferings, and cold. I was not inclined to march against the enemy; moreover, his Cossacks had already given him the alarm ; he was prepared ; he received us as well as he could. He was nevertheless beaten and thrown back on his masses, which were in positions parallel to the road, and extended in some sort from Smolensko to Krasnoi ; they attacked us in flank, they ought to have been able to defeat us. Fortunately the illusion of our glory still continued ; we were protected by the remembrance of our victories. Kutusow saw from a distance our columns which were defiling on the road, but did not venture to attack them. He decided at last on running the risk ; but a peasant informed him that Napoleon was at Krasnoi, that the guard occupied all the neighbourhood. This news damped his courage : he revoked the orders that he had despatched.

We had long before taken the measure of his capacity ; we always took it into our account ; it was one of our resources ; he might nevertheless change his mind, rush to arms, and destroy us. We all perceived it ; but we had no news from Eugene. Davoust and Ney were in the rear; we could not leave them. The temperature moreover became every day more severe ; the Russians also suffered ; they had slumbered hitherto, they might slumber still. Napoleon resolved to take the chance of it ; he waited. Every thing turned out as he had foreseen. Milloradowitz wished to intercept the fourth corps, but he could not reach it. Five thousand infantry, who had neither horses to clear away the assailants, nor cannon to defend themselves with, constantly repulsed the multitudes of soldiers which were rushing on them, made head against all this advanced-guard, and escaped. Davoust followed ; the enemy flattered themselves that they could take their revenge on the Marshal, but the Emperor prevented it. He extended his line on the left of Krasnoi, brought some troops into action, and opened a pretty well sustained fire of artillery. Kutusow, alarmed at the sight of the 14 or 15,000 men who had been drawn together, recalled his detached corps : the Marshal passed over, and came to take part in the action. The end was attained, the firing ceased, and the retreat commenced. The enemy tried to prevent it ; but the first regiment of the voltigeurs of the guard repulsed all their attacks ; neither the cavalry, the infantry, nor grape shot could move it : it perished on the spot. This heroic resistance struck the Russians ; they discontinued the pursuit. As soon as we were out of one embarrassment, we fell into another. We in number from 14 to 15,000 men, had ventured to place ourselves in line against Kutusow's 20,000 ; we had extricated ourselves, without a reverse, from a situation where we ought to have been all taken; but our provisions, our rear was lost. Minsk had been surprised; the army of Moldavia covered the Beresina; Ney was still behind: never had our situation been so terrible. Napoleon, who was astonished at this disastrous complication of affairs, despatched orders to resume the offensive, and to take Polosk. Success appeared to him easy. " If the Duke de Belluno shew energy, the enterprise cannot fail; the character of the troops that he commands ensures it. It is Ney that I am uneasy about; what is to become of him." This Marshal was in an unparalleled situation; all the valour, the *sang froid*, and perseverance of that intrepid warrior were necessary to extricate him; he had received on the night of the 16th or 17th news of Eugene's battle, and Davoust's departure. These two events could not move him. " All the Cossacks of Russia," said he, on learning it, " should not hinder me from executing my instructions; I will not depart from them a tittle." He concluded his arrangements, and proceeded to march: 6,000 infantry, three hundred horses, and twelve pieces of cannon composed all his force. He was annoyed by the light troops of the enemy which hovered round his flanks; he was marching in close order, ready to receive any attack. At three o'clock, his vanguard reached Katowa, and halted in sight of the corps of Milloradowitz. The weather was foggy; neither party could see what troops were before them. Ney crosses a ravine which separated him from the enemy's troops, breaks through the first line, routs the second, and would have defeated the whole army if the ravages of the artillery had not prevented him. He was obliged to sound a retreat; but his attack had been so impetuous that they dared not pursue him. He lighted night-fires, as if he intended to stop all night: the Russians imitated him. As soon as he had taken some rest, he removed his quarters, and resolved to interpose the Borysthenes as a line of separation between him and the enemy's troops, which were too numerous for him to be able to force: he rushed into the stream, on the ice, and reached the opposite bank; but new dangers were awaiting him there.

The Cossacks covered the plain; they charged us, and kept up a furious fire of grape shot. Ney, who could not make any return to this destructive cannonade, hastened his march, dispersing, overthrowing every thing that dared oppose him. He marched for a wood which was not far distant; he was on the point of reaching it, when a battery was unmasked on him and disorganized his column. The soldiers waver and throw down their arms, but the Marshal soon restores them to their courage; his words, his voice, his example, encourage the most timid: they rush on; the enemy's artillery fly; we are masters of the wood. But there were neither roads nor paths through this thicket; it was intersected by so many ravines, and there were so many obstacles, that it was with infinite difficulty that it was traversed: nearly all the *matériel* was left in it. The Cossacks became the more daring; for two days they never ceased renewing their attacks: but they had themselves been obliged to make a circuit, their cannon was in arrear, they had no artillery; a few voltigeurs did justice on them. Ney was close upon Orsza: the night was advanced; he marched in silence: he flattered himself that he had at last ridded himself of the enemy. On a sudden he perceives the fires of bivouacs, he discovers the camp of a numerous army. He did not know whether he should rejoice or tremble, whether they were Russians or French, when a fire opened upon him removes his uncertainty: the reconnoitring parties are received with discharges of musquetry; explosions, cries, drums, are mingled and confounded together; one would have thought that we were to give battle to all Russia. Furious at seeing danger return at the moment when he thought that he had escaped from it, the Marshal makes an effort to open a passage; he rushes towards the fires—but the camp is deserted: it is a trick, a stratagem. Platoff had, it appears, taken us for his own troops; he had thought to frighten us with shadows. The Duke disdained to follow a few Cossacks, who had been employed in this phantasmagoria; he continued his march, and three leagues further on reached the fourth corps.

CHAPTER XXXVI.

While this was going on, we had left Krasnoi. Napoleon marched on foot at the head of his guard, and often talked of Ney; he called to mind his *coup d'œil,* so accurate and true, his courage proof against every thing, in short all the qualities which made him so brilliant on the field of battle. —" He is lost. Well! I have three hundred millions in the Tuileries, I would give them if he were restored to me."—He fixed his head-quarters at Dombrowna. He lodged with a Russian lady.

who had the courage not to abandon her house. I was on duty that day: the Emperor sent for me towards one o'clock in the morning; he was very much dejected; it was difficult for him not to be so; the scene was frightful. He observed to me, "My affairs are going on very badly; these poor soldiers rend my heart; I cannot, however, relieve them."—There was a cry of " To arms!"—Firing was heard; every thing was in an uproar. " Go, see what it is," Napoleon said to me with the greatest *sang froid;* "I am sure that they are some rogues of Cossacks who want to hinder us from sleeping." It was in reality a false alarm. He was not satisfied with some personages whom I abstain from naming.—" What a set of tragedy-kings, without energy, courage, or moral force! Have I been able to deceive myself to such a degree? To what men have I trusted myself? Poor Ney! with whom have I matched thee?"

We set off for Orsza, and fixed our quarters at a Jesuits' convent. Napoleon despaired of ever seeing the rear-guard. Neither did we see any more the Russian infantry; it was probable that they had taken some position: they ought to have let nothing escape. The next day we pushed on two leagues farther; we halted in a wretched hamlet. It was there that the Emperor learnt, towards the evening, of Ney's arrival, and his having joined the fourth corps. It may be easily conceived what joy he experienced, and in what manner he received the Marshal on the next day. We reached Borisow; Oudinot had beaten Lambert; the fugitives had joined Tchitschagoff, and covered the right bank of the Beresina. Napoleon was uneasy: we had neither a bridge-train nor subsistence. The main army was advancing, and the troops from Moldavia blockaded the passage: we were surrounded on every side: the situation was frightful, and unheard-of. Nothing less than the talents and the great decision of the Emperor was necessary to extricate us from so great a difficulty: no Frenchman, not even Napoleon, could expect to escape.

This prince stopped a short time at Borisow, gave orders for the false attack which saved us, and marched towards Oudinot's head-quarters a few leagues distant. We slept a little on this side of the place, at a country house which belonged to a Prince Radzivill. General Mouton and myself passed the night there on a handful of straw; we thought on the morrow, and our reflexions were not cheerful. We set off on our journey at four o'clock: we were in one of the Emperor's calêches. We perceived the fires of the Russians; they occupied the opposite bank; the woods, the marshes, were full of them; they reached beyond our range of sight. The river was deep, muddy, all covered with floating pieces; it was here that we were to cross or surrender. We augured badly of success. The General explained himself with frankness: he had often done it before Napoleon, who treated him as a malcontent, but nevertheless liked him much.

We arrived at Oudinot's head-quarters: day was just beginning to dawn; the Emperor conversed a moment with the Marshal, took some refreshment, and gave orders. Ney took me apart; we went out together; he said to me, in German, "Our situation is unparalleled; if Napoleon extricates himself to-day, he must have the devil in him." We were very uneasy, and there was sufficient cause. The King of Naples came to us, and was not less solicitous. "I have proposed to Napoleon," he observed to us, "to save himself, and cross the river at a few leagues distance from hence. I have some Poles who would answer for his safety, and would conduct him to Wilna, but he rejects the proposal, and will not even hear it mentioned. As for me, I do not think we can escape." We were all three of the same opinion. Murat replied, "We will all get over; we can never think of surrendering." While conversing, we perceived the enemy were filing off; their masses had disappeared, the fires were extinguished, nothing more than the ends of the columns, which were lost in the wood, were seen, and from five to six hundred Cossacks that were scattered on the plain. We examined with the telescope; we were convinced that the camp was raised. I went to Napoleon, who was conversing with Marshal Oudinot.— "Sire, the enemy have left their position."— "That is impossible." The King of Naples and Marshal Ney arrived, and confirmed what I had just announced. The Emperor came out from his barrack, cast his eye on the other side of the river. " I have outwitted the Admiral (he could not pronounce the name Tchitschagoff); he believes me to be at the point where I ordered the false attack; he is running to Borisow." His eyes sparkled with joy and impatience; he urged the erection of the bridges, and mounted twenty pieces of cannon in battery. These were commanded by a brave officer with a wooden leg, called Brechtel; a ball carried it off during the action, and knocked him down. "Look," he said, to one of his gunners, "for another leg, in waggon No. 5." He fitted it on, and continued his firing. The Emperor made sixty men swim across, under the command of Colonel Jacqueminot. They ventured imprudently in pursuit of the Cossacks; one of them was taken and questioned, and informed the Russians where Napoleon was. Tchitschagoff retraced his steps, but it was too late; Napoleon, his guard, Ney, Oudinot, and all the troops which these Marshals retained, had passed. The Admiral, confused by having been duped, forgot the marshes of Lemblin. The bridge, which extended a league and a quarter over this swampy ground, was our only escape; if it had been destroyed, he would have had our fate still in his hands: but Witgenstein commenced the firing on the left bank; he occupied the right; his soldiers were wallowing in plenty; a handful of men, sinking under the burthen of a wretched life, might have been trampled under foot. He neglected the defile, Eugene hastened to get possession of it; we were sure of our rear, we waited for Tchitschagoff.

We were 8000, fainting from fatigue and hunger: he had the army of Moldavia. The issue of the combat did not appear doubtful to him; he advanced with the ardour of victory; the action commenced; the troops were intermixed; the ground was heaped with the dead. Ney directs, animates the charges; every where the Russians are surrounded. They rally; they bring up fresh forces: but Berkeim comes up; the cuirassiers rush on their columns—all are cut to pieces.

Napoleon was surrounded by his guard, which he had drawn up in order of battle at the entrance of the forest; it was still fine, and of an imposing appearance. Two thousand prisoners defiled before them; we were intoxicated with so noble a result: our joy was but of short duration, the account given by some Russians damped it. Partonneau had been taken; all his division had laid down their arms; an aide-de-camp of Marshal Victor came to confirm this sad news. Napoleon was deeply affected with so unexpected a misfortune—"Must this loss come to spoil all, after having escaped as by a miracle, and having completely beaten the Russians." The combat was still very warm on the left bank: from four to five thousand men opposed to the enemy's army an obstinate resistance. "Go and see what is the state of things; ascend the right bank, examine what is passing on the left, come and give me an account of it." I went and saw brilliant charges of infantry and cavalry; those which General Fournier conducted were particularly conspicuous by their simultaneousness and impetuosity. But the disproportion was immense; we were forced to give way; the horrors of the bridge began: it is useless to recall this scene of desolation.

We left the dreary banks of the Beresina, where

we had acquired so much glory and experienced so many misfortunes: we marched on towards Wilna. We discoursed of nothing, we were occupied with nothing, but the arrival of the Austrians; the lowest soldier, dreamed of nothing but Schwartzenberg. Where is he? What is he doing? Why does he not appear? I will not permit myself any reflexion on the movement of this prince, then our ally.

For a long time we had no news from France; we were ignorant of what was going on in the Grand Duchy; we were informed of it at Malotechno. Napoleon received nineteen despatches at once. It was there, I believe, that he determined on the plan of quitting the army, but he did not execute it till at Smorgoni, eighteen leagues from Wilna. We reached that place. The Emperor sent for me towards two o'clock; he carefully closed the doors of the apartment that he occupied, and said to me: "Well, Rapp, I set out this night for Paris; my presence is necessary there for the good of France, and even for the welfare of this unfortunate army. I shall give the command of it to the King of Naples."— I was not prepared for this mark of confidence, for I frankly avow that I was not in the secret of the journey.—"Sire," I answered, "your departure will cause a melancholy sensation among the troops; they do not expect it."—" My return is indispensable; it is necessary to watch over Austria, and keep Prussia within bounds."—" I am ignorant of what the Austrians will do; their sovereign is your father-in-law: but for the Prussians, you will not keep them: our disasters are too great; they will profit by them."— Napoleon walked up and down with his hands behind his back; he kept silence for a moment, and replied: "When they know that I am at Paris, and see me at the head of the nation, and of 1,200,000 men which I shall organize, they will look twice before they make war. Duroc, Caulincourt, and Mouton, will set off with me, Lauriston will go to Warsaw, and you will return to Dantzic; you will see Ney at Wilna, with whom you will stop at least four days: Murat shall join you; you shall try to rally the army as well as you are able. The magazines are full, you will find every thing in abundance. You will stop the Russians; you shall strike a blow with Ney, if it is necessary. He will have already the Loyson division, composed of 18,000 fresh troops; Wrede also is bringing up to him 10,000 Bavarians; other reinforcements are on the march. You will go into cantonments."

Napoleon departed. I received orders from the Major-general, who informed me in a letter what Napoleon had already told me himself; he sent me at the same time a private letter from the Emperor, in which he repeated, " Do all you can to rally the army at Wilna, remain there four days at least; then you will go to Dantzic." The next day I set off. The cold was so intense, that when I arrived at Wilna, I had my nose, one of my ears, and two fingers frozen. I stopped at General Hogendorp's, and went straight to Marshal Ney's quarters; I informed him of Napoleon's orders, and of the conversation which I had with him at the moment of his departure. The Marshal was greatly astonished at Napoleon's estimate of the number of his troops. " Just now," he said to me, " I beat the call to arms, and I was not able to raise five hundred: every one is frozen, fatigued, and discouraged; no one will make any further effort. You have the appearance of being in pain; go and rest yourself; to-morrow we shall see."—The next day I went to him: the King of Naples had just arrived with the guard. We conversed much about our situation. Ney wished for a retreat, he thought it indispensable. " It is forced on us: there are no means of stopping a day longer." He had not ended before the report of cannon was heard. The Russians arrived in force; they were fighting at the distance of half a league from us. All at once we saw the Bavarians returning in confusion: they were *pêle-mêle* with those of our troops that had been dragging behind: confusion was at its height; as Ney had foretold, it was impossible to do any thing with our troops. The King of Naples came to us: he still hoped to make some resistance; but the reports which he received from the heights of Wilna undeceived him. He immediately ordered a retrograde movement, and went towards the Niemen. " I advise you," said the Prince, " to set off without delay for Dantzic, where your presence will soon be wanted. The least delay may cause you to fall into the hands of the Cossacks: that would be an untoward accident, which would be profitable neither to the army nor to the Emperor."

I followed this advice: I hired two Jews who conducted me to the Niemen. My equipages, which had hitherto fortunately escaped all disaster, were already on the road.

We soon arrived at the fatal heights where we were obliged to abandon all the remainder of our *matériel.* It was impossible to ascend it.—Our horses were worn out in unsuccessful attempts;

we assisted them, we urged them, but the ground was so slippery, so steep, that we were obliged to give up the undertaking. I consulted with my aide-de-camp on the steps which it was best to take. My Israelites proposed that we should follow a cross road, which had, besides other things, the advantage of being shorter: they begged me to trust to them; they would answer for me. I believed them: we sat off; on the next evening we were across the Niemen. I suffered horribly; my fingers, my nose, my ear, were beginning to give me great uneasiness, when a Polish barber pointed out a remedy, rather disagreeable, but which succeeded. I arrived at last at Dantzic; the King of Naples followed at some days' march distance; Macdonald, whom the Prussians had so unworthily betrayed, was coming after us. " It is only by a miracle," he informed me, " that myself, my staff, and the seventh division, have not been destroyed: we were delivered up; our legs saved us." He sent me his troops, which were incorporated with those that I had under my orders. The Russians appeared almost immediately. General Bachelet had a very smart engagement with them. They spread themselves around the place, and the blockade began.

CHAPTER XXXVII.

DANTZIC appears made by nature for a fortress: washed on the north by the Vistula, protected on the south-west by a chain of precipitous heights, it is defended on all other sides by an inundation, which is spread by means of two rivers which traverse it, the Radaune, and the Mottlaw. Struck with the advantages of so fine a situation, Napoleon had resolved to render it impregnable; he had caused some immense works to be began. *Têtes-de-pont*, forts, intrenched camps, were to protect it from insult and overlook the course of the river; but time had been wanting, and most of the works were either imperfect or scarcely traced out. No magazine was bomb-proof, no shelter sufficiently solid to keep the garrison in security; the casemates were uninhabitable, the quarters were in ruins, and the parapets tumbling down. The cold, still very severe, had frozen the waters; and Dantzic, the situation of which is naturally so happy and so strong, was nothing more than a place open at every point.

The garrison was not in a better state; it was composed of a confused mass of soldiers of all kinds and of all nations: there were French, Germans, Poles, Africans, Spaniards, Dutch, and Italians. The greater number, worn out or diseased, had been thrown into Dantzic because they were unable to continue their march: they had hoped to find some relief there; but destitute of all medicines, of animal food and vegetables, without spirits or forage, I was obliged to send away those who were not absolutely incapable of leaving the place. Nevertheless I had 35,000 left, out of which there were not above 8 or 10,000 fighting men; even these were nearly all recruits who had neither experience nor discipline. This circumstance, indeed, did not much alarm me; I was acquainted with our soldiers; I knew that for them to fight well they only wanted an example. I was resolved not to spare myself.

Such was the deplorable state in which the place and the troops charged with defending it were found. It was necessary first to provide for the most important point—to shelter ourselves from attack. The thing was not easy; the snow covered the fortifications; it obstructed all the covert ways, all the avenues: the cold was extreme; the thermometer was more than twenty degrees below zero *, and the ice was already several inches thick. Nevertheless there was no time for hesitation; it was necessary to resolve to be carried by assault, or to submit to fresh fatigues almost as excessive as those we had experienced. I concerted with two men whose devotedness was equal to their intelligence; these were Colonel Richemont and General Campredon, both were attached to the engineer corps of which the latter had the command.

I gave orders to raise new works, and to clear the waters of the Vistula. This undertaking appeared impracticable, on account of the severity of the season; nevertheless the troops undertook it with their accustomed zeal. Notwithstanding the cold which overwhelmed them, they never suffered a murmur or a complaint to escape them. They executed the tasks which were prescribed to them with a devotion and constancy beyond all praise. At last, after unparalleled difficulties, they surmounted every obstacle; the ice, broken by hatchets and moved with levers towards the sea, assisted by the force of the stream, opened in the middle of the river a channel from sixteen to

---

* Of Reaumur. *Translator*.

seventeen metres broad, and two leagues and a half in length. But we were destined to see difficulties return as soon as they were overcome : scarcely had an unexpected success crowned our efforts, when the cold set in with redoubled severity; in one night the Vistula, the ditches, were covered with a sheet of ice almost as thick as the one we had broken. In vain were boats moved up and down incessantly, to keep up by agitation the fluidity of the water; neither these precautions nor the rapidity of the river could preserve it. It was necessary to resume those labours, which had cost us so much, and which a moment had destroyed. Day and night were employed in breaking the ice ; we could not nevertheless prevent its forming again a third time : but more obstinate even than the elements which combined against us, our soldiers opposed their courage to these obstacles, and at last succeeded in triumphing over them.

On all the remainder of the front of the plain the same zeal was shown and the same difficulties occurred : the earth, frozen several feet deep, resisted the spade and braved the efforts of the pioneers ; nothing could separate this compact mass ;—even the axe rebounded. It was necessary to have recourse to fire to melt it ; great piles of wood, placed at distances from each other, and kept up for a long time, were the only means which enabled us to make excavations and to raise the necessary palisades. With great labour and perseverance, we had at last the satisfaction of seeing in a state of defence works that had only just been begun. The Holm, Weichselmunde, the entrenched camp of Neufahrwasser, and the multitude of forts which protect the approaches of Dantzic, were put in a situation to be able to offer a noble resistance; and, if this town was not raised to the degree of strength of which it was susceptible, it was at least capable of supporting a siege, the duration and adventures of which are not amongst those events which do most honour to foreign arms.

These fatigues were more than human power could support. Bivouacking, privations, continual service, aggravated their severity: disease, consequently, was not slow in making its appearance. From the first days of January every sun took from us fifty men: at the end of the following month we were losing as many as a hundred and thirty; and we counted more than 15,000 sick. From the troops, the epidemic had passed to the inhabitants: it committed among them the most dreadful ravages; no age nor sex was spared; those who were afflicted by poverty, and those who were surrounded by ease and luxury, were alike its prey. All gave way, all perished; the young, first entering on the path of life—the old, whose career was nearly run. Grief reigned in every family; consternation was in every breast. Dantzic, at other times so lively, now plunged in a melancholy silence, only offered in every direction to the saddened eye the pomp and processions of funerals. The sound of the bells, the hearses, the images of death reproduced under every form, aggravated a situation already so deplorable. The minds of the troops began to be shaken. I hastened to cut up the evil by its root; I interdicted these funeral solemnities which the piety of the living consecrates to the dead.

I had not waited for the epidemic to rage in all its violence before I opposed it. As soon as the first symptoms had been observed, I had caused hospitals to be opened, medicines, beds, and every thing which is necessary for this part of the service to be purchased. A wholesome and plentiful food would have been more efficacious; but we were so badly provisioned, that we could scarcely furnish for each day's allowance two ounces of fresh meat. A little salt meat, some dried beans, composed all that we had in our power to offer to men worn out by long privations. This state of things was cruel; I could not, however, remedy it any way. I had, in vain, despatched a vessel for Stralsund, in order to draw from Swedish Pomerania, which we still possessed, food and medicines; the sloop, charged with my despatches, assailed by a violent tempest, was driven on shore. We were approaching the Equinox: the Baltic was already agitated by storms: it was not possible to make a second attempt.

Courage was the only resource we had left. It was only at the point of the sword that we could obtain the means of subsistence; but, whatever was the devotedness of the troops, prudence did not warrant conducting them against the enemy, exhausted as they were by disease and misery. It was necessary to resign ourselves to fate, and patiently hope that the gentle influence of the fine season would come to recruit our strength: this was not far distant; all the signs which announce it were already showing themselves. The weather was milder, the ice was beginning to melt, the breaking up of the frost was near, and we flattered ourselves that the inundation would relieve, to a certain degree, the fatigues that we were suffering; but that which was expected to solace our misfortunes was always that which raised them to their height.

The Vistula cleared itself with violence: since 1775 there had never been an example of such impetuosity in the current: the finest part of Dantzic, its magazines, its arsenals, became a prey to the waves; the country was covered with water; nothing presented itself, for the extent of several leagues, but the afflicting spectacle of trees torn up by their roots, of houses in ruins, of men, of cattle floating lifeless and in confusion among the loose ice. Our destruction appeared inevitable: all our works were demolished; our palisades carried away, our sluices broken, our forts opened and undermined by the waves, left us without the means of defence before a numerous enemy. We could no longer communicate with the Holm, a position so important, and of which the fortifications were nearly annihilated. The island of Heubude was in a deplorable state: our posts of the Werder, those of the Nerhung, had been submerged. To complete our misfortunes, we were threatened, when the Vistula should resume its course, with seeing the inundation which habitually surrounded the place dried up.

CHAPTER XXXVIII.

But the Allies did not well second the elements which were fighting for them. Instead of at once coming to the attack, they wasted their time in miserable intrigues: there were proclamations on proclamations, some for the magistracy, some for the inhabitants, some for the soldiers. Some were excited to revolt, others to desert: the brave Poles, the Westphalians, the Bavarians, were, in turns, solicited, pressed, and menaced. This paper-war gave me little uneasiness; I knew the fidelity of my troops; I had the greatest confidence in them. I gave them a proof of it; as soon as the proclamations reached us, I had them read at the head of the regiments. This open conduct pleased them; they were grateful for it; they only had the greater contempt for an enemy who seemed to hold their honour more cheap than their courage, and they themselves often brought to me these fine productions of Russian genius, without having even read them.

The besiegers persisted in remaining inactive before the place: I occasionally roused them from the lethargy into which they were plunged. These gentlemen threatened us rather insolently with an assault; they had even, towards the end of January, ordered a great number of ladders in the villages of the Werder. I resolved to make them see that we were not yet reduced so low. On the 29th I put some troops in motion in the direction of Brantau; General Granjean debouched from Stries with four battalions, a troop of cavalry, and two field-pieces; he routed, in his excursion, some bands of Baskirs and Cossacks: this was the prelude to a more serious action.

I knew that fresh troops had arrived before the place, and that they were spread about in the Nerhung, and occupied in force Bohnsack and Stries: I sent to reconnoitre them. General Detrées was charged with this expedition. He routed, at first, every thing which presented itself in his way; but his riflemen abandoned themselves too much to the pursuit, and had nearly become victims of their rashness: a cloud of Cossacks fell on them, and would have cut them to pieces if Colonel Farine had not saved them. We were less fortunate at another point: our advanced posts had orders to keep under arms, to observe the movements of the enemy, but not to engage in action: Colonel Heering, who commanded at Stolzenberg, could not contain himself; he imprudently descended into the plain, and attacked the Cossacks with thoughtless impetuosity; his troops, surprised in a defile, could not withstand the shock of the cavalry, and were broken. This piece of folly cost us 250 men. The enemy grew warm: this trivial success had given them confidence. Towards three in the afternoon, their columns presented themselves before Langfuhr, and succeeded in establishing themselves there. Thirty men posted in front of this village were taken prisoners: they had gone into a house, and had made a long resistance; the ground was heaped with dead, but, seeing no chance of relief, they were obliged to lay down their arms, for want of ammunition. I immediately gave orders to retake this position: General Granjean began to march with eight battalions, four pieces of artillery, and some cavalry: the attack was completely successful; the Russians were routed and put to flight. They endeavoured to return to the charge, but, always broken, always overwhelmed by our cavalry, they appeared at last decided on retreating. We were not slow in following their example. The field of battle was nearly deserted, when the Neapolitans left in Langfuhr were suddenly assaulted by swarms of Cossacks, supported by a numerous infantry. General Husson and the Commandant Szembeck came up rapidly with a Polish battalion, charged the enemy with the bayonet, and made a dreadful slaughter of them.

This check calmed the petulance of the Allies; there was no more question about ladders or assaults. On my side, I left them quiet: I was not in a condition to give them frequent alarms. My troops were exhausted: on their legs night and day, worn out by disease, pierced with cold, badly clothed, still worse fed, they could with difficulty sustain themselves:—nothing equalled their wretchedness but the resignation with which they supported it. Soldiers with their noses and ears frost-bitten, or wounds still open, cheerfully performed the service of the advanced posts. When I saw them defiling on parade, muffled up in furs, their heads wrapped in bandages, or walking with the help of sticks, I was affected even to tears. I should willingly have given some relief to men so unfortunate, but yet so constant: the Russians did not suffer it. They had imagined that their proclamations had produced all the effect they expected from them; that we were fighting among ourselves, and that the people were in a state of revolt: they resolved to profit by such a fine conjuncture, and to take us.

It was now the month of March; on the 5th, at daybreak, they poured like swarms on my advanced posts, they covered, they inundated all my line, and spread themselves in multitudes in the villages which it included. At the report of so sudden an attack, I gave the necessary orders, and proceeded towards Langfuhr with the General of division Granjean. We had scarcely gone a few steps when we heard the charge furiously sounded: it was the chiefs of battalion Claumont and Blaer, who were charging with the bayonet a column of Russians of 3 or 4000 men, and dispersing them. We doubled our speed in order to assist them, but the attack had been so impetuous that we could not arrive in time: we reached the village just as the acclamations of the soldiers announced their victory. I hastened to congratulate them on this fine feat of arms, which it really was, as less than 800 men had completely routed four times their number of infantry and cavalry. They had even nearly got possession of their cannon; three Neapolitan voltigeurs were already cutting the traces of the horses that had been killed, when they were charged in their turn and obliged to leave their prize.

Fortune was less favourable to us in other

points: General Franceschi supported himself with difficulty in advance of Alt-Schottland, he gave ground, defending it, however, foot by foot: he followed his instructions, and saved time. The brave Colonel Buthler came in haste to his assistance. Scarcely had the Bavarians arrived at the first houses of the village, when they rushed with impetuosity on the enemy, repulsed him, charged him with the bayonet, and succeeded in preventing his advance; but while they were making a resistance on one side, the Russians threatened them on the other. After three unsuccessful attacks, they had at last triumphed over the fine resistance of the chief of battalion Clement, and had made themselves masters of Stolzenberg: they were already debouching from this village, and were about to take us in flank. This movement should have been decisive; I hastened to prevent it. I gave orders to the sixth Neapolitan regiment to occupy on the right a small hill which strengthened our position. General Detrécs conducted the attack, charged, and took the summit; the enemy hastily attempted to retake it, but could not succeed. Quite covered with bruises, with his clothes full of holes from bullets, Colonel Degennero opposed an invincible resistance, and forced them to retreat. In the mean time, General Bachelu, with four battalions under his orders, mounted the heights on the right of Schidlitz: on a sudden he rushes on the Allies, attacks them in flank, and overthrows them. In vain they endeavour to fortify themselves in the houses; our voltigeurs, led on by Lieutenant Bouvenot and the sub-officer Tarride, break through the window-frames, destroy the doors, kill, take, or disperse all that they meet, and get possession of one piece of artillery: a Russian General animated his troops to defend it, but the impulse was given; three brave fellows, the sub-lieutenant Vanus, the Quarter-masters Autresol and Hatuite, rush furiously upon it, and get possession of it.

It was three o'clock in the afternoon, and the Allies still occupied Schottland and Ohra; notwithstanding his courage, the chief of battalion Boulan had not been able to dislodge them. I resolved to try a second time a manœuvre which had so well succeeded;—I turned them. While I led on a false attack by the head of Schottland, General Bachelu masked his march, and went towards Ohra; he was followed by three battalions of infantry, a hundred and fifty, horses and a light battery. Our troops boiled with impatience; as soon as they heard the charge begin, they uttered cries of joy, sprang forwards against the enemy, broke his ranks, and completely routed him. He rallied, and returned to the charge; but the grape-shot was redoubled: the bayonet carried disorder among his ranks. He flies, he endeavours to escape through every outlet, but finds none that are not intercepted. Necessity rouses his courage, he rallies, debouches, and rushes on us. The confusion becomes terrible. He struggles to escape from disgrace, our soldiers to consummate the victory; on either side, they press on; they attack with fury. An adjutant-major of the 29th of the line, Delondres, rushed into the middle of the Russians; a few brave fellows followed him: death and confusion waited on his steps; but soon overpowered by their number, exhausted by large wounds, he is obliged to lay down his arms: but his spirits return; he recovers himself; indignation gives him strength: he attacks his escort, takes it, and comes to bear a part in the victory: it was no longer disputed. Our troops, who had come forth at the noise of the firing, had ranged themselves in front of Ohra, and commenced a destructive firing, which overpowered the enemy:—he gave way, broke his ranks, and only escaped death by invoking the clemency of the conqueror.

In a moment the streets were heaped with the dead. Five hundred men laid down their arms:

most of them belonged to that army of Moldavia which we had almost destroyed at the passage of the Beresina.

The enemy fled in every direction. In the Nerhung, at Neufahrwasser, every where, he expiated by defeat the success which he had gained by surprise. Major Nongarède had only to shew himself, to disperse clouds of Cossacks who were skirmishing without success with some weak Neapolitan posts which we had in the rear. Some detachments of dragoons gave chase to the Russians who had ventured in front of Saspe, and took Brasen.

We again occupied the positions that we held before the attack: unfortunately they had cost us dear. We had 600 men *hors de combat;* it is true that most of these soon recovered from their wounds. Of this number was Major Horadam, Colonel d'Egloffstein, and General Devilliers, who will be found to figure so often in this narrative.

The enemy had suffered more; 2000 of their troops lay on the dust, we had between 11 and 12,000 prisoners in our hands, and one piece of artillery.

This day was one of the most glorious of the siege: it was a fresh example of what courage and discipline may effect. Under the walls of Dantzic, as at the passage of the Beresina, worn out by want or by disease, we were still the same; we appeared on the field of battle with the same ascendancy, the same superiority.

CHAPTER XXXIX.

THE Russians might have been *satisfied*. It was not likely that they would return soon to the charge. However, the transactions of the 5th had convinced me of the necessity of different measures, which I was unwilling to take. They had only succeeded in penetrating as far as the foot of Bichofsberg, where Colonel Figuier was keeping a strict look out, by the protection of an old convent of Capuchins: this neighbourhood was too dangerous; I caused the old edifice to be pulled down. Some houses in several villages, and particularly in Schottland, were fortified. We had retaken this place, but with great difficulty: the resistance had been so great, that it was at one time a question whether we should not burn it. I rejected this cruel expedient: I could not make up my mind to ruin inhabitants who had already suffered so much during the first siege. I thought it more honourable to drive off the Russians at the point of the bayonet, and I succeeded; but I did not like to run this perilous risk again.

In the mean time the epidemic was far from subsiding: it appeared, on the contrary, to gather fresh strength every day. Six thousand men had already perished; 18,000 men were lying inanimate in the hospitals. General Franceschi, whom death had spared so many times on the field of battle, had just expired. Every hour, every minute, increased our losses, and carried off our most valiant soldiers. Substantial food would have saved them; but our provisions were coming to an end. We had no longer any quantity of animal food or cattle; straw even was wanting for the beds of our sick: I resolved on seeking for some remedy for evils which so many brave men were enduring. The attempt was dangerous; but they well deserved that I should expose myself to some dangers in order to relieve them.

For a long time I had purposed sending an expedition against Quadendorf, where it was supposed there were abundant resources. I had hitherto deferred it because the troops which were at my disposal appeared to me insufficient; but necessity spoke more forcibly than all these considerations: I hesitated no longer. General Devilliers crowned the heights of Wonneberg and of Pitzendorf; his right supported on Zigangenberg, and the left by the brigade of General Husson. He commenced without delay an alternate fire of artillery and musquetry. While the enemy returned this harmless fire as well as they could, General Heudelet debouched by the valley of Matzlaw, and got possession of the post charged with its defence. General Bachelu marched in front. Twelve hundred men, and six pieces of cannon, under the command of General Gault, were advancing in the second line, and formed the reserve. Five hundred Russians wished to prevent our entrance into Borgfeld. They were trampled under foot: all who escaped the bayonet perished by the edge of the sabre: all were put to death. The enemy came up with their masses, and were not more successful. Overpowered, broken before they were in a state of defence, they found safety only in flight. They were not allowed time to place their artillery in battery; pursued without intermission, they were obliged to leave the field without firing a single round: the Poles were irresistible; chiefs and soldiers, all rushed on the Russians with a determination and boldness of which there is no example. A drummer, the brave Mattuzalik, knocked down one of the enemy with his drumsticks, and compelled him to surrender.

While we drove them before us, General Heudelet threatened their rear. As soon as the enemy perceived this movement, it was no longer a flight, it was disorder, confusion, of which it is difficult to form an idea. They deserted their wounded and their hospitals; they evacuated, with all speed, Schweiskopff, Saint-Albrecht, and did not halt till they reached the other side of Praust, which our voltigeurs entered pell-mell with them.

On arriving at Saint-Albrecht, I learned that the Russians were still maintaining their ground on the banks of the Mottlau. I made arrangements to prevent their receiving any relief while we attacked them. Major Scifferlitz, with a battalion of the 13th Bavarian, assisted by a company of Westphalians and the flotilla, was charged with this attack. It took place with perfect concert and great impetuosity: 300 Russians were laid in the dust with their chief, who had fallen under the blows of the brave Zarlinwski; the remainder were drowned or taken. A hundred of them were escaping through the inundation, when they were overtaken by Lieutenant Faber, who charged them at the head of some brave troops, up to the neck in water, and brought them back. A mere boy, young Kern, animated our soldiers; he went before them; excited them; he threw himself into the thickest of the fight. His comrades paused, and hesitated to follow him. He turned to them with the boldness which courage inspires; "Forward! Bavarians!" he exclaimed, and they were carried away by his impulse.

The day was drawing to a close: the Russians displayed such large numbers of troops in front of Quadendorf, that I did not judge it right to continue the attack. We returned to Dantzic, after having caused the enemy an immense loss, and having taken from them 350 men. This was almost the only result of so brilliant a sally. Scarcely did it procure us a hundred head of cattle. We had been anticipated: all that the villages had contained had been removed to the rear.

Independently of the attempt to procure provisions, I had another object in view, which did not succeed better. Since the commencement of the blockade I had no channel of communication with the French army: I was not aware of its force, or of its fortune. I had put every means in operation in order to get some information on these points; but the hatred was so general and so rooted, no bribery had been able to overcome it.

I hoped that the burgomasters would be more tractable, but they knew nothing but the reports that were circulated by the Russians. I remained in a state of the most complete ignorance of every thing that was going on around me.

After all, whatever might be the course of events, the place was to be defended, and defended to the very last moment; that is to say, we had to live as long as possible with the resources that we still possessed. I redoubled my economy; and, as something is generally gained by an interchange of ideas, I formed a commission which was exclusively charged with the care of the provisions. Count Heudelet was the president; it was of very great service. It applied itself in a particular manner to ameliorate the condition of the hospitals. It made purchases of linen, of medicines, and substituted for butter, which was no longer to be procured, gelatine. All the wine and fresh meat we had was reserved for the sick; and in order that they might not fail us, the commission seized, after a valuation on both sides, the cellars and the cattle which were found in the place. The troops no longer received any animal food but the flesh of horses, which had been obtained in the same way. But all the cares of the commission could not subdue the epidemic: it might be said that this cruel pest was inflamed in proportion to the opposition it met. Continually more violent, more irremediable, it burst forth with fresh strength in those places that it had already attacked, and assailed those that had before escaped. Weichselmunde, Neufahrwasser, previously free from its attacks, now became a prey to its ravages. The troops, the population, from one extremity of our lines to the other, struggled in the agonies of a cruel disease. Those who escaped, and those who fell, equally deserved pity. Given up to all the convulsions of delirium, they wept, they groaned, they dwelt on the remembrance of their battles and their pleasures, which no longer existed but in their dreams.—Now calm, now furious, they called on their country, their parents, the friends of their childhood; they prayed for, they shuddered at, the destiny of the brave men who had perished;—torn alternately by contrary passions, they breathed out the remnant of life in the horrors of despair.

The more remedies were lavished, the more the sufferings increased. The evil spread by means of those very efforts which were used to destroy it. Every day of the last fortnight of March carried off more than 200 men. The epidemic gradually ceased to be so destructive; but it was not till the end of May that it was subdued altogether. It had by that time swept away 5500 inhabitants, and 12,000 brave soldiers. Among this number was General Gault: an excellent officer, a soldier full of courage—he deserved a better lot.

Disease was making war on us for the benefit of the Russians, while they themselves disturbed us but very little. The expedition of Borgfeld had cooled their courage; they made intrenchments, they fortified themselves, they were only engaged in defensive measures. Nevertheless, as it was absolutely necessary to give some signs of life, they every now and then endeavoured to surprise my advanced posts. Annoyed by these insignificant attacks, I wished in return to break their slumbers as they were breaking ours. They had above Brentau a signal which furnished me with the means. Our business was to burn it: I intrusted the management of it to two officers, whose intelligence and courage I had experienced. They were the chiefs of battalion Zsembeck and Potocki. On a dark night they went forth from Langfuhr, and marched for a long time without being perceived: discharges of musquetry at length apprised them that they were discovered; they immediately rushed on and overthrew the enemy. Potocki advanced towards Brentau, and dispersed a numerous body of infantry which opposed his passage. Forty men threw themselves into a kind of block-house: a voltigeur followed them, and summoned them to surrender; he was killed. The Poles, quite furious, immediately inundated the redoubt, and exterminated all the Russians that it contained.

Whilst these things were going on in the village, Zsembeck made himself master of the signal. He set fire to it, and immediately descended into the plain, overthrew and cut to pieces the detachments which he found in his way, and pushed on as far as the walls of Oliwa, where he threw some shells. At the same time the brave Devillain, quarter-master to the eighth, swept, with a dozen hussars, all that part of our advanced posts. He charged with so much boldness that the Cossacks were terrified and broken. Success encouraged him; he extended himself to the right, reconnoitred, searched the wood, and did not join our troops till the moment they were retiring.

Meanwhile all the signals were on fire. The Russian army ran to arms, and expected every moment to see itself attacked; it passed in this state the rest of the night and the whole of the next day. We repaid them in a mass the alarms which they had given us in detail.

The political horizon became every day more cloudy. Prussia had thrown aside the mask; she made war against us by insurrection. This event could not be hidden from the soldiers, the Russians had too great an interest in informing them of it. I consequently threw no obstacle in the way of its being made known. Immediately attempts to seduce the soldiers again began to be resorted to. The enemy thought that the confidence and attachment of our troops were shaken. The disproportion between the means of attack and defence, money, promises, every thing was brought into play to engage them to desert. A bounty was offered as a recompense for shame : I was justified in offering one as a reward for fidelity. I promised a reward of 200 francs to any one who should deliver up a man convicted of seducing our soldiers. This measure had its effect. Most of the emissaries that the besiegers had in the place were pointed out to me. According to our laws they had incurred the pain of death; but men in general are less wicked than unfortunate. Nearly all of them were fathers of families who had yielded to necessity. I delivered them up to the derision of the soldiers; I ordered their heads to be shaved, and dismissed them. This device kept them at home; I was freed from them without having recourse to executions.

The garrison appeared very little disturbed by the increase which it had learned the enemy had received. Nevertheless I wished it to judge of itself what it was still capable of. It was near Easter. The weather was mild, the sky clear. I appointed a review; it took place in the face of the army which was besieging us. At daybreak the inhabitants, the sick even, occupied the heights of Langfuhr; they spread themselves on the glacis and avenues, and crowned all the ascents from the plain which separates Stries from Oliwa. The troops were not long before they appeared. Seven thousand men, followed by a numerous artillery, all in magnificent condition, successively ranged themselves in order of battle. They manœuvred, they defiled, with unparalleled precision. The Russians, astonished at so much boldness, did not venture to trouble us: they, also ranged in order of battle, were spectators of our movements, without throwing any obstacle in the way. It would have been, however, a fine opportunity for them; not a piece was loaded; I had particularly prohibited the use of cartridge. The bayonet alone was to punish them, if they were rash enough to give the slightest insult.

This measure was, perhaps, rather a bold one, but it was necessary to exalt the courage of the soldier, and to convince him of the contempt that the boasting of foreigners deserved.

CHAPTER XL.

After parading, the question was how we should subsist; this was much less easy. The enemy had rifled all the villages, and had left neither forage nor cattle; no more resources were to be had, unless we sought them at the distance of several leagues. I had gained experience at Borgfeld, and I acted accordingly. I had obtained exact information on the facilities and the obstacles which an expedition into the Nerhung presented; I knew the number, the position of the troops, and their complete security. I made my arrangements. Twelve hundred chosen men, three hundred and fifty horse, a company of light artillery with eight pieces of cannon, commanded by General Bachelu, advanced towards Heubude. The enemy, driven in, endeavoured in vain to defend Bonhsack. Bachelu does not give him time to recollect himself, charges him, routs him, and drives him back in confusion as far as Woldern. The enemy's principal forces occupy this village. Near five thousand men receive him and support him; but, always carried forward by the same impetuosity, our troops come up running, and prevent him from deploying. They presently commence the attack: a part of them spread as sharpshooters, over the downs and the plain, the rest remain in line and commence a destructive fire. Our artillery, our cavalry, come up, and complete the defeat: it was so prompt and so decided, that the artillery did not attempt to fire a single round; it escaped with all speed from the field of battle. A column of Lithuanians ventured to stem the torrent. Colonel Farine rushed on it with his dragoons, and compelled it to lay down its arms. The reserve was still untouched. The brave Redou marches towards them; he watches them, seizes the moment when they are retiring, charges them, and takes them prisoners: at the same time Captain Neumann goes in pursuit of the fugitives, flies from left to right, scatters confusion in all directions, and with a handful of soldiers gathers up some hundreds of the Allied troops, whom he obliges to surrender. This advantage cost him two wounds. The sub-lieutenant Schneider was still more hurt, and alone received twelve lance-wounds.

I had myself followed the movement of General Bachelu: I advanced as far as Woldern; but the Russians were flying in such disorder, that it appeared to me useless to follow them any farther. The troops that had defeated them, were quite sufficient to pursue them. As soon as I learnt that they had driven them back more than twelve leagues, I stopped their march. They fixed their quarters, and employed themselves in taking away the forage and cattle that we found in the places that we had got possession of.

The reserve that I had with me was useless, owing to the promptitude and dexterity with which General Bachelu had conducted this expedition. I ordered it to cross the Vistula. It landed in front of the fortress of Lacosta, and marched towards the dyke, which the enemy still occupied. At the same time the gun-boats came up the river and commenced the attack. The Russians soon gave way, and dispersed. We extended ourselves without any obstacle over the whole extent of the Werder.

We remained four days in these different positions. General Bachelu, on the right bank of the river, rifled that part of Nerhung that he had taken; whilst with the aid of our boats we drew, from the left side, all the resources that we could get. Five hundred head of horned cattle, four hundred head of sheep, twelve hundred quintals of hay, eight hundred of straw, and two thousand three hundred decalitres of oats, were the result of this expedition. The enemy tried to intercept our convoys; but the *sang-froid* and dexterity of Lieutenant Hoékinski and of the Commissary Belisal, triumphed over all obstacles. The attacks of the Russians even turned to our advantage, and brought us a hundred head of oxen, which the intrepid Brelinski took from them after having defeated them. The army employed in the siege did not attempt to disturb us. Immoveable in its lines, it only appeared occupied with the demonstrations our troops were making on the side of Langfuhr, and Newschottland. Its uneasiness was so great, that the noise of a heavy shower of rain was mistaken for our advance;—it thought itself attacked, set on fire its signals on the left, and spread alarm as far as Pitzendorf.

We had revictualled our hospitals; but our own situation was not changed. Two ounces of horseflesh, and one ounce of salt beef, still formed our daily ration. As soon as I was out of one difficulty I fell into another. I had procured some provisions, but the military chest was exhausted; it had not been able to meet the expense of paying for the provisions we had carried off. I was obliged to issue bills payable on the raising of the blockade. Nevertheless it was necessary to secure the pay of the soldiers, to cover the expenses of the artillery, and the engineer department; without which the place would fall of itself. To what expedient, what means to have recourse in this extremity? There was but one. I was unwilling to adopt it; but every thing gave way to necessity: I demanded a loan of 3,000,000 from the inhabitants.

The inhabitants of Dantzic were indignant at this measure. They complained, murmured, and threatened some commotion. The enemy became more pressing. The fleet, the land forces, all assumed a more hostile attitude. It was at this conjuncture that Baron Servien, condemned to death for decoying soldiers, accused the senator Piegeleau, of being at the head of a conspiracy formed in the interest of Russia. The reputation of this magistrate was untarnished, but the charges were so detailed, so precise, and the consequences of imprudent security so serious, that I ordered him to be arrested. His innocence was soon established. I had for a short time doubted the honesty of this respectable man : it was my duty to make him an acknowledgment. I made it in the way which appeared to me best fitted to calm the impression of this unpleasant adventure. The citizens had remained quiet, and the frequent skirmishes, which had appeared to me suspicious, were owing to the increase of troops which had arrived before the fortress.

The Duke of Wurtemburg had just taken the command of it. More enterprising, more restless, than General Levis, he did not allow my advanced posts breathing-time; if he failed in one point, he tried another. Driven back at Langfuhr, put to flight at Zigangenberg, he threw himself on Ohra. As badly received in that position as in the former ones, he did not the less return to the charge; he attacked at one time Stolzenberg, Schidlitz, and the post of the barrier : defeated at all these points, he tried again, and again was defeated. No check discouraged him; he tried a last effort; he rushed during the night on my troops, who were refreshing themselves after their fatigues, and took some houses, which he set fire to; but at the sight of the two battalions which ran to arms, he was alarmed, and retreated.

The patroles and sentinels were continually engaged. These combats, in which individual courage is put most to the test, were all to our advantage. The Cossacks did not shine at all in them. Three of them combined for the purpose of overpowering a dragoon of the 12th, called Drumes: this brave fellow waits for them with firmness; knocked down by a blow from a lance, he rises, seizes the end of the weapon, draws his adversary to him, and lays him dead on the spot. Héquet, another dragoon of the same regiment, resisted four of these barbarians: although wounded, he knocked down one, killed another, and put the rest to flight. I could cite a thousand traits of the same kind.

These continual attacks harassed my soldiers. I could not suffer them to be insulted by the Cossacks. We took arms: General Granjean commanded the right, General Devilliers the centre, and the left was under the direction of Count Heudelet. The unexpected appearance of our columns froze the enemy with dread. Their horses were grazing freely on the plain, their infantry was at rest in the camps: they did not expect this attack. At the moment we were beginning to move, I received the authentic news of the immortal victories of Lutzen and Bautzen: I communicated it, I proclaimed it, I spread it abroad. Joy, intoxication, enthusiasm, are at their height ; all these sentiments are shewn at once ; our troops are impatient for the fight they burn to conquer. From left to right the cry of " Forward !" is re-echoed. The signal is given. Immediately the artillery is unmasked : the troops approach the enemy, the combat begins, the ground is covered with heaps of dead. Captain Preutin pours his fire upon the enemy, and forces them to evacuate Schœnfeld. The Polish horse-artillery comes up at a gallop, places itself within half gunshot distance, and overthrows every thing in its way. Major Bellancourt and the chief of battalion Duprat press on and bear down the fugitives: they disperse them as often as they rally. Defeated at the centre, the enemy throws himself on our left, and threatens Ohra. Major Schneider opposes a stout resistance. This excellent officer defends himself at one point, while he attacks at another, and makes up by his courage for the insufficiency of the means at his disposal. Generals Brissau and Husson run to his assistance. The Russians, overpowered, cannot stem the torrent; they are put to flight, and do not stop till they reach the heights behind Wonneburg. They soon change their plan, and rush on our right wing, which receives them with admirable firmness. Colonel d'Engloffstein, Major Horadam, Lieutenant-colonel Hope, emulate one another in exertions. Sergeants Vigneux and Auger also set an example of courage. I rush to the midst of this bloody contest: I order the Poles of the 10th to advance, with five pieces of cannon which were in reserve. The combat grows warmer, and becomes more and more terrible. The Russians at last give way, and escape in confusion from the camp of Pitzkendorf. I did not think it right to pursue them: sufficient for the day are the evils thereof. They had about 1800 men put *hors de combat*. I caused the firing to cease. On our side we reckoned four hundred killed or wounded.

The Allies, conquered in two consecutive battles, had solicited an armistice. The war had been carried back to the Oder. We were once more the arbiters of fortune. Our glory was so much the more pure, as it was entirely the result of that impetuous courage which supplies the want of experience, and does not give way before any obstacle. Mere recruits had triumphed over the combined forces of Prussia and Russia. Captain Planat brought us the news of it at the moment when the defeated besiegers were seeking safety in flight. Napoleon had added to his despatches proofs of his munificence: he condescended to grant me the ribbon of the order of *La Reunion.* He authorised me to make promotions, to confer marks of honour, and to point out the superior officers that I thought fit for advancement. His victories had exalted the courage of the troops; the soldiers once more swore by his genius; they saw him again triumphing on the banks of the Vistula. His despatch was conceived in the following terms.

" Monsieur le Comte Rapp,

" The Major-general acquaints you with the situation of affairs. I hope that peace will be concluded in the course of the year; but if my expectations are disappointed, I shall come to raise your blockade. Our armies have never been more numerous or in a finer condition. You will see by the journals all the measures which I have taken, and which have secured me 1,200,000 men under arms, and 100,000 horse. My relations with Denmark are very amicable, where Baron Alquier still continues my minister. I need not recommend you to be deaf to all insinuations, and at all events to keep the important fortress which I have confided to you. Inform me by the return of the officer what soldiers have most distinguished themselves. The promotion and the decoration which you shall think they have deserved, you may consider as conferred; and you may bestow decorations of the Legion of Honour to the number of ten crosses of officers, and a hundred of knights. Make choice of the men that have rendered the most important services, and send me the list by return of the officer, in order that the Chancellor of the Legion of Honour may be instructed of the appointments. You may also fill up in your ranks all the vacant appointments, as far as the rank of Captain inclusive. Send also an account of these promotions. On this I pray God, &c.

"NAPOLEON."

"Neumark, June 5, 1813."

CHAPTER XLI.

THE sovereigns had fixed on the conditions of the armistice. Every fortress was to be re-victualled once in five days, and to have a league of ground beyond its lines; but the Duke of Wurtemberg took on himself to elude this engagement. He contested my statement of our positions; he disputed about the limits. After several conferences, we came to a provisional arrangement, and we remitted the question to persons appointed to settle it. There then arose new difficulties; at one time they alleged want of provisions, at another want of conveyance. The allowances, at all times incomplete, were constantly in arrears; at last they were entirely suspended. The Duke stood in need of a pretext; he found one: he pretended that we had broken the truce, because we had done justice on some band of robbers which infested our rear. His letter, which could have been transmitted to me in two hours, was two days before it reached me. So many subterfuges made me indignant: I went straight to the point; I told him that I would have no more tergiversation, and that he must fight or fulfil the conditions stipulated on. He replied by talking of the cause of nations and of kings. This language was curious; I expressed to him how much it astonished me, coming from the mouth of a prince, whose sovereign had been our ally for five years, and whose brother was still fighting for us. This last example touched him a little. He replied peevishly, " That a Russian General-in-chief did not think himself inferior in any respect to a king of the Confederation, since it only depended on the Emperor Alexander to raise him to that dignity, and that then he might be a king as well as another; that he would, however, only be so under this slight condition, that it should not be at the expense of any power or person."

The troops ran to arms: but the Duke was unwilling to take the consequences of this rupture. He offered to continue the supplies. They ought to have been sent on the 24th, but they did not come till the 26th, and were never complete. Tainted meat, and flour so very bad that we did not venture to make any use of it till we had made experiments on it, were the only provisions that the Russians furnished us with. They were not more faithful as to the quantity: we did not receive above two-thirds of what was guaranteed to us by the treaty.

The Prince de Neuchatel told me that it was necessary to hold out till the month of May following. The thing was quite impossible; I had neither provisions nor troops sufficient for so prolonged a defence. I pointed it out to him; my despatch was precise. Every thing that was possible we were ready to undertake, but good intentions do not create means.

"Dantzic, June 16, 1813.

"My Prince,

"I received the letter which your Highness did me the honour to write me from Neumark, of the 5th of June. M. Planat has also sent me a collection of *Moniteurs*, containing the detail of the decisive battles gained by Napoleon over the combined forces. I had had, from the day before M. Planat's arrival, intelligence of the brilliant successes of the armies of Napoleon. This good news has produced on the garrison the best effect: it has seen that I had not flattered it with vain hopes; and the patience and courage of which it has given proofs have found the reward that they were entitled to expect.

"The armistice has also been transmitted to me, and I write to your Highness particularly on this subject. I ought not to conceal that this suspension of arms, in the state things are in, must be more disadvantageous than advantageous to the garrison; for disease still occasions us a loss of 1100 men a month, the consequence of which will be that by the 1st of August we shall have lost 1700 men.

"Our provisions, moreover, will be consumed; and, if the Duke of Wurtemberg does not show a better disposition towards us than he has done, we shall not be able to save, as otherwise we should have done, a part of the provisions that he is bound to furnish us. Till the month of October my situation will not give me any uneasiness, but beyond that period it will be a painful one indeed; for we shall want men to defend the immense range of our fortifications, provisions for the defenders, and we shall have no more to hope for from resources within or without.

"The account of the composition for the rations since the blockade will shew your Highness that I have carried into execution, in the distribution of the provision, the rigid economy which our situation demanded, and that to this end I have employed all the resources of which I could avail myself: but these resources are exhausting; and it would be useless to reckon on those which might be derived from the expulsion of the inhabitants; indeed, it is only necessary, in order to be convinced of this painful truth, to recollect that two years ago Napoleon called by requisition on the inhabitants of Dantzic, for 600,000 quintals of corn—an order which was most rigorously carried into execution. At that time only 23,000 quintals were left for the subsistence of its inhabitants. Since that period they have lived on this quantity, and some trifling portions which had been concealed from the strictest searches.

"I have given above an account of the loss which disease still produces every month. The accounts of the situation of the troops present an effective force of 20,558 men; which supposes, according to the estimates (but too accurate) which I have already given, that the garrison will be reduced, at the end of the armistice, to 20,000 men, from which number must be deducted at least 2,000 who will be in the hospitals, even supposing that want does not increase the ravages of disease. What would be our condition, then, by the month of May, when the progress of mortality which the actual state of things supposes will have mowed down so many of our men? It results from the calculation which we are able to make, (admitting that winter diseases do not materially increase the number of deaths, and allowing for a loss of 1000 only per month,) that the sum total of the loss would be, by the 1st of May, 8000 men, omitting altogether those who may perish in actions, or who may die from the consequence of their wounds. There would only remain, then, by the month of May, an effective force of 11,000 men, of whom there will certainly be 3000 in the hospitals: how is it possible to defend fortifications so extensive with so feeble a garrison?

" I have already given orders for the construction of works intended to defend the entrance of Mottlaw, an extremely weak point when the rivers are frozen. I am going on besides with every thing which can secure my communication, but, I repeat, men are wanting for the defences. Your Highness must not doubt that, if it becomes necessary, I will do every thing which honour and my devotion to the Emperor can suggest, to maintain myself in some point or other of Dantzic.

"The state of the magazines will prove to your Highness that our resources are very limited. You will, no doubt, think that I shall manage them with all the care which the desire to make an honourable defence inspires me with: it is with this object in view that I have added to the commission for the management of provisions, which the law has appointed in places in a state of siege, a considerable number of members in addition to those which it requires.

"I have put them under the presidency of the General of the division Count Heudelet. This commission is instructed to lay before me all the measures which may tend to economy and to the welfare of the soldiers; it has rendered great service, and I am sorry that I did not give it at an earlier period the attributes which it now possesses.

"The article of finances merits very particular

attention on the part of the Emperor and your Highness. All the funds which have been left at my disposal have been consumed, and I have been obliged to have recourse to a forced loan, which I imposed on all those who were still able to yield any thing. This loan has been put into execution with great severity towards those who pretended not to be able to contribute to the common defence; but notwithstanding all the pains which were taken in respect to this, and all the measures which were resorted to in order to conduce to similar results, up to the present time, only 1,700,000 francs have been raised, and there will be great difficulty in levying the rest.

" The expenses of the pay of the army, those of the constructions in the engineer department, as well as those which concern manual labour (for all the materials which are in the place will be taken, as has been done for these two months past, by requisition, to be paid for on demand at the raising of the blockade); the sums for the artillery; those for the hospitals, for the different branches of the service, for provisions, that is to say, in short, for every thing that is necessary for manual and daily labour; for the constructions in the marine department, clothing—all these expenses, of which I have ordered an estimate to be made, amount to more than 900,000 francs per month.

"A foreign commercial house has offered to provide funds here, provided that the paymaster-general guarantee him reimbursement at Paris. It would be a great security of tranquillity, if I saw this affair settled; but I should prefer that the funds were sent to me, for otherwise some circumstance might happen which would stop the stipulated payment in the second month. Your Highness is well aware that there are no means of dispensing with punctual payment of all the expenses alluded to above, especially with a garrison composed like the one which I command; I beseech you, then, to solicit from his Majesty measures which may secure the payment of the sums which I stand in absolute need of.

" I ought not to close without observing to your Highness that the quantity of powder which now remains in our magazines is not nearly in proportion to what would be necessary for a siege.

"To conclude, Monseigneur, I have thought it right to make beforehand all the observations which occur to my mind on the insufficiency of men for the defence, on the inadequacy of the means of subsistence, on the funds necessary to meet our expenses, in short, on our supplies in every department which are at all in proportion to our approaching wants. I beseech your Highness, then, to lay before the Emperor the painful situation in which we shall be placed, if his Majesty does not come to our aid. What remains of the garrison is in other respects excellent, and the performance of its part may be relied on, by means of a few rewards well applied for unlimited devotion. It will do all that the Emperor can expect from his best soldiers, and will justify the confidence which his Majesty has placed in it, and the favour which he has bestowed on it by placing it among the number of the corps of his Grand Army.

" I am, &c.

(Signed) " COUNT RAPP."

The armistice was meanwhile approaching its termination. The troops, the ammunition, the artillery for the siege were arriving in abundance before the place. We soon had 300 pieces of cannon of large calibre, and 60,000 fighting troops before us. The disproportion was immense; but we had conquered when enfeebled by disease, we might hope to conquer again. Nothing but the means of subsistence was wanting. The Russians were so convinced of this that they gave chase to the smallest craft which went fishing. Their gun-boats had even captured some of the craft which had not gone beyond the limits. I immediately despatched a flag of truce to the Admiral. I represented to him that the sea ought to be free for a league from the shore, and that I should know how to make the conditions of the armistice respected, if they again attempted to infringe them. He promised to conform to the conditions, and no more to molest our boats. He did not, indeed, molest them; but that very evening he carried off our unfortunate fishermen, who had retired, without suspicion of what was to happen, to their huts. He dreaded the abundance which a few pounds of fish would produce in the fortress. The peasants and the course of the waters were not better treated. They entrapped the former, and turned the latter in another direction. It appeared to them as if every thing was put in motion to get us food; that it was coming on us in every direction. It was in vain for me to protest; indeed, never were pretences or excuses wanting. At last the Prince of Wolkonski announced to me the recommencement of hostilities; I received this news with sincere satisfaction. Our relations were too disagreeable for me not to desire to see them ended.

CHAPTER XLII.

THE enemy was full of confidence; he fought, he intrigued, he flattered himself with the hopes of taking the place by storm or reducing it to ashes; but through the vigilance and intrepidity of my soldiers all his attempts failed. His incendiary rockets were wasted on our ramparts; his attacks were repulsed, and his emissaries discovered. Several of these wretches had already introduced themselves into our magazines, and were preparing to set them on fire. I perhaps ought to have made an example of them; but I dreaded lest this example might be dangerous: I feared that it would give a knowledge of the crime to those who were then ignorant of it, and that it would spread alarm amongst the troops. I pretended to believe that they had endeavoured to pilfer some provisions, and I dismissed them; but I issued such severe proclamations against theft, that I kept malevolence at a distance.

After three days of humiliation and fatigue the

besiegers succeeded at last in getting possession of the wood of Ohra. Driven from it almost immediately, they re-appear with new forces, and drive in our detachment. The battalion on duty takes a second time its arms, and rushes to its relief. Major Legros attacks the wood; two companies of grenadiers march on the village; the troops meet each other, they charge, they drive, they overthrow : the struggle becomes frightful. Captain Capgrau seizes by the hair a Prussian officer : whilst he throws him on the ground, he himself is on the point of being killed ; a soldier already touches him with his bayonet. Lieutenant Sabatier turns aside the blow, closes on the Cossack, and runs him through with his sabre ; but at the moment he saves his chief, he receives in the throat a wound which compels him to quit the field of battle. In the wood, in the village, every where, the Russians are defeated : Captain Duchat kills four himself; Commandant Charton, Lieutenants Devrine and Blanchard, mow them down in heaps ; a crowd of brave fellows rush into the midst of them and increase the disorder. Francou, whose valour a short time afterwards was so famous, Martin, Couture, Rochette, Schlitz, Lepont, Bennot, Soudè, Paris, Belochio, all sub-officers of the light troops, the carabineer Richida, the drummer Breiquier rush even to the centre of their columns, and give them up to the swords of our soldiers.

Fresh troops take the place of those who are defeated, and establish themselves in the wood; our heroes led on by Lieutenant Joly Delatour, rush forward, attack and defeat them. The enemy, nevertheless, do not lose courage; they form again into ranks, and present themselves a third time: but always overcome, always cut in pieces, they at last discontinue their attacks.

Early the next day the enemy throw themselves on Stries and Heiligenbrun, and take possession of Langfuhr. Our advanced posts fall back on two blockhouses, situated on the right and left of the village. The Russians pursue them, and prepare to attack them; but the Poles fire on them with such rapidity and precision that they are forced to retreat. They return in greater force, they cover, they inundate the defiles of the Jesch Kental; they threaten Heiligenbrun, they debouch by Stries; all my line is under fire. These manœuvres left no doubt as to their intentions; it was clear that they had serious views on Langfuhr; I determined to anticipate them, and march out to meet them. I assembled my troops, the left in the village, the centre in the ravines of Zigangenberg, and the right extending as far as Ohra. Twenty-four pieces of cannon, commanded by General Lepin, are placed in the middle between the two wings. They immediately commence a firing: the enemy's redoubts, his masses, his camp at Pitzkendorf, every thing is ploughed up by our ball, we dismount two of his pieces. The Poles, the Bavarians, the Westphalians, and 250 horse, commanded by General Farine, debouch at the same time. The brave Szembeck, already engaged with the Russians, was driving them from Duvelkam; as soon as our soldiers perceive this defeat, they grow warm, and they are encouraged; they rush on the redoubts at Pitzkendorf. The allies, driven back on their works, endeavour in vain to defend themselves; young Centurione at the head of his hussars, overcomes every obstacle, but falls covered with wounds. At the sight of this excellent officer carried off at so tender an age, the thirst for vengeance kindles the courage of our men: infantry and cavalry pour pellmell on the redoubts. The trumpeter Bernardin, the chasseur Olire, the Quarter-master Boucher, throw themselves into the midst of the Russians; Lieutenant Tirion, already wounded, goes straight to the officer who commands them, and takes him prisoner. From that moment it is no longer a battle—it is slaughter, it is carnage, all perish at the point of the bayonet, or only owe their lives to the mercy of the conquerors. Whilst our soldiers are giving themselves up to the fire of their courage, a cloud of Cossacks rush on them, and threaten to cut them in pieces; but General Cavaignac moves up so promptly with the reserve of cavalry, the troops charge with such zeal, the Commanding-Adjutant de Erens, the chiefs of squadrons Bel and Zeluski, Captains Gibert, Fayaux, Vallier, Pateski, and Bagatho, display so much intelligence and skill that the enemy is completely routed, and disperses in the most frightful confusion.

The cannonade grew warmer and warmer. The Russians still occupied the Johanisberg, the ground in front of Pitzkendorf, and made a furious attack on Langfuhr. I detached against them a battalion of the Vistula, which was supported by the Neapolitans commanded by General Détrées, having under his orders General Pépé, who has since been rendered so famous by the events which have occurred in his own country. The brave Szembeck commenced the attack; it was made with great regularity and impetuosity. The Russians, routed at the point of the bayonet, overthrown by destructive charges, seek safety by flight. The Poles pursue them with increased boldness; the drummer Hhade seizes one of them by the cartouche-box, pulls him from the ranks and disarms him. Captain Fatczinsky forgets that he is wounded, rushes into a house which they occupy, kills their chief, and makes thirty of them prisoners.

The Neapolitans are not less impetuous; they press forward in pursuit of the fugitives, drive them on and fire upon them. General Pépé, Colonel Lebon, the Commandants Balathier, and Sourdet, Captains Chivandier and Cianculli direct and excite their courage, and give at once both precept and example.

On the opposite side of the mountain the conflict was not less obstinate or bloody. At the appointed signal, Colonel Kaminsky had marched on the Russians and had dislodged them; he drove them before him—the pursuit was hot. Reinforcements arrive; our adversaries endeavour to stem the torrent, but the Poles pursue them with impetuosity. Roseizensky, Drabizelwsky, Doks, Zaremba, Zygnowiez, followed by men devoted to their leaders, rush on them and cut them in pieces.

We were masters of Johanisberg. The weather was terrible; the enemy was flying at a distance. I ordered a retreat to be sounded—it was done in the most perfect order. At six o'clock every thing was tranquil. But the Russians were not long before they made their appearance again. They attack at the same time the Belvedere and the heights of Heiligenbrun; they keep up a very smart firing; but they are nevertheless unable to obtain the slightest advantage. Colonel Kaminsky, and Commander Szembeck display a courage and skill which disconcert them. They withdraw, but at the same time two battalions, supported by a numerous cavalry, march on the village of Stries. Kaminsky rushes to its defence. The Russians return immediately to the charge; they scale the heights, they attack the Belvedere, push on, and press their attacks. All their attempts fail against the excellent arrangements of Major Deskur, and the valour of the chiefs of battalion Johman and Robiesky.

This was not the first diversion they had tried. They had already driven in our advanced posts from Schidlitz to Ohra: Major Schneider, attacked in front and flank, only maintained this suburb by courage. He perceived a numerous column which imprudently entered the great broad-street: he charged it, poured a shower of grape-shot on it, and destroyed it. General Husson came up with the reserve. We resumed the offensive; in an instant the wood and the village are taken, and the Russians thrown into dreadful confusion. The chief of battalion, Boulanger, disarmed eight of them; a sergeant who had been wounded by a musquet-ball, the brave Vestel, disarmed three: the sub-officer Cornu rescued one of our men, and took his escort prisoners.

I was once more master of the Johanisberg and of Langfuhr, but this success could not be durable; it was evident that the Russians, continually returning to the charge with fresh troops, must in the end succeed. Moreover, these two positions were so far separated from each other, that they could neither injure me much, nor be of much use to me. I gave, in consequence, orders to evacuate them, if the Allies presented themselves in force. But their audacity had given place to timidity. They were afraid of removing from the heights; they dared not take possession of a village that had been abandoned. Impatient, nevertheless, to get possession of it, they engage in a general action to make themselves masters of a post which I had resolved not to defend. The troops take arms; the fleet supports them. The whole of my line is attacked: eighty gun-boats fire in concert, and pour their shot on Neufahrwasser. Schelmulle, New-Schottland, Ohra, Zigangendorf became a prey to the flames. The enemy's troops spread themselves as a torrent in the plain; they overthrow or set fire to every thing that opposes their passage: I came up in the midst of this terrible confusion. But already the courage of the Russians had declined; they were repulsed by a handful of brave men under the command of Major Poyeck, and left the approaches of Kabrun filled with heaps of dead bodies. I gave orders to pursue them: the impetuous Gibert rushed forward with his chasseurs. Captain Maisonneuve joined him; they charged: the disorderly multitude was repulsed and driven back on Schelmulle. This party of the Russians, joined by the troops which occupied the village, received, without being broken, the destructive vollies of Captain Ostrowsky; but almost immediately turned by Captain Marnier, one of the bravest officers in the French army, they fled, disbanded themselves, and sought for refuge amidst the ruins of buildings which they had given to the flames.

The struggle was not less warm at Langfuhr: attacked by 12,000 Russians, our posts fought and struggled in the very midst of the immense columns of the enemy. Sergeant Szhatkowsky stood in need of all his courage to escape from the Cossacks. Employed on a work in front of the village, with thirteen men, he was surrounded by these irregular troops; he immediately rallied his workmen, faced on one side, attacked on the other, and constantly marching and fighting, at last disengaged himself without losing a man.

The Russians, humiliated by their losses, marched on the village. Two houses, which I had put in a state to resist a *coup de main*, defended its entrance: our adversaries attacked them in flank, pressed on, and attempted an escalade; but a destructive fire threw them into confusion, and compelled them to retreat. To increase their misfortunes, the Neapolitans appear, and attack them. Colonels Lebon and Dégennero pressed on, broke through the cavalry, and penetrated into Langfuhr. The cavalry returned to the charge with greater numbers and audacity; it took advantage of impediments, seized the right moment, and charged our battalions as they were scattered up and down the streets. A bloody conflict ensued; the brave Paliazzi fell, pierced with ten lance wounds: Captains Nicolaü, Angeli, Dégennero, are covered with wounds, and are compelled to leave the field of battle. In vain the intrepid Grimaldi, in vain Lieutenants Amato, Legendre, Hubert, Pouza, Gomez, and Zanetti endeavoured to stem the torrent; numbers prevailed: we were compelled to retreat. A few brave fellows, engaged too far in front, were unable to follow, and were cut off; but far from giving way to despair, their courage increased at the sight of danger; they rallied round the Adjutant-major Odiardi. They advance, they turn, they retrograde, and at last reach the fortified houses. Already were they attacked for the second time; the Allies, enraged at the resistance, threw themselves on the pallisadoes; tore them from the ground, and appeared about to triumph over all these obstacles: but, laid in the dust as soon as they were open to our fire, they soon despaired of success: unable to take the houses, they set fire to them. Our brave fellows are not disconcerted: some continued the firing, others subdue the flames; and the enemy is not advanced farther than before. A thick smoke hid from our view the two houses; I was still ignorant whether our troops occupied them, or whether the Allies had made themselves masters of them. Reports announced the latter; I resolved, nevertheless, to make an attempt to know; but the balls, fired from off the houses, were falling on us in showers: I concluded that they were lost. One circumstance in particular rendered it probable: the firing had ceased, while the flames were still raging. I was unwilling, however, to believe that they had been given up; I ordered a fresh reconnoissance. The neighbourhood of these two posts was heaped with dead bodies, clad in white capotes. Deceived by the colour of the dress, the officers whom I had sent were persuaded that the Bavarians had perished; all asserted it, all were convinced of it. The loss of such brave men was melancholy, and deserved not to be admitted on appearances. I charged one of my aides-de-camp, Captain Marnier, to ascertain the real state of the case: this mission could not be disagreeable to him; he had, at the battle of Uclès, summoned a Spanish division to lay down its arms, and had taken it: the spears of the Cossacks would not stop him. At daybreak he set out from Kabrun, with eight men who requested to follow him; he proceeded, running, to the house on the right. Immediately the barriers were opened, the detachment joined him, and made its retreat, in spite of the Russians who rushed forward to intercept it.

That on the left still remained; but the greatest difficulty was overcome. I was certain that it still existed: I issued orders that it should be relieved. A battalion advanced; no sooner was it perceived by these admirable soldiers, than they placed their wounded in the midst of it, and rushed forth on the Allies. Several received wounds; the brave Dalwick was struck by a ball, which shattered his left shoulder, but he continued to fight with ardour. The contest became more and more bloody. The Bavarians, inflamed with the noble desire to save their countrymen, and animated by the example of two intrepid officers, Adjutant-major Seiferlitz and Lieutenant Muck, threw themselves precipitately on the enemy, broke through them, and at last brought off in safety this handful of devoted soldiers. They made a kind of triumphal entry: every one was anxious to see them, and to congratulate them: all spoke of their constancy, and boasted of their resignation. Alone, abandoned to their own resources, without provisions, without ammunition, parched with thirst, suffocated by the smoke, they had braved the threats, repulsed the summons, and rejected with disdain the insinuations of the enemy. Captain Fahrebeck in particular was loaded with encomiums; his *sang-froid* was admired, his courage extolled; his firmness and his prudence were the subject and the theme of every one's conversation. It was natural that I should testify to these brave fellows how much I was satisfied with them: I inserted in the order of the day the perils that they had faced, the risks they had run; and I lodged the wounded in my own hotel. Every day I visited them; every day I made myself acquainted with their situation, and assured myself that their wants were supplied. An officer, who was in my confidence, M. Romeru, was moreover instructed to lavish on them the cares and the consolation which I was not able to give them myself.

As soon as the enemy was master of Langfuhr, he began to labour; works upon works were constructed: his exertions were unremitted. His design was to narrow my position more and more, and ultimately to compel me to shut myself up in the fortress. This plan was admirable; the only question was how to execute it; this was a more difficult affair. I had covered the fronts of Oliwa and Hagelsberg by a formidable entrenched camp; nine works composed it: the lunette of Istria occupied the culminating point of the heights, which command the fort and defile of Hagelsberg; it was flanked by the batteries Kirgeur and Caulincourt. A selection was afterwards made among the hillocks situated between these works and the road of Langfuhr, of those which were most advantageously situated, and they were fortified. The following was the arrangement of these redoubts: going on the right from Caulincourt, the redoubt Romeuf, the battery Grabowsky, the redoubt Deroy, the battery Montbrun. In fine, to complete this line of fortifications and to extend it as far as the Vistula, two batteries more were established; the one called Fitzer, across the road of Langfuhr, the other known by the name of Gudin, was little farther distant; it rested on an artificial inundation, which extended as far as the dyke on the left of the Vistula, and formed the right of all our line, which still enclosed two batteries which were placed on the other side of the river. All these works were palisadoed, provided with barracks, and powder magazines. I ordered moreover two barrack camps to be erected; the one to hold four hundred men, towards the extreme left behind Kirgeur, and the other a hundred and fifty, behind Montbrun. The part of this line which extends from Montbrun to Gudin was connected by a kind of covered road; that which extended to the left was sufficiently protected by the badness of the ground. I thought, moreover, that it was necessary to secure the power of acting on the offensive in a part of these works.

Ohra was also put in a state of defence. A mass of houses, which communicated with each other, and the doors and windows of which had been carefully walled up; parapets and palisadoes, which had no other outlet but a tongue of land, bounded by two beds of water, rather deep, formed an advanced retrenchment, known under the name of the *first entrenchment* of Ohra; the second, situated four hundred yards in its rear, was composed of the same materials, and was supported on a large Jesuit's convent, which had been fortified. The heights and defiles which approach the suburb were fortified; the redoubt with which they were surmounted prevented the enemy from turning us, and soon became famous under the name of the batteries and lines of Friuli.

Whilst we were executing these works the enemy frequently skirmished with our advanced posts: Schidlitz, Ohra, Stolzenberg, were in turn the object of his attacks. Repulsed at every point, he attempted to surprise Heubade ; but he there met with more than his match. The Commandant Carré, an old soldier, full of vigilance, and acquainted with all kinds of stratagems, perceived his columns, succeeded in making them engage each other, and retired without loss from a critical situation.

Quite ashamed at this cruel mystification, the Russians flatter themselves with the prospect of taking revenge at Kabrun. They surround it, they scale it, but received by a destructive firing, directed by Captain Nazzewski, they withdrew leaving the ditches filled with dead. They march once more on Schidlitz: put to flight the first time, they return to the charge with fresh vigour and impetuosity; but Adjutant-major Bouttin, Captains Kleber and Feuillade, raise to such a degree the courage of our soldiers, that they throw themselves on the Allies, and defeat them.

The fleet also was not idle: on the 4th, at daybreak, it appeared, drawn up in line of battle; it had failed two days before in two consecutive attacks, and completely wasted more than seven thousand rounds of cannon-shot. Shame, thirst after vengeance, every thing incited it to fight: it was the explosion of a volcano. The frigates and the gun-boats thundered forth at once, and covered us with a shower of shells: but far from being discomposed, our batteries are managed with increased coolness and regularity. Officers and soldiers, all soar above danger, and only think on victory. A gunner, engaged in spunging a gun, had an arm carried off; Captain Pomerenski takes up the spunging-rod and performs duty. Sergeant Viard serves a piece which fires red hot balls, and points it as at the polygon; Lieutenant Milewski manages and superintends his own, sinks one gun-boat, damages others, and compels them to leave the scene of action. Captain Leppigé, Sergeant-major Zackowski, Sergeant

Radzmiski, Corporal Multarowski, set the most admirable examples of coolness and skill. Captain Henrion, Lieutenant Hagueny, Captain of the frigate Rousseau, the seamen Despeistre and Costo, the Corporals Davis and Dubous stick to their cannon, and do not cease to fight them till the enemy fly. The fleet, convinced of the inutility of its efforts, makes to sea, with the satisfaction of having fired nine thousand rounds in order to kill two men. It had also dismounted two of our pieces; but it had lost two gun-boats, nine others were seriously damaged, and its frigates were full of holes from our shells and ball.

We very soon had a more formidable enemy to contend with. The Vistula suddenly rises, overflows, or breaks down the dykes, and escapes with impetuosity. The place, the fortifications, become a prey to the waves. The bridges are carried away, the sluices destroyed, and the banks broken up; the waters, now without impediment, rush into the ditches, and undermine the bastions. Those of Bœren, and Braunn Ross were in ruins, and it was to be feared, that, when the Vistula should return to its natural bed, the inundation could not be kept up; but the engineer department was not negligent in this critical juncture, they succeeded in re-establishing the breaches, by means of great dexterity and perseverance; and when the water subsided, the inundation kept up by the branches which run through the Werder scarcely experienced any change of level.

The turn of the Russians had now arrived: they had profited by the embarrassment which the swelling of the waters caused us; they had raised battery on battery; and on the 15th of November they unmasked a score lined with guns of the largest calibre. The fleet also came up to try its powers against our forts. Masses of infantry were ready to give the assault as soon as the palisadoes should be destroyed; three bomb-vessels and forty gun-boats pour in a dreadful fire upon Newfahrwasser. Danger, far from dejecting, only animates our soldiers; they swear they will conquer, they swear they will punish the assailants. The troops of the line keep close to the cannon, the artillery points them, as at a review; they damage and dismast a crowd of gun-boats. Of a sudden, a terrible explosion is heard: a ball had pierced the Sainte-Barbe, the sloop disappeared. The same explosion was repeated. We congratulate, and encourage each other, we are eager to imitate the heroes who fire with such admirable precision. Three vessels become nearly at the same time a prey to the flames, and the first line of ships retires all covered with wreck. The second takes its place, without being more successful, and the divisions thus succeed each other every three hours, without slackening the fire. At last, disheartened by the obstacles which were opposed to it, by the courage of our soldiers, the excellent arrangements of Colonel Rousselot, and the vigilance of Major François, the fleet retires to repair its losses. Twelve hours fighting, and 20,000 discharges of cannon, had no other result than the killing and wounding of half a dozen of our men, and the damaging of three of our gun-carriages. This was the last attempt. A few months earlier it would have been infallible, but in war the very moment should be seized.

The troops were more successful. They attacked our posts in advance of Ohra, and got possession of that of the Etoile on the heights at the right of the village. Major Legros does not allow them time to establish themselves; four chosen companies, under the command of Captains Valard and Aubry, march without delay to the point of attack. They take the Russians by surprise, and cut them in pieces. In vain do they appear with fresh troops; repulsed, put to flight, they disperse, though without losing courage; they make a fresh attempt, but met by a destructive discharge of musquetry, they disband and fall under the fire of two companies placed in the village of Stadtgebieth which annihilate them.

CHAPTER. XLIII.

The season became every day more severe. The rains were incessant, and produced a fetid fog which the sun, without heat, could scarcely dissipate. But what was still worse, the scarcity still continued to increase. Horses, dogs, cats were eaten, we had exhausted all our resources, our salt even failed us. It is true that industry supplied the deficiency. Some soldiers conceived the idea of boiling some old planks which had formerly belonged to a storehouse; the trial succeeded. We sprung this new mine, and the hospitals were supplied. The population was reduced to the last extremity, it lived on nothing but *malt* and *bran*, and it had not even enough of these to satisfy its wants. In this state of distress I thought the philanthropic allies would not repulse their fellow-countrymen. I drove out of the fortress the prisoners and the beggars, all, in a word, who had no provisions. But the Prussians were inexorable, and but for the inhabitants of Saint-Albretch, they would have left them to perish from want. Others went to the quarters occupied by the Russians, and were not better received. Without shelter, without food of any kind, they would have perished under the eyes of these liberators of humanity, if I had not taken pity on their wretchedness. I gave them some relief, and sent them to their homes. Several begged to be employed in the fortifications, and they received half or a quarter of a loaf of ammunition bread for their wages. In the mean time the enemy had completed their works. From time to time they tried their batteries, and seemed to perform a prelude to a more serious action. On the 10th, accordingly, they all began to fire towards the close of the day. The town, the Holme, the entrenched camp of Newfahrwasser are inundated with shells, grenades, and red hot balls. The fire breaks forth, and consumes the convent of the Dominicans. The Russian prisoners who were kept in the building were on the point of perishing, when our soldiers rushed in and saved them from death. The flames continuing to increase in violence, wreathed round the neighbouring houses, and threatened to reduce them to ashes. At the same time the Allies presented themselves in strength before our posts of Ohra, and drove them back as far as Stadtgebieth. I came up with Count Heudelet. The enemy, overthrown at the point of the bayonet, attempted in vain to return to the charge; General Husson and Major Legros repulsed all their attacks. A mistake augmented their losses. Two of their columns took each other for the enemy, and engaged accordingly. They recognised their friends by the cries of the wounded, but more than 300 men were already laid in the dust. On our side we had a hundred *hors de combat*.

Early the next day the enemy appeared before the houses beyond Stadtgebieth. Driven back twice, he set fire to them. Although twice wounded, Captain Basset was unwilling to give them up, but it was not long before the progress of the flames compelled him; he retired fighting all the way. The Allies, being masters of the village, pushed on, without halting, to the level of the Etoile, and took it. The posts which remained on the descent of the hill were henceforth too weak, and I called them in. The enemy at last took possession of this position, but he paid sufficiently dear for a mere embankment of earth.

The farther he advanced towards Langfuhr, the more perilous his situation became; taken in flank and in rear, thundered on by the batteries of the Holme, he was soon unable to debouch from the redoubts he had raised at Kabrun. Confused at having mistaken the true point of attack, he concentrated his forces, and marched on the heights of Ohra. He tried every means to get possession of them, and I neglected none to defend them. I improved, I extended my works. I made every one contribute his skill and information. Superior officers of each department of the army, under the presidency of General Granjean, consulted on the measures which the security of the place required. They put our provisions and our ammunition out of the reach of the ravages of fire. They portion out the provisions, and organize the engine department, and get mills in readiness; so that if the shells should destroy what we already possessed there were others to supply their loss. In the mean time the Allies continued their bombardment. Fire succeeded fire, and threatened to reduce every thing to ashes. On a sudden the batteries ceased, the firing was suspended. At this unexpected silence, the inhabitants resumed their courage; they ran, they fled to the relief of the quarters that were on fire. Poor people! there was nothing to save from the flames but a few walls; the place was on the brink of its ruin.

The enemy had only stopped the firing in order to resume it with greater fury. As soon as his arrangements were made, he opened it with violence. The batteries of the Etoile, those of Johannisberg, Kabrun, Schellmule, Langfuhr, fire rounds upon rounds, and overwhelm us with shells, rockets, and red hot balls. Fires break out, the edifices are falling to ruins. Dantzic presents the appearance of a volcano whose eruptions issue forth, disappear, and again shew themselves in every direction. The two banks of the Mottlaw, the Butter-Marck, the Poggenful, the Speicher-Insell, all are destroyed. In vain do the troops run to their assistance, an unintermitting shower of projectiles triumphs over their efforts, and a loss of several millions aggravates the misfortunes of this wretched population.

Our forts and our villages were not in a better condition. Ohra in particular was nothing but a heap of ashes. Five batteries were blazing against it without intermission; clouds of riflemen, sheltered by the inequalities of the ground, overwhelmed us with shot, and impeded the working of our guns. The first entrenchment, almost annihilated by fire and balls, still held out. Major Schneider defended it with a degree of valour and prudence which still promised a long resistance; but it was on the point of being taken by approaches and I gave it up. I also relinquished the head of Schidlitz. The enemy had tried some days before to make themselves masters of it. Three companies had presented themselves before our posts, but being vigorously charged by Captain Leclerc and Lieutenant Kowalzky, they were routed, and sought their safety in flight. This lesson was not thrown away; the Allies returned with more considerable forces, and established themselves there. A very serious accident befel us soon after. A shell burst in a magazine of wood, and set it on fire. Powder is not quicker; in an instant every thing is in a blaze. The flames, propagated by a strong wind, spread themselves from point to point, and present a heap of fire which no effort can extinguish. A sad spectator of so cruel a disaster, I hoped at least to save the distant buildings. My expectation was still deceived, and we had the misfortune to see the greatest part of our provisions consumed before our eyes. Officers and soldiers, all were plunged in mournful silence, all beheld with amazement this scene of desolation, when of a sudden a terrible discharge of musquetry is heard. The enemy were attacking the lines of Frioul, and were getting possession of them. Captain Chambure flies to their relief. This valiant officer commanded a chosen troop called the *free company*, or the *enfants perdus;* he rushes into the redoubt, and cuts the Russians in pieces. Not a man escapes: those who avoid the bayonet perish under the fire of the chiefs of the battalion, Clauron and Dybowski. Lieutenant Conrad gives a proof on this occasion of singular firmness. With a shoulder fractured by a ball, he throws himself into the thickest of the fight; Chambure extricates him: "You are wounded," he said to him, "this is no longer a place for you, go, and announce to the general that we are in the redoubt."—"Captain," replied the intrepid lieutenant, "I have still my right-hand, you have only your left,"—and he continues to fight.

Defeated on the left, our assailants throw themselves on the right, and drive us back as far as our forts. I did not judge it right to resume the attack, in a dark night; I waited till the next day. Two columns, commanded by Generals Breissau and Devilliers, marched at the same time on Stolzenberg and Schidlitz; the Russians occupied them in force; but our troops fought with so much zeal—Major Deskur, the Chiefs of the battalions, Poniatowski, Crikicowski, and Carré, Captains Fahrebeck, Perrin, Kalisa, and Rousin, led them on with so much skill and valour, that the Allies were broken, and left the field of battle heaped with their dead. Unfortunately, our success was dearly bought: General Breissau, so estimable for his talents and courage, was dangerously wounded. In vain all the aid of art was lavished on him; he expired after a month of acute suffering.

Our troops were victorious; but what a spectacle awaited them within the fortress; rubbish and ruins were the only remains of our magazines. One alone had escaped the fury of the flames. Indebted for its preservation to Colonel Cottin, and the second in command of the staff Marquessac, it had only been secured by dint of their zeal and perseverance. The chief of squadron Turckheim, who had also given so many proofs of zeal, and Lieutenant Fleurz, had also succeeded in saving 4000 quintals of corn: all the rest was in flames; every thing else had perished. We did not preserve two months' provisions, which the flames, continually more active, and an unceasing bombardment, threatened with destruction.

The Russians advanced slowly, but yet they advanced.—They had got possession of different posts, and marched in mass on Stolzenberg. Too weak to offer an effectual resistance, our soldiers had evacuated it. General Husson assembled a few troops, and sounded the charge. It took place with remarkable impetuosity. Captain Milsent, and Adjutant-Major Rivel, moved forwards at the head of some of our bravest soldiers, came up with the enemy and defeated him.

Captain Chambure was preparing a more severe lesson for our assailants. He embarked in a dark night, deceived the vigilance of the fleet, and landed opposite to Bohnsack. He surprises the village, sets fire to the habitations and magazines, slaughters the men and horses, and returns to his boats. They were no longer on the shore. The trumpets were sounding, the call to arms was heard; death appeared inevitable. Nevertheless, he does not lose courage, he calms the soldiers, throws himself across the enemy's entrenchments, and arrives safe and sound at the moment it was thought he was destroyed. He soon begins another march, and proceeds to Brœsen; he falls unexpectedly on the troops which occupy it, defeats them, and does not retire till he has burnt their camp. Scarcely has he returned, when he rushes upon a more perilous enterprise.—He penetrates into the enemy's trenches, defeats and drives in their posts, and returns to shelter himself behind our batteries. Lieutenant Jaimebon, seriously wounded at the beginning of the attack, fought as if he had not been affected by the pain; it was so acute that the fear alone of discouraging the soldiers was capable of stifling his groans. He died five days afterwards: honour be to his memory!

The *free company* became every day more audacious. Trenches, palisadoes, were trifling obstacles; it penetrated every where. In the middle of a dark night, it stole along from tree to tree, the whole length of the avenue of Langfuhr, without being perceived by the Russians. On a sudden it leaped into their works, killed some of the Russians, drove out the others, and pursued them as far as Kabrun. The brave Surimont, the intrepid Rozay, Payen, Dezeau, Gonipet, and Francore, threw themselves on the redoubt, and carried it. A hundred men were put to the sword, the others owed their escape only to flight.

We carried on with our besiegers a war of surprise and bravery; they combated us by stratagems and proclamations. Their batteries were unceasing, and our magazines were destroyed. Our troops, wasted and harassed by labour and want of sleep, had nothing to renew their strength but a little bread and an ounce of the flesh of our horses; if we might give that name to the wretched skeletons of animals, which, rejected by the cavalry and waggon train, had turned the mill, till being unable to stand any longer they were led to the slaughter-houses. It was to men so fatigued with fighting and suffering, that the Russians promised repose and abundance. Every attempt to decoy them was used. Gold, silver, threats, the anger of their sovereigns, the voice of their country, were offered and invoked. The Duke assisted his emissaries;—he wrote, intreated, protested, assailed officers, and soldiers. Desertion began to prevail among our foreign troops, they even refused to do any duty. The Bavarians, the Poles themselves, too well acquainted with our misfortunes, feared to make a sacrilegious use of their arms, and remained in a state of inaction. We were reduced to our mere national troops, that is to say, to less than 6000 men; and we had an extent of more than two leagues to defend. I resolved to inform the Emperor of this painful situation. This was not an easy task; all Germany was in a state of insurrection; the sea was covered with the enemy's squadrons. But no dangers, no obstacles, deterred Captain Marnier; he undertook this adventurous expedition, captured a vessel, sailed along with the English fleet and escaped from it.

The Duke of Wurtemburg attempted to seduce every one. I was not myself free from his attempts. He exalted his resources, depreciated mine, spoke of France, of Siberia, and proposed to me to give up the fortress.—His threats and his offers were addressed to a wrong quarter: I convinced him of this, and I heard no more of them. More suitable means were brought into play; the fires were increased, and the bombardment, continually growing more furious, was kept up night and day. The town, the Bischfberg, the redoubts of Frioul were battered to pieces. Supported by so tremendous a fire of artillery, the Russians expected to carry us by assault. They advanced provided with hatchets and ladders, and rushed on the Gudin battery. Captain Razumsky commanded it; he received them with discharges of grape-shot, and overthrew them. They nevertheless rallied, and attempted an escalade; but overpowered by a destructive firing, they dispersed at the sight of Major Deskur, and left their arms and ladders in the possession of the valiant Captains Zbiewski, and Propocki. They attempted, with as little success, to make themselves masters of the Fitzer battery, in the avenue of Langfuhr. Colonel Plessman, Captain Renouard, and Adjutant Stolling, made a resistance which they could not overcome: three times they return to the charge, as often are they defeated.

The redoubts of Frioul were meanwhile in a deplorable condition; without parapets and mines, overwhelmed by shell and grape-shot, they presented no means of defence: I ordered them to be deserted. The greatest part of the fortifications was still untouched, but our provisions were approaching to their termination.

The season when the ice appears was arrived. Twenty thousand men would have been necessary for me to withstand the progress of the besiegers, to guard the forts, to secure the inundation, and to keep the course of the water free. The contest was too unequal; to have continued the defence would merely have been to spill blood for the pleasure of spilling it.

I conceived I had found a plan which was consistent both with my duty and with humanity. I calculated the number of days that the remainder of our provisions would last us; I proposed to suspend hostilities, and to surrender the fortress at the end of that term, if the course of affairs did not alter the arrangement. Negotiation began, the firing ceased. General Houdelet and Colonel

Richemont went to the enemy's camp and concluded a capitulation, in which the power of returning to France was particularly guaranteed to us. A part of the articles had been already executed; the Russian prisoners had been sent back, the forts had been given up, when I learnt that the Emperor Alexander refused his ratification. The Duke of Wurtemberg offered me to put things in their former condition. This was a mockery: But what could we do? We had no more provisions. It was necessary to be resigned. He managed things as he wished, and we took the road to Russia.

Affected by our misfortunes, our allies wished to have suffered them in common with us. The Poles broke their arms in pieces; the Bavarians swore never to turn them against us. But duty bids the affections be silent. It became necessary to separate. General Prince de Radziwill and Colonel Butler, both so distinguished by their character and by their achievements, led them back to their country.

Thus ended, after one year's fighting, a defence, in which we had to encounter every calamity and every obstacle;—a defence, which is not one of the least proofs of what the courage and patriotism of French soldiers are able to effect.

CHAPTER XLIV.

We were conducted to Kiow. We were there informed of the prodigies performed by that handful of brave men who had not despaired of the safety of their country. They had triumphed at Montmirail, at Sezanne, at Champaubert, in every part where the enemy had dared to await them. All Europe fled before them; the coalition was dissolved. The obstinacy of a soldier snatched from us the fruits of victory. It became necessary to fight and conquer again; but ammunition failed us; the corps did not arrive, the generals were haranguing the troops to make them capitulate. Every thing was lost; our glory, our conquests vanished as a shadow; even the signs of them were repudiated.

The end of the coalition was attained. Our captivity was no longer profitable; we were set at liberty. We returned to France: what a spectacle did she present! The body of emigrants had invaded the army and the anti-chambers; they were bending under the ensigns of command and decorations. The first person that I met at the Tuileries was a chief of a battalion, whom I had formerly assisted and protected: he was become lieutenant-general; he did not know me again. Another, who was with me a long time at Dantzic, had not a better memory. This last person I had received at the recommendation of the Duke de Cadore, I had experienced his sickening adulations: he used to style me *Monseigneur*, your *Excellency;* he would willingly have called me the *Eternal*. In proportion as I told him how much these fooleries displeased me, he increased them; he even conceived the idea of attending at my *levee*. If it had depended on him I must have conceived myself a sovereign. His malversations delivered me from this obstinate flatterer; they became so glaring that the government was on the point of proceeding against him. I saved this gentleman from the shame of punishment; but I made him retire: he went to exercise his industry at . . . . . He soon became acquainted with our reverses, was alarmed, took post, and never stopped till he was on this side of the Rhine: his fear had served him better than courage could have done. He had large epaulets, and four or five decorations. This was well for the opening of his career:—promotion does not go on so quickly on the field of battle. He withdrew as soon as he saw me: apparently his costume embarrassed him. I met a third, who, also, did not feel quite at ease in my presence. Formerly attached to Josephine, he had given proof of a truly exquisite foresight; in order to be provided against all unforeseen cases which might occur in promenades and journeys, he had provided himself with a silver gilt vessel. When a circumstance required it, he drew it from his pocket, presented it, took it, emptied it, wiped it, and put it away with care. This shewed the very instinct of domesticity.

But all these worthies, so ardent for the treasury, for decorations and commands, soon shewed the amount of their courage. Napoleon appeared, they were eclipsed. They had flocked to Louis XVIII., the dispenser of favours; but they had not a trigger to pull for Louis XVIII. in misfortune. We tried a few dispositions; but the people, the soldiers had never been accomplices of the humiliations of France; they refused to fight against the colours that they adored, and the Emperor peaceably resumed the reins of government.

Generals Bertrand and Lemarrois wrote to me to come to the Tuileries; I returned to Paris. A new invitation was waiting for me at my hotel;

the grand-marshal informed me that his Majesty wished to see me. I did not like to keep him waiting; I went just as I was, quite sure that Napoleon would know how to appreciate duty and affection. I was introduced immediately.

Napoleon. " You are there, Monsieur General Rapp; you have been much wanted? Whence do you come?"

Rapp. " From Ecouen, where I have left my troops at the disposal of the minister of war."

Napoleon. " Did you really intend to fight against me?"

Rapp. " Yes, Sire."

Napoleon. " The Devil!"

Rapp. " The determination was compulsory."

Napoleon. (In an animated tone.) " F . . . . . ! I was very well aware that you were before me. If an engagement had taken place, I would have sought you out on the field of battle: I would have shewn you the head of Medusa: Would you have dared to fire at me?"

Rapp. " Undoubtedly,—my duty . . . ."

Napoleon. " This is going too far. But the soldiers would not have obeyed you; they have preserved more affection for me. Besides, if you had fired a single shot, your peasants of Alsace would have stoned you."

Rapp. "You will agree, Sire, that the situation was a very painful one: you abdicate, you leave us, you engage us to serve the King; you return. All the power of old recollections cannot deceive us."

Napoleon. "How is that? What do you mean to say? Do you think that I have returned without alliance, without an agreement?..... Moreover, my system is changed: no more war, no more conquests; I wish to reign in peace, and promote the welfare of my subjects."

Rapp. "You are pleased to say so; but your anti-chambers are already full of those flatterers who have always encouraged your inclination for arms."

Napoleon. "Bah! bah!.... Did you often go to the Tuileries?"

Rapp. "Sometimes, Sire."

Napoleon. "How did those folks behave to you?"

Rapp. "I have no reason to complain of them."

Napoleon. "The King appears to have received you well on your return from Russia?"

Rapp. "Quite so, Sire."

Napoleon. "Without doubt. Cajoled first, then sent about your business. This is what would have befallen you all;—for, after all, you were not their men; you could not suit them: other titles, other rights were necessary to please them."

Rapp. "The King delivered France from the Allies."

Napoleon. "Very true; but at what price! and his engagements, has he kept them? Why did he not hang Ferrand for his speech on the national domains? It is that, it is the insolence of the nobles and priests which made me leave the island of Elba. I might have come with three millions of peasants who ran to me to tell their grievances, and offer their services. But I was certain of not finding resistance in my way to Paris. The Bourbons are very fortunate that I have returned: without me they would at last have had a dreadful revolution.

"Have you read Chateaubriand's pamphlet, which does not even allow me courage on the field of battle? Have you not sometimes seen me stand fire? Am I a coward?"

Rapp. "I have felt, in common with all honourable men, indignation at an accusation as unjust as it is mean."

Napoleon. "Did you sometimes see the Duke d'Orleans?"

Rapp. "I only saw him once."

Napoleon. " He is the only one who has discretion and tact! The others have bad men about them and are very ill-advised. They do not like me; they will now be more furious than ever; there is good reason for it. I am arrived without striking a blow. They are now about to cry me down as *ambitious;* that is their eternal reproach: they have nothing else to say."

Rapp. " They are not the only persons who accuse you of ambition."

Napoleon. " How ..... am I ambitious? When people are ambitious are they as fat as I am?" (He struck his stomach with both hands).

Rapp. " Your Majesty jokes."

Napoleon. " No: I have wished that France should be what she ought to be; but I have never been ambitious. Besides, what do these folks think of? It becomes them well to assume importance with the nation and the army. Is it their courage on which they pride themselves?"

Rapp. "They have occasionally shewn some— in the army of Condé for instance."

Napoleon. " What is that order that I see on you?"

Rapp. " The Legion of Honour."

Napoleon. "The Devil! They have had, however, the sense to make a handsome decoration of it. And these two crosses here?" (He touched them).

Rapp. "Saint Louis and the Lily." (He smiled).

Napoleon. "What do you think of that.... Berthier, who did not like to remain. He will return; I forgive him all; on one condition however—it is, that he will wear his *garde du corps* uniform to appear before me. But enough of this. Well, General Rapp, we must serve France once more, and we shall rescue ourselves from the condition in which we are."

Rapp. "Confess, Sire, (since you have had the goodness sometimes to permit me to speak to you freely), confess that you were wrong in not making peace at Dresden? every thing was repaired if you had concluded it. Do you recollect my reports on the spirit of Germany? you treated them as pamphlets; you blamed me."

Napoleon. "I could not make peace at Dresden; the Allies were not sincere. Besides, if every one had done his duty at the renewal of hostilities, I should again have been the master of the world. I had already gained to my side 32,000 Austrians."

Rapp. "It is only a moment since your Majesty had no ambition, and now we hear again of the sovereignty of the world."

Napoleon. "Ah! well, that's true.—Besides, Marmont, the senators . . . . . My plan was arranged so as not to let a single ally escape."

Rapp. "All these misfortunes are the consequence of the reverses at Leipsic: you might have prevented them by accepting peace at Dresden."

Napoleon. "You are ignorant what such a peace would have been:" (and suddenly growing warm,) "Would you be afraid to go to war again; you, who have been my aide-de-camp for fifteen years? On your return from Egypt, at the death of Desaix, you were nothing but a soldier; I have made a man of you: now you may pretend to any thing."

Rapp. "I have never let slip any opportunity of shewing my gratitude to you for it; and if I am yet alive, it is not my fault."

Napoleon. "I shall never forget your conduct in the retreat from Moscow. Ney and you are of that small number who have the soul thoroughly well tempered. Besides, at your siege of Dantzic you did more than impossibilities."

Napoleon fell on my neck and pressed me with vehemence against him for at least two minutes. He embraced me several times, and said to me, pulling my mustachios—

"Come, come, a hero of Egypt and Austerlitz

can never forsake me. You shall take the command of the army of the Rhine, while I treat with the Austrians and Russians. I hope that, in a month's time, you will receive my wife and son at Strasburg. It is my pleasure that from this evening you perform the duty of my *aide-de-camp*. Write to Count Maison to come to embrace me; he is a brave man, I wish to see him."

Napoleon related a part of this conversation to some persons about him. He told them that I had spoken to him with too great liberty, and that he had pulled my ears. Fortune smiled on him. The courtiers came round him in multitudes:—it was enthusiasm, devotion: they boiled with zeal. These protestations had not, however, all the effect they had promised themselves. Many were rejected; one particularly, who persisted in obtruding his services, was repulsed with severity. Loaded with favours, gold, and dignities, he had overwhelmed his unfortunate benefactor with insults; he was treated with loathing and contempt. These gentlemen boast at present of an incorruptible fidelity. They find fault with the indulgence of the King in the saloons of the Faubourg Saint-Germain. They would like to see all those who were employed during the hundred days led to the scaffold. Chance has served them, appearances are for them; let it be so: but the generals, the ministers of Napoleon, the officers attached to his person, know full well what to think of these stoics of the anti-chamber. Sooner or later the royal government will be enlightened: there is wherewithal to supply the place of the red book.

Napoleon sent for me on the 29th of March, and informed me that I must set out for the army of the Rhine. He gave me the grand eagle of the Legion of Honour, which he had destined for me after the siege of Dantzic. He told me that within fifteen days my forces should be raised to 40,000 men, (I had 15,000 at the commencement of hostilities); I observed to him that this was very little in comparison with those that we were going to have on our hands; that the Congress (its declaration was already known) threatened us with a deluge of soldiers. "The declaration you allude to is false," he replied angrily; "it was fabricated at Paris: however, go. Lecourbe will command in Franche Comté; Suchet in the Alps; Clausel on the Garonne. We have great chance of success. Gerard goes to Metz: he has just tormented me to give him that Bourmont, I yielded to him with regret: I never liked that man's countenance."

"The propositions I have made to the Sovereigns have been coldly received. Nevertheless all hopes of arrangement are not destroyed. It is possible that the energy with which opinion is pronounced, may incline them to sentiments of peace. I am going to make another attempt. This is the letter that I write to them:

" Sir, my Brother.

" You will have learnt in the course of the last month, my return to the coasts of France, my entry into Paris, and the departure of the family of the Bourbons. The true nature of these events must already be known to your Majesty. They are the work of an irresistible power, the work of the unanimous wish of a great nation which knows its duties, and its rights. The dynasty, which force restored to the French people, was not made for them. The Bourbons have not consented to link themselves either to their opinions or their manners. France had a right to separate herself from them. Her voice called for a liberator. The hope which prompted me on to the greatest of sacrifices had been deceived. I came, and from the point at which I reached the shore, the love of my people has borne me even to the bosom of my capital. The first wish of my heart is to repay so much kindness by the maintenance of an honourable peace. The re-establishment of the Imperial Throne was necessary for the happiness of the French: my most earnest wish is to render it, at the same time, useful to the consolidation of the repose of Europe. Enough glory has shone by turns around the colours of different nations; the vicissitudes of fortune have often enough made great calamities follow great successes. A finer arena is open to-day to Sovereigns, and I am the first to descend into it: after having presented to the world the spectacle of great combats, it will be more pleasant henceforth to know no other rivalry than that of the advantages of peace; and no other struggle than the holy contest, whose people shall be most happy. France hastens to proclaim with frankness this noble end of her wishes. Jealous of her own independence, the invariable principle of her policy will be the most unbounded respect for the independence of other nations. If, happily, such are, as I trust they are, the personal sentiments of your Majesty, a general calm is secured for a long time, and justice seated on the confines of the different states, will suffice alone to guard their frontiers.

"I am with esteem, &c."

But all overtures were useless. He was above human stature; he secured the supremacy of France; this was the grievance which nothing could counterbalance; I was convinced of it. His destruction was resolved on.

I set out for Alsace: the hostile attitude of foreign courts had excited general indignation in that province: all generous minds, all who abhor a foreign yoke, were preparing themselves to repulse this league of kings, who, under pretext of fighting with one man, only sought to enrich themselves with our spoils. The inhabitants, by concert and by a spontaneous movement, had rushed to the heights which command the defiles, to the roads or passages, and laboured at the construction of entrenchments; women and children put their hands to the work. They diverted and animated each other, by singing patriotic songs. There was between all the citizens a rivalry in zeal and devotion; some raised redoubts, others cast balls, mounted old muskets, and fitted the cartouches. In fine, every hand was in movement, every one wished to labour in the common defence.

An affecting scene, and worthy of ancient times, took place at Mulhausen, when I arrived there. A ball was given, the most distinguished persons of the town were met, the assembly was brilliant and numerous. Towards the close of the evening, war and invasion of the territory were talked of; every one communicated his advice, every one told his hopes and his fears.

The ladies were talking together, and conversed on the dangers of their country. On a sudden one of the youngest proposed to her companions that they should swear, never to marry any Frenchman who had not defended the frontiers. Cries of joy, clapping of hands, resounded from every part of the room. The looks of all present were directed towards the ladies; the rest of the company came up, and crowded round them. I went with the throng, I applauded this generous proposal, I had the honour of administering the oath, which every one of the fair patriots came to receive at my hands.

This trait recalls the marriage of the Samnites, but it has something perhaps still more admirable in it: that which was an institution among the people in question, was with us the effect of a spontaneous resolution; with them patriotism was in the law, with us it was in the hearts of our fair countrywomen.

CHAPTER XLV.

All this zeal however did not fill up my ranks; the time was passing away, and the recruits did not come in. The allies formed themselves in corps on the left bank of the river; they could cross at any time; my situation was become very critical. I communicated to the Emperor the accounts of my number and situation. He could not conceal his surprise. "So few men! Alsace, the patriotism of which is so ardent! No matter—victory will soon raise battalions. There is nothing to despair of; war has its chances, we shall get through it!"—Napoleon had ordered me, four days before, not to leave a single soldier of the line in the fortified places; to take from the depôts all who were in a condition to serve; to inundate and make good the lines of Weissembourg, and to keep up carefully my communications with Bitche. I was engaged in these measures; but he found that I did not proceed with sufficient celerity; he wrote to me.

"Monsieur General Rapp,

"I have received your letter of the 12th of May; I see by the statement you have annexed, that the 18th regiment of the line, of which your army has two battalions, 1200 men strong, can furnish you with a third battalion, of 600 men; order it to set off immediately from Strasburg to join you. The 32d can only supply a reinforcement of 200 men to your active battalions, which will raise them to 1200 men. The 39th and 55th can furnish you their third battalions; order them to join you. The 58th can furnish you with 200 men, to make its two battalions complete. The 103d can complete its two first battalions to 1200 men; the 104th the same. The 7th light regiment can furnish you with its third battalion ; in the same manner the 10th light regiment. You can then, with a little activity, reinforce your infantry with 4000 men. I am surprised that there has not been more voluntary enlistment in Alsace for these regiments. The 39th of the line is recruited in the Upper Rhine; that department ought at least to have furnished 2000 veteran troops, which, divided between the 39th, 32d, and 18th, ought to raise the third, and even the fourth battalions, to their full numbers. The 10th light, which is recruiting in Upper Saône, ought to receive many recruits. The 57th, which is recruiting in the Doubs, ought also to receive a great number. The 7th light, the 58th, and the 104th, which recruit in the Lower Rhine, ought to be complete. Inform me for what reason all the men that you have at your depôts, are not immediately clothed, and do not fill up your ranks. Let me also know what men are announced for these regiments, from the different departments. Do you expect that by the 1st of June your third battalions will be complete, and that each regiment will amount to 1800 men, which will make 7000 men for each of your divisions? Are you satisfied with the generals of division, and of brigade, under your command? What will be the condition of the 2d chasseurs, the 7th and 19th dragoons, all of which have their depôts in your division, by the 1st of June? These three regiments had at their depôt 400 men, and 300 horses: they must have received an increase since. By the 1st of June, with active measures, this division ought to have 1500 horse. The third division has also all its depôts in your arrondissement: it has 1200 men at its depôt; it ought, then, to furnish you with 2000 horses.

"Paris, May 14th 1815." "NAPOLEON."

I immediately replied to the questions which he had put to me; I explained to him the deplorable state into which the army had fallen : arms, horses, clothing, it was necessary to have every thing renewed. I could not have more than 22,000 men at my disposal by the 1st of June. The picture was not brilliant, but the Emperor made so admirable an use of his resources, that we were never justified in despairing. He put fresh funds at my disposal; he stimulated my zeal, begged me to neglect nothing to increase my forces, and to reconnoitre all the defiles. His despatch deserves to be known.

" COUNT RAPP,

" I received your letter of the 18th of May. I have allotted 13,000,000 francs for clothing in the distribution of May. Orders for considerable sums have been sent to each corps of your army: be assured that they will be paid. I cannot reconcile to my mind that you will not be able to have at your disposal by the 1st of June more than 22,000 men, when the force at the depôts is 4000 men. Send for the third battalion of the 18th regiment, the third of the 39th, the third of the 57th, the third of the 7th light, the fourth of the 10th light, which will raise you one regiment of four battalions, four of three battalions, and four of two battalions, or twenty-four battalions in all. Hasten the clothing; money is in the course of being transmitted to you, and will not be wanting. The enumeration of your cavalry, which you have sent me, is not correct. How is it that the 6th cuirassiers has only its third and fourth squadrons at the depôt? What is then become of its fifth squadron? The same observation for the 19th dragoons. You have 1787 men, and only 427 horses; but you do not inform me how many men there are in detachment to take the horses of the gendarmes, how many there are to be remounted at the depôt of Versailles, how many horses the regiment is to receive from the contracts it has made, or how many the departments are to furnish. If you are sufficiently active, you ought soon to have 1500 or 1600 of these 1700 men mounted, which, joined to those now composing the squadrons, will increase your cavalry to near 4000 men. You look at these matters too lightly; remove the obstacles by your own exertions; see the depôts, and augment your army. Keep spies on the look out to know what is passing on the other side of the Rhine, and principally at Mentz and Thionville; and make yourself acquainted with all the openings of the Vosges.

"NAPOLEON."

"Paris, May 20th 1815."

CHAPTER XLVI.

I WENT to occupy the lines of the Lauter. Twenty-three years before we had defended them; but then they were in a good condition, the left bank of the river was protected; we had 80,000 fighting men, a corps of reserve, and the army of the Upper Rhine assisted us. Nothing of that sort existed now. The lines were merely a heap of ruins : the banks and the sluices, which formed their principal strength, were nearly destroyed, and the places which supported them were neither armed nor even secure against a *coup de main*. We scarcely reckoned 15,000 infantry, which were divided into three divisions, under the orders of Generals Rottembourg, Albert, and Grandjean. Two thousand horse, under Count Merlin, composed all our cavalry. From Weissemburg as far as Huninguen on one side, and to Belgium on the other, the frontiers were completely unprotected. In this state of things Germesheim became an important position; defended by a considerable garrison, and twenty-four pieces of cannon, it could not be carried but by main force. I despaired not of success, and I made, as soon as the news of hostilities reached me, a general reconnoissance, in which I got possession of Haun, of Auwailler, and of all the villages of the Queich. The chief of squadron Turckheim took at a gallop that of Gottenstein, and the Bavarian detachments which occupied it.

On the 21st, towards midnight, all the arrangements were made, and the columns of attack were already in march, when news of the disaster of Waterloo was announced. The columns were immediately recalled. I well knew that the enemy would lose no time in crossing the river; I hastened to take the administrative measures that circumstances required, and to put in a state of defence the fortresses which were under my command. I threw a battalion of the line into Landau, whither I ordered the treasuries of the country to be removed. But already, as I had foreseen, the troops of the coalition had passed the Rhine at Oppenheim and at Germesheim, and had spread themselves in every direction; our soldiers were obliged to fight their way in order to arrive at their destination. We retreated behind the Lauter; and the rumour of the invasion of the

Upper Rhine by the Grand Army under the command of Schwartzenberg having reached me at the same time, I despatched, post haste, two battalions to reinforce the garrisons of Neuf Brisack and of Schelestadt.

The Russians, Austrians, Bavarians, Wurtemburgers, Badeners, and a multitude from other nations, assembled to the number of more than 60,000 men, under the orders of the Prince-Royal, now King of Wurtemburg, soon outfronted the feeble corps under my command.

I had first determined to defend Alsace foot by foot, retiring towards the Vosges, the Meurthe, the Moselle and the Marne: but I learnt that the army of the Moselle, which supported me on my left, had marched towards the north; that the enemy's columns already occupied Sarrebruck, and inundated Lorraine: this movement then was no longer practicable. On the other hand, a hasty decision, in such an unexpected juncture, might be attended with the most serious consequences. I temporized, in hopes of receiving orders to regulate my movements. But after the despatch which informed me of our misfortunes, I did not receive another till the entry of Louis XVIII into Paris.

In the evening of the 24th the Wurtemburg cavalry attacked my advanced posts, the chasseurs of the 7th and the dragoons of the 11th took arms, rushed on the enemy, and cut them in pieces. The next day the army continued its movement of concentration; I fixed my quarters in advance of the forest of Haguenau, the right of the army at Seltz, the centre at Surbourg, and the left, being my cavalry, on the road to Bitche, which the enemy had already invested.

This position was only a temporary one—it was too extended: I only took it to avoid retiring suddenly behind the town, and thus allowing the enemy to penetrate between that place and Saverne, which Lieutenant-general Desbureaux occupied with a battalion of the line, some partisans, and a few lancers.

General Rottembourg was intrusted with the task of observing the Rhine on our rear and on the right.—I had only been able to allow him a brigade, which I had left at Seltz; out of this I was obliged to withdraw the 40th regiment the moment the Austrians appeared. There only remained with him the 39th, whose second battalion formed the advanced posts, and the reserve. The first, a company of sappers and eight pieces of cannon, composed the line of battle for more than half a league of ground. The situation, without being bad in itself, had nothing particularly encouraging in it. The small town of Seltz, supported on the Rhine, is situated on the two banks of the Seltzbach. This river is pretty secure for about 400 yards, but farther up it is fordable every where, and the woods on its banks render the passage of it still more easy. On the other hand, I feared a landing which the enemy could easily effect behind the right, and to which I could make but a feeble opposition, whilst all my attention was wanted to the front, which, as I have said, extended to a great distance.

In this alternative General Rottembourg decided on keeping a watch on the Rhine only by means of patroles, and he sent a company to guard the fords from the mill at Seltz to Nideradern. He placed his artillery on a small eminence on the right bank, to the left of the town; and what remained of his soldiers he sent forward to support the second battalion, which occupied the advanced posts and the wood.

At eleven o'clock the enemy, having assembled his masses, commenced the attack by a well-sustained fire of musquetry, which he supported with eight pieces of cannon. The opposition of our troops was obstinate, and for a long time was effectual, but at last this small advanced post was compelled to retreat into the wood. It maintained itself there with heroic courage, and resisted for a long time the efforts of from 8 to 9000 men, aided by a numerous artillery. In fine, after a few hours of the finest resistance, this handful of valiant troops retreated in the greatest order, and rejoined the first battalion.

Emboldened by this success our adversaries brought down their masses. They debouched by the main road, and marched on Seltz, of which they thought to get possession without difficulty. We allowed them to come up under the fire of our batteries; as soon as they could play, a tremendous discharge carried death into their ranks. Encouraged by their numbers, they nevertheless continued to advance, and the combat recommenced with more vigour than before. But, constantly repelled by the valour of our soldiers, and mowed down by the French artillery, the Austrians in the end gave way, and retired in confusion into the wood. Their movements from that time became uncertain, and they hesitated a long time what they should do. Our cannon continued to carry destruction into their ranks. Attack was not more dangerous than inaction; they again advanced, and succeeded in getting possession of the part of the town situated on the left bank. But this triumph cost them dear: a few shells, thrown on the houses of which they were in possession, compelled them to leave them, and to regain, in a great hurry, their first place of shelter: our batteries fired with increased fury, and the fugitives suffered an immense loss.

This was not the only attack in which they failed. At the commencement of the action they had advanced by the main road from Weissembourg to Haguenau on Surbourg, which was occupied by a battalion of the 18th, under the command of Colonel Voyrol. This village was valiantly defended: for more than two hours the enemy could not penetrate into it; but they at last brought up forces so considerable, that under the apprehension of seeing the position turned, General Albert ordered it to be evacuated. Our soldiers withdrew behind the Saare, where they joined the remainder of the regiment. Attacked in this position by some chosen troops of the Austrian army, they remained immoveable. Wearied with so many fruitless attacks, and convinced that they could not succeed in forcing men who appeared determined to die at their post, nor in getting possession of the avenues of the forest, the Allies at last decided on retreating.

We had three hundred men killed and wounded. The Austrians, by their own account, had lost

2000 men, and had two pieces of cannon dismounted.

Our troops had scarcely taken a few hours rest, when I was obliged to put them again on their march. The Allied army of the Upper Rhine was advancing on Strasburg; I had received this news during the action. I had not a moment to loose: I marched immediately towards that place, and the result has shewn whether this measure was proper.

CHAPTER XLVII.

It was during this retreat that the soldiers heard of the disastrous battle of Waterloo, and the Emperor's abdication, which, to that moment, I had carefully concealed from them. These events produced an universal discouragement, and desertion soon found its way among them. Fatal projects entered the minds even of those who were least carried away by passion. Excited by malevolence, some wished to return to their homes; others proposed to throw themselves as partisans into the Vosges.

I was immediately informed of these intentions. I directly foresaw what terrible consequences they might produce. I issued an order of the day; it succeeded; their minds were tranquillized, but it was not long before anxiety revived. When we reached Haguenau, the ... regiment, formerly so illustrious, loudly proclaimed the design of quitting the army, and of repairing with its artillery into the mountains. The cannon were already harnessed, and one battalion had taken up its arms. I was informed of it; I rushed to the spot; I took in my hand the eagle of the rebels, and placing myself in the midst of them, " Soldiers," I cried, " I learn that it is proposed among you to desert us. In an hour's time we shall fight; do you wish the Austrians to think that you have fled from the field of honour? Let the brave swear never to quit their eagles or their general-in-chief. I grant permission to the cowards to depart." At these words, all exclaimed, " Long live Rapp! long live our general!" Every one swore to die by his standard, and tranquillity was restored.

We immediately began our march, and reached the Souffel, two leagues in advance of Strasburg. The fifteenth division had its right on the river Ill, its centre at Hoenheim, its left at Souffelweyersheim, and extended to the road from Brumpt; the sixteenth occupied Lampertheim, Mundolsheim, the three villages of Hausbergen, with its left resting on the road from Saverne: lastly, the seventeenth was in columns on the road from Molsheim, with two regiments of cavalry; two others were placed in the rear of the fifteenth division at Bischeim. Such was the situation of our troops on the morning of the 28th, when the enemy attacked with impetuosity the village of Lampertheim, which was occupied by a battalion of the 10th, under the command of General Beurmann. This battalion alone sustained for a long time the attacks of 8000 infantry, and the continued firing of six pieces of cannon. However, as the number of the assailants was continually increasing, it withdrew behind the river, and, conformably to its orders, stationed itself at Mundolsheim.

The enemy's columns, from 40 to 50,000 men strong, advanced immediately by the roads from Brumpt and Bishweiller. All these arrangements, and the masses of cavalry which covered the first of these roads, announced that their project was to separate the divisions of Generals Rottembourg and Albert, in order to overwhelm the latter. I did not mistake the design of the Allies, but I had not the power of uniting my troops, which had

GENERAL RAPP. 367

deployed in an immense plain, and were already engaged throughout the whole line. There only remained one expedient; I adopted it immediately, fortunately it was a most fatal one for the enemy. I closed the 10th regiment into columns, in the very midst of the firing; I ordered the 32d to advance; and I moved it *en echelon* after having formed it into a square. The rest of the division of Albert remained in reserve on the height of Hiderhausbergen.

Defending the ground foot by foot, General Rottembourg changed the front of his division, throwing his left wing into the rear, and proceeded to cover the villages of Hoenheim, Bischeim and Schittigheim, threatening the flank of the troops which were engaged between these two divisions. This was according to his orders.

The 103d was placed on the road from Brumpt, and the 36th left Souffelweyersheim to support it; but scarcely had it begun to march when the Allies attacked the village. I immediately despatched a company to defend this important position. Our soldiers advanced to it, running, but our adversaries had taken possession of it before they could arrive. Captain Chauvin supported with extraordinary courage the fire of a cloud of sharp-shooters, and thus gave time for General Fririon to come up.

This officer left a battalion and four pieces of cannon to cover the road, and advanced in charging time with the rest of his forces. General Gudin seconded this movement, and manœuvred on the road from Bischweiler: the Austrians gave way, and withdrew; but the reinforcements which they every moment received left our troops no chance of maintaining their position. On the other hand, the assailants had outflanked the 10th, and the moment had arrived for effecting the movement which I had ordered. Consequently the 16th division wheeled back its left wing perpendicularly to the rear, while it preserved the head of Hoenheim, from whence our artillery raked the enemy in flank and rear. At the same time the gallant General Beurmann, attacked on every side and already surrounded, sallied forth from Mundolsheim at the head of the 10th, and retreated without disorder towards the division.

The Austrians on their side advanced on the road from Brumpt with enormous masses of cavalry and infantry, supported by a formidable artillery. They penetrated between the two divisions, and arrived without obstacle on four pieces of cannon which had been continually pouring discharges of grape-shot on their columns. They were taken; but the enemy presented his flank to the troops of General Rottembourg, and to two regiments of cavalry which were on his front. I took advantage of this circumstance: put myself at the head of the 11th dragoons, and the 7th horse chasseurs. I made a rapid charge: I routed the first line, penetrated the second, and overthrew every thing that offered me any resistance. We made a dreadful slaughter of the Austrian and Wurtemburg cavalry. At the same time the 32d came up at the charge in close columns, and prevented them from rallying. They were thrown back on their own infantry, whom they put to flight.

General Rottembourg, on his side, pushed forward his right wing, and opened on the enemy, who defiled in confusion before his columns, a most destructive fire of artillery and musquetry; in an instant the field of battle is covered with the slain, and the immense army of the Prince of Wurtemburg is routed. The defeat was so complete that baggage, which was two leagues in the rear, was attacked and plundered, and the Prince himself lost his equipages. The confusion extended itself as far as Haguenau, and would have gone still farther if 30,000 Russians, who came up from Weissembourg, had not by their presence encouraged the fugitives. The night which came on, and the risk that there would have been in adventuring against forces so superior to our own, prevented us from profiting by our successes. We could not retake our artillery, the enemy had made haste to remove it to his rear.

It cost him very dear to keep it. He had from 1500 to 2000 men killed, and a still more considerable number wounded. On our side there were about 700 killed and wounded. Of this number were two Captains of light artillery, Favier and Dandlau, both wounded in defending their cannon, and Colonel Montagnier, who performed such signal service on this occasion.

The enemy's General revenged himself for this defeat by devastation. The day after the battle he set on fire the village of Souffelweyersheim, under pretext that the peasants had fired on his troops. This was not the fact, and the name of the Prince of Wurtemburg will remain for ever sullied by an action which plunged a multitude of families into misery.

Whether the vigour with which we had repulsed all their attacks had given them a distaste for making new ones, or from some other motive, our adversaries remained some days without undertaking any thing. I took advantage of this repose to provision Strasburg, and to fortify myself in my positions. I also had time to give to all commanders of places, who were under my command, the most precise instructions.

Meantime the allied army continued to increase; fresh corps arrived every day to swell its numbers: very soon 70,000 men deployed before us, and pressed us on every side. Flags of truce came one after the other, without having any marked object in view. I proposed to the enemy's General a suspension of arms, during which I might send an officer to Paris, and receive orders from the government. The Prince of Wurtemburg refused, without however renouncing the system of communication that he had adopted.

It was about this time that he sent for the pastor of Wendenheim, a respectable man and an excellent patriot. " Are you acquainted," he said to him, " with General Rapp?"—" Yes, my Lord." —" Will you undertake a mission to him?" " Assuredly, if its object is in no respect contrary to the interests of my country."—" Well then, go, and tell him that if he will deliver up Strasburg to me for the King of France, wealth and honours shall be showered on him."—" My Lord, General Rapp is an Alsacian, and consequently a good Frenchman; never will he consent to dishonour his military career. I consequently beseech your Highness to entrust some one else with this message." At these words the venerable pastor bowed and departed, leaving the Prince astonished and confused at having proposed in vain this piece of meanness. Nevertheless, his Highness was not discouraged. On the 3d of June, he despatched General Vacquant to me, with a flag of truce, to demand of me in the name of the King of France the surrender of Strasburg. In order to inspire more confidence, the Austrian officer wore an enormous white ribband and the decoration of the lily. I asked him whether he came from the King; he replied that he did not. "Well then," I said to him, " I will not give up the place till my soldiers shall have eaten the thighs of Austrians, as those I had at Dantzic ate those of Russians." Importuned by the insignificant communications which the commander of the allied forces was every day sending me, I endeavoured to penetrate into his motives. With this object a general *reconnoissance* was made on the 6th on the Austrian positions. Our soldiers took some posts of cavalry, cut others to pieces, and returned to the camp, after having made all the enemy's army get under arms.

Having heard, two days after, a heavy cannonade in the direction of Phalzburg, I resolved to make a second reconnoissance, as well to make myself precisely acquainted with the forces that

I had before me, as to hinder the Prince of Wurtemburg from detaching troops against that place. Albert's division and the cavalry marched against the entrenched camp, which the Austrians had formed all the way from the strong position of Oberhausbergen to Hiderhausbergen. The attack commenced at three o'clock in the morning: it was impetuous, and crowned with the most complete success. The enemy's cavalry were repulsed and put to flight by the brigade of General Grouvel; the principal villages were taken at the point of the bayonet, and the entrenchments carried by force. Several officers were taken in their beds, and others at the very moment they were rushing to arms. Some generals escaped in their shirts, and owed their safety only to the darkness which protected them.

The 10th light infantry, commanded by the gallant Colonel Cretté, displayed in this affair the same valour as at the battle of the 28th. The 18th, under the orders of Colonel Voyrol, one of the most intrepid officers in the French army, made itself master of the village of Mittelhausbergen, where he withstood for a long time numerous forces, and incessant attacks on every point.

The signal for retreat having been given, General Albert ordered the 57th to form in *echelon* towards the attack on the right, and the 32d towards that on the left. We retired in the best order. The enemy endeavoured to disturb us; he attacked our troops. The 57th received him without wavering, and opened a fire at musquet-length which disorganized his columns. Twice the allied cavalry returned to the charge, twice was it repulsed with loss. General Laroche, who led it on, was wounded, and fell under the feet of the horses; he would have perished if the French had not come to his assistance. " Friends," cried he, " I once served in your ranks, save me." He was immediately taken up, and restored to his own men. A troop of cuirassiers had nearly surprised the 18th in its retrograde movement, but the chief of the staff, Colonel Schneider, having skilfully opposed to it a battalion that he had by him, broke their shock, and saved the regiment from an inevitable defeat.

The Allies, convinced that they could not succeed in cutting us off, left us peaceably to continue our march. Our troops returned to their camp, after having accurately ascertained the immense superiority of the forces that they had to contend with. Both parties entered into cantonments. A military convention was signed a few days afterwards, and hostilities ceased throughout all Alsace.

CHAPTER XLVIII.

INACTIVITY soon engendered sedition. Other armies, other corps, which had not the excuse of being misled by a political combination, had trampled under foot military discipline. Is it strange that, in the midst of the general effervescence, my soldiers should for a moment have forgotten themselves? this episode is painful to me. I ought neither to write it, nor omit it. I can well bear the blame which Joubert, Massena, and so many other Generals, whom I do not pretend to equal, have incurred. The following are the terms in which this act of disobedience is related by an anonymous writer:—he has not thought proper to tell every thing, but it is my own conduct that is concerned; I must imitate his reserve. I submit, moreover, to the judgment which he has delivered.

" The Austrians, despairing of ever getting possession of Strasburg by force of arms, endeavoured to form an understanding with a party in the town. They succeeded by their sagacity in the application of the two means which act the most powerfully on the heart of men—gold and terror. They decoyed some by the attraction of riches, they subdued others by making them dread the vengeance of the government. When they were in this manner assured of all those whom they thought open to seduction, they hastened to execute their perfidious designs.

"From the commencement of the campaign our soldiers had been in a state of irritation, well calculated to promote the secret views of the enemy: they were acquainted with the disastrous affair of Waterloo, they knew all the details of it; but they had too much confidence in the skill of that celebrated man, with whom they had five times triumphed over all Europe—they had too often seen him, by sudden inspirations, regain his hold of victory when she was escaping from him, to believe that his military genius had on the sudden abandoned him; they were perpetually thinking of this disaster, and they could never think of it without rage. Persuaded as they were that our troops had continued the same, and that they had to do with the same enemies, such a defeat appeared to them inconceivable. Not knowing the true cause of it, they attributed all our misfortunes to treason. Traitors had given intelligence of our plans; traitors had commanded false manœuvres, traitors had raised the cry of *sauve qui peut!* There were traitors among the generals, among the officers, among the soldiers; and who knew whether there were none but in the army of the north? Who knew whether the corps, of which they were a part, their regiment, their company, were not infested with them? Could they reckon on their chiefs, on their comrades? Every one was suspected, it was necessary to distrust every one!

"Such was the language in which anger found vent, which malevolence caught up, magnified, envenomed, and which every soldier in the end repeated and believed. This idea soon became the medium through which every thing was explained. Accustomed to keep the field, they saw themselves with pain compelled to retreat before an enemy whom they despised. It would have been natural to attribute his progress to an immense numerical superiority. They chose to explain it otherwise; their chiefs were in correspondence with the Austrians. Several circumstances, as unfortunate as they were unavoidable, concurred to give to this opinion an appearance of probability, in the prejudiced eyes of these soldiers. The first of these was the order which General

Rapp received, to disband the army, and to dismiss each soldier separately, without money and without arms. The next was, an injunction sent to him by the government to deliver to the Russian commissioners ten thousand musquets taken from the arsenal at Strasburg. These two despatches obliged him to enter into a correspondence with the Allies. The frequent interchange of messengers which took place on this occasion produced a bad effect on their minds. The mystery which the General was obliged to observe, to conceal from the troops the removal of the fire-arms, increased the irritation; malevolence raised it to its height. It was loudly said that Count Rapp had sold himself, that he had received several millions of francs from the Austrians to introduce them into the fortress, and that if he discharged the soldiers individually, and without arms, it was in consequence of an agreement to deliver them up to the enemy.

"As soon as these seeds of discontent had been once sown in the different corps, they were developed of themselves; the instigators had nothing more to do than to observe their progress, to combine the incidents calculated to augment the disorders, and to render inevitable the catastrophe which they were preparing.

"Although General Rapp was far from suspecting such a plot, he had taken, in some way, all the measures that he could take to frustrate it. As soon as the ministerial despatch relative to the disbanding the troops reached him, he had despatched with all speed to Paris one of his aides-de-camp, the chief of squadron Marnier. This officer saw the ministers repeatedly, and represented to them into what violence the army would be led, if the whole amount of the pay due to it was not discharged; but he could only obtain, notwithstanding the most earnest solicitations, a bill for 400,000 francs, on the chest of the war department. His return with this trifling sum, destroyed all the hopes that had been excited. The General-in-chief, who saw the troops getting more and more exasperated, left nothing untried to allay the storm. The want of money was the principal cause of dissatisfaction. To put an end to this source of discontent, Count Rapp endeavoured to raise a loan in Strasburg. The inhabitants having demanded of him a security, he solicited from the minister of Finance authority to pledge the stores of tobacco in the town: the minister refused it. Nevertheless, by the interposition of General Semelé, who commanded the fortress, a sum of 160,000 francs was obtained. Such slight supplies could not satisfy the soldiers, who were inflamed by false reports, and among whom the insurrection was not slow in breaking out. It was sudden and general, and presented a character quite peculiar. I will enter into all the details of it, because they will serve to make the spirit of the French soldiery better known.

" On the 2d of September, about eight in the morning, about sixty subaltern officers of different regiments met in one of the bastions of the place. They agreed on a plan of obedience to the orders for the disbanding of the army, but on conditions, from which they resolved not to swerve. This declaration began in the following manner.

" In the name of the army of the Rhine, the officers, sub-officers, and soldiers, will obey the orders issued for the disbanding of the army only on the following conditions:

" Art. I. The officers, sub-officers, and soldiers, will not leave the army till they have received all the pay that is due to them.

" Art. II. They will set out all on the same day, carrying their arms, baggage, and fifty cartridges each," &c. &c.

"As soon as this document was drawn up, they repaired to the General-in-chief to communicate it to him. The General, who was at the time unwell, was taking a bath. Astonished at this unexpected visit, he gave orders that they should be admitted. Five officers immediately entered the bathing room; they explained the object of their mission, and declared that the army would not submit to be disbanded till those conditions should have been fulfilled. At the word conditions the General in a rage sprang out of the bath, and tearing the paper out of the hands of the speaker, cried, "What, Sirs, do you wish to impose conditions on me? you refuse to obey! conditions on me!"

"The tone of his voice, the look of Count Rapp, and perhaps the attitude in which he presented himself, struck the deputation. It retired in confusion, and each of the officers returned to give an account to his regiment of the bad reception they had met with.

"The sub-officers, who were assembled to the number of about 500, were waiting for the General's answer. They clearly perceived, when they were made acquainted with it, that such a man was not easily intimidated, and that they were not likely to be more successful in such an attempt than their chiefs. But their determination was taken; they came and ranged themselves in line of battle in the palace-yard, and demanded to be introduced to the General-in-chief. An aide-de-camp came down to know the purpose which brought them there; they refused to enter into any explanation with him. 'Who is the chief of the troop?' asked the officer.—'No one! Every one!' they all replied together. He called into the centre of the court the oldest of each regiment; he remonstrated with them on the act of disobedience that they were rendering themselves guilty of. A thousand voices at once interrupted him. 'Money! money!—we will be paid what is due to us; we know how to get ourselves paid!'

"The chief of the staff Colonel Schneider, whose courage they had so often admired in the midst of danger, arrived at this conjuncture, and endeavoured, but with as little success, to quiet them. 'Money!' they again repeated, 'money!' Wearied with uttering their cries, and holding out useless threats, and not being able to get at the General-in-chief, they dispersed, after having fixed on a rendezvous. The greatest part went to the parade, where they immediately proceeded to the election of the new chiefs whom they had determined on having. One of them, called Dalouzi, sergeant in the 7th light regiment, well known for his ability, his courage, and particularly for a soldier-like oratory which was peculiar to him, was unanimously elected. 'You want to be paid,' he said to his comrades, 'and it is for this that you are here.'—'Yes!' they replied with a common voice.—'Well then! if you will promise to obey me, and to abstain from all confusion, to respect property, to protect persons, I swear by my head that you shall be paid within twenty-four hours.' This speech was received with cries of joy, and the sergeant was appointed General. He immediately chose for the chief of the staff the drum-major of the 58th; a second sub-officer was charged with the office of governor of the fortress; a third with the command of the first division; another with that of the second, and so on. The regiments had colonels, the battalions and squadrons chiefs, and the companies captains; in short, a complete staff was formed.

"The other sub-officers had returned to the barracks, where the soldiers were waiting with impatience for the result of the step that had been taken. The drum was immediately beat to arms, and all the corps, infantry, cavalry, and artillery, marched in order and in double quick time to the parade. The organization was scarcely ended when they arrived there. As soon as they appeared, the new chiefs went and took command, and marched the troops to the points they had orders to occupy.

"In the mean time General Rapp, astonished to see so serious an insurrection break out, had dressed himself in haste, in hopes of ascertaining the motives of these seditious movements, and of succeeding in quieting them. But the different operations of which we have just given an account had been effected with such celerity, that at the moment when he set out, accompanied by his adjutant-general and a few officers, several columns, followed by a numerous populace, were already debouching through all the streets leading from the square of the palace. As soon as they perceived the General, the troops hastily put themselves in order of battle, and charged bayonets to hinder him from passing. Immediately furious cries were heard in the rear ranks. "Fire! he has sold the army.—Fire then!" Some wretches, scattered among the troops, excited them by their gestures and voices to massacre this brave man. Rage spread from man to man, and confusion was soon at its height. The soldiers, enraged, loaded their musquets; the ranks were doubled, eight pieces of cannon arrived at a gallop, and were immediately loaded with grape-shot.

"Every time that General Rapp addressed those who menaced him, vociferations commenced, and irritating cries were uttered with increased violence. Musquets were repeatedly levelled at him, and the pieces of cannon were constantly directed against his person, and the gunners followed all his movements. 'Stand aside!' they exclaimed, 'that we may fire on him.' A howitzer was constantly kept so directly pointed at the group which surrounded the General, that he perceived it. He ran to the cannoneer who was holding the match, 'Well! what would you do, wretched man? (he said to him) do you wish to kill me? Fire then, here I am at the mouth of your gun.' 'Ah, General,' the soldier exclaimed, letting the match fall from his hand, 'I was at the siege of Dantzick with you, I would give you my life; but my comrades will be paid, and I am obliged to do as they do;' and he resumed his match.

"Wearied with senseless questions, with appeals without any object, deafened by the clamours of the multitude, the mass of which was continually increasing, the General decided at last on returning to the palace.

"The troops followed him, and the different avenues were immediately occupied by eight pieces of cannon, a thousand infantry, and a squadron of cavalry. This guard called itself the Exterior guard of the palace. A battalion came and established itself in the court, and took the name of Interior guard. Nearly sixty sentinels were placed in pairs at all the gates, and on the stair-case which led to the apartment of Count Rapp; there were also some for a few moments at the door of his bed-chamber. The telegraph and the mint were immediately taken possession of. To shew that they had no bad designs, a detachment was sent to the hotel of the Austrian General Volkman, who was in the place, and was put at his disposal. The drawbridges were raised, and there was no communication with any one out of the fortress without a permission signed by the new commander. The drum-major of the 58th repaired with a trumpet to the head-quarters of the Allies, and signified to them that if they respected the truce, the garrison would not commit any act of hostility, but that if they endeavoured to take advantage of the misunderstanding which existed between the chief and the soldiers, it would know how to oppose a noble resistance.

"Meanwhile Dalouzi had established his staff at the Parade, and had appointed two commissions, the one for the provisions, composed of quarter-master-sergeants, and the other for the finances, composed of sergeant-majors: they constituted themselves permanent, deliberated on the measures best calculated to maintain the public tranquillity, and to put the town in a state of security against surprise. The posts of the citadel and those of the interior were doubled; guards were even placed at some old posterns, which, till then, had been neglected; the outer line was strengthened, the troops bivouacked in the squares, and in the streets; in fact no precaution was omitted which the most suspicious prudence could suggest. In order to prevent the excesses to which malevolence might excite the soldiers, it was forbidden, under pain of death, to enter any of the places where brandy, wine, or beer, was sold. The same punishment was denounced against all who should be guilty of plunder, riot, or insubordination. Lastly, still better to secure the public tranquillity, it was resolved that the army should be informed of its situation every six hours.

"These arrangements having been made, the receiver-general, and the inspector of reviews, were sent for. The latter made a calculation of the sums necessary for the present year's pay, the other presented the account of what he had in the chest; after which, Dalouzi convoked the town council, to whom he declared the motives which had made the garrison take arms, and requested the mayor to take means to get funds necessary to pay the arrears.

"He then despatched to Count Rapp a deputation, composed of the new governor and of five or six general-sergeants: 'Well, what do you want of me again?' cried the General in a tone of indignation and contempt.—'You are unworthy to wear the French uniform. I believed that you were men of honour; I am deceived. You allow yourselves to be seduced by wretches. What do you wish to do? Why do these guards surround the palace? Why is this artillery pointed against me? Am I then so formidable? Is it believed that I wish to escape? Why should I escape? I fear nothing—I do not fear you. But to the point, what do you want of me?' He repeated this question. The agitation of Count Rapp while pronouncing these words was a striking contrast to the melancholy air of the deputation. These sub-officers, ashamed of keeping a chief whom they loved, and whose valour and fidelity were so well known to them, a prisoner, kept a profound silence. They were on the point of withdrawing, when one of them spoke: 'General', he said, 'we have learned that the other corps of the army have been paid; our soldiers also are resolved to be paid; they are in a state of revolt, but they obey us. We only ask what is due to us, the slight indemnification for so much blood and so many wounds; we only ask for what is indispensable to enable us to perform our march and withdraw to our homes. The troops will not return to order, it is a thing firmly resolved on, until every one be paid.'—'There is not enough money in the chest,' replied the General. 'It was my intention to have you paid, stoppages and all. I despatched an aide-de-camp to Paris; he saw the ministers, but they could only give him 400,000 francs. It is this sum, together with that in the chest of the paymaster, which I will order to be divided among the different regiments.'—'The army will be paid, my General.'—'I have told you all that I have to say to you; withdraw, and return as soon as possible to order.—If the enemy unfortunately should be acquainted with what is going on here, what will become of you?'—'All this has been foreseen, my General: a regiment of cavalry and twelve pieces of cannon, have set out to reinforce the division which is at the camp. It is easy for you to get us paid ; and you have every thing to fear on the part of the soldiers, if in twenty-four hours from this time their request is not complied with.'—' What is it to me what you and your soldiers may do ? I repeat that you shall only have the funds which are destined for you. Do not hope that whatever happens, you can compel me to do what my duty prohibits.'— ' General, the soldiers can conduct you to the citadel, they can even shoot you ; we answer for them now, but if you do not cause us to be paid · · · ·'—' I have nothing more to say to you, quit my house. If you shoot me, so be it ; I prefer death to shame. You are the enemies of order, you are the instruments of malevolence and of a conspiracy which you yourselves are not acquainted with. The enemy perhaps is in concert ; I make you responsible for every thing that may happen. You have heard me ; begone! I am ashamed to converse with rebels !'

"The word conspiracy made a very deep impression upon them : they remained silent for some time. They began again, however, and one of them said, that if there were among them any who had secret intentions, they were ignorant of it ; that for themselves they only wanted their pay ;

but that paid they would be, and that they were going to bring to him the civil authorities, in order that he might give directions for raising the funds: after which they withdrew.

"Whilst the council was consulting on the means of securing public tranquillity, and of liquidating the pay in arrear, the army had effected different movements; it had marched and countermarched, always at a running pace, without uttering a word, without venting a threat against the officers whom it had put under arrest. This silence, rather extraordinary for French soldiers, had something sinister about it at which the inhabitants were alarmed. Nevertheless the troops at last became calm, but they held no communication with the towns-people; they even refused to answer their questions. In the streets, in the squares, groups were continually seen forming, which dispersed after they had communicated in a very low tone either orders or opinions. The whole town was plunged in melancholy disquietude: fatal epochs were recalled to their recollection—they feared to see them revive: every one trembled for his property—for his life. Never was there a more terrifying scene than that which this large city then presented.

"The General-in-chief having learned that the

inhabitants had consented to raise the necessary funds, and that they yielded to fear what they had for so long a time refused to his entreaties, despatched the adjutant-general to the civil authorities to settle with them about the distribution of the loan. This officer was conducted to the townhall by a corporal and six men who did not quit him. He finished his accounts, and returned to the palace under the same escort.

"In the mean time, the Generals and chiefs of corps, employed in turn threats and entreaties to bring back the mutineers to their duty. The men, who loved their superiors, and who would not have dared to fail in duty before their faces, had recourse to artifice to escape from the ascendancy and the representations which they dreaded. When an officer went in one direction, care was taken to oppose to him in the front rank soldiers of a different corps and description, and while he harangued these, the others vociferated from behind. If, in spite of this tactic, he succeeded in getting at one of his own men, and reproached him: 'Me, my Officer,' the other replied with hypocritical mildness, 'I am not doing any thing, I am not speaking a word;' and he immediately buried himself in the crowd. The troops soon adopted a general measure to free themselves from these importunate solicitations, and all those who had any important command were ordered to keep to their homes.

"The alarms of the citizens were soon tranquillized, the retreat was sounded a long time before night, and from that moment patroles succeeded one another without interruption. Several orders of the day were read at each post. They recommended tranquillity and obedience, and promised that the payments should be made within twenty-four hours. One of these orders was thus worded:

'Every thing is going on well, the inhabitants are raising the money, and the payments have begun. (Signed,) GARRISON.'

"The town was ordered to be illuminated, in order that it might be more easy to keep up a strict watch.

"The secret instigators of the insurrection did not fail to perceive that a degree of wisdom presided in all the councils, which rendered their case desperate, that their end was baffled if they did not succeed in again inflaming the minds of the soldiery, and in exciting some commotion in which blood might be spilt.

"With this view, about five o'clock in the

afternoon, a horse chasseur arrived at full gallop on the parade, announcing that three waggons full of gold had just been stopped belonging to General Rapp, who was sending them out of the city under the protection of the Austrians. 'These three waggons,' he added, 'have been taken to the covered bridge, and here is the receipt I am bearing to our commander-in-chief;— General Rapp must be shot; he is a traitor, he has sold us to the enemy.'

" Whatever irritation still remained, this speech produced little effect. The troops used their chief roughly to compel him to levy contributions, but they did not entertain any suspicion against him. His reputation as a man of honour remained unblemished, and his integrity was no more doubted by them than his courage. Such open provocations to murder excited distrust, and the soldiers became more circumspect. Some, however, propagated alarms, and wished that his person should be secured; but the army had the good sense to repel suggestions the complete perfidiousness of which it did not perhaps at first perceive.

" As soon as one expedient failed, the conspirators attempted another, and left nothing untried to spill blood, persuaded that if it had once flowed, it would be easy to make it flow again. The General's coachman was driving from the palace to the stables a cart laden with straw. The sentinels made some objections to allow it to pass: it however went on, but scarcely was it out, when some ill-disposed persons cried, Treason, and pretended that under the pretext of removing straw the military chest was carried off. Immediately the multitude rushed on the cart and on its load, in order to search it the better. Nothing was found; they loaded it again, demanding nevertheless that it should go back: the horses took fright, set off, and ran over a child.

"At this sight fury redoubled, the guards were forced, the multitude rushed tumultuously into the court of the palace, seized the coachman, and massacred him without pity in the hands of an officer who had come forth to defend him. The disorder was not meant to stop at the death of a servant; but groupes of soldiers came up, forced the most infuriated to restrain themselves, and thus the blow once more failed.

"All the attempts to get General Rapp massacred by the hands of his troops having failed, recourse was had to extraordinary means of assassinating him. As soon as night was come, a multitude of individuals succeeded each other, and used force to introduce themselves into his bed-chamber. But the aides-de-camp and some officers defended the door with courage, and preserved their chief from insult.

"In the midst of this effervescence an event suddenly happened to cool the soldiery, and contributed to restore them to order. The enemy's line drew its cantonments closer round the town, at the very moment the insurrection broke out, and also received considerable reinforcements. This coincidence of the measures adopted by the Austrians with an event which they ought not to have been acquainted with, gave much room for conjecture: thus the outer division immediately doubled their main guards; fresh troops and artillery came from the town.

"The enemy, intimidated, durst not make any attempt. Perhaps he was also awaiting the result of the plots which he had framed in Strasburg; perhaps he feared to enter into an engagement with an army so much the more formidable, as it had put itself under the necessity of conquering; and as it continued, for all that related to the military arrangements, to receive its orders from General Rottembourg, whose courage and skill the Austrians had experienced more than once during this campaign. The enemy, therefore, remained in position, and appeared to be waiting till the favourable moment should arrive. On its side, the army was on its guard against the tricks prepared for it, and pursued, with calmness and firmness, the only end which it had in view, the discharge of the pay in arrear.

"General *Garrison* redoubled his vigilance to preserve public tranquillity, and went forth attended by his staff, all dressed in their uniform and on horseback, to secure the execution of his orders. As soon as he appeared the drums beat to arms, the guards were turned out, and rendered him all the honours due to a Commander-in-chief.

"Thus Strasburg presented the appearance of the most perfect order in the midst of disorder; and the most severe discipline reigned in an army in a state of revolt.

"The loan having been raised, the pay-officers, according to the numerical order of the regiments, were conducted under a good escort to the paymaster-general, where they received the sums necessary for the pay of their corps. But they were enjoined not to make any individual payments until all the regiments should have received what was owing to them. Thus passed the first day: there was less agitation on the second. Still there was an attempt to make the troops believe some rumours calculated to produce disturbance, but little attention was paid to them. Towards evening, the orders given to the sentinels of the palace became less strict; the aides-de-camp had leave to go out under escort. A file of grenadiers was appointed to escort them where they wished, and to conduct them back again.

" During the night the posts were all renewed. Individuals, in the uniform of sub-officers, presented themselves once more to penetrate into the General's apartments, to satisfy themselves, as they said, that he had not escaped. The altercations between them and the officers of the staff were warmer than ever; the latter, nevertheless, in the end prevailed. In fine, the division of the funds was effected towards nine o'clock in the morning. Immediately the call to arms was sounded, the army assembled, withdrew its posts, raised the siege of the palace, and repaired to the parade. General Garrison, accompanied by all his staff, drew up the troops in line, and addressed to them the following proclamation. We give it *verbatim.*

" ' Soldiers of the Army of the Rhine,

" ' The bold step which has just been taken by your sub-officers to obtain justice, and the complete discharge of your pay, has compromised them with the civil and military authorities. It is in your good conduct, your resignation, and your excellent discipline that they hope to find safety; that which you have maintained up to the present time is the best guarantee of it; and of this they hope for a continuance.

" 'Soldiers, the pay-officers have in their possession all that is owing to you; the garrison will return to its former situation, the posts will remain till the General-in-chief shall have given orders in consequence. On their return from the parade, the sergeant-majors and quarter-masters shall repair to their pay-officers, and shall take note before paying the troops from MM. the Colonels, in order to keep back what is not due.

" 'The infantry is to be disbanded—it will take superior orders; and the cavalry, still having no order, will wait its lot, in order to give up, at least before setting off, the horses, arms, and all that belongs to the Government, in order that it may be said they are Frenchmen: they have served with honour, they have obtained payment of what was due to them, and have submitted to the orders of the King, under the glorious title of the Army of the Rhine.

" 'By order of the Army of the Rhine.' "

"The Sergeant-General, after having delivered this speech, which the army heard in silence, made the two divisions of infantry, the cavalry, and artillery defile before him, and went in great pomp to display at the offices of the Prefect and Mayor the white flags that had been made by his orders. The troops then returned to their barracks, and submitted themselves to the authority of their respective officers.

"As soon as they were restored to liberty, the Generals, Colonels, and superior officers were anxious to repair to Count Rapp, to express to him the pain they had experienced at seeing the army thus unmindful of the rein of discipline. They even caused a protest against the seditious movements which the army had given way to, to be printed, which they all signed, and which contained expressions very flattering to the General-in-Chief.

"Two days after, they laid down their arms at the arsenal, and all the corps were disbanded. Dalouzi, as leader of the revolt, had incurred the penalty of death; but he was pardoned on account of the good order that he had maintained in the midst of the insurrection."*

---

* Summary of the Operations of the Armies of the Rhine and Jura, 1815.

The army was dissolved; my command having expired, there was nothing to keep me any longer in Alsace. But the good souls of the Faubourg Saint-Germain had imagined that we were a source of terror to Europe. On the field of battle I believe we were, and the Allies did not disallow it. In other respects this was thinking too highly of us. With regard to plots and conspiracies, it is not we who deserved the palm. I, nevertheless, went to meet that which they wished to allot to me. I wrote to the King, I did not attempt to disguise my sentiments from him. If I had been able to throw the whole coalition into the Rhine I would have done it; I did not conceal it. My letter was thus worded.

" Sire,

" I do not endeavour to justify my conduct. Your Majesty knows that the bent of my mind and my military education have always led me to defend the French territory against all foreign aggression : I could not, above all, hesitate to offer my life in defence of Alsace, which gave me birth.

" If I have preserved the esteem of your Majesty, I desire to finish my career in my own country; if it were otherwise, I should be the first to demand to go and pass my days abroad : I could not live in my country without the esteem of my sovereign."

"I only ask this; I have need of nothing more."

This letter was of use. Marks of regard that had escaped the Monarch kept malevolence within bounds. I passed some months at Paris without being disturbed; but the race of emigrants had filled the chambers and harangued at the tribune. Their vociferations against all the men distinguished for their talent and courage whom France can boast of, gave me such a disgust that I withdrew. I went into Switzerland, where at least aristocracy did not present the scandalous spectacle of the rage of the present time combined with the meanness of the past. The ordinance of the 5th of September was issued a short time afterwards: I returned to Paris, where I live quietly in the bosom of my family, and where I have experienced happiness which till then was unknown to me.

Here the Memoirs terminate. We will only add a few words.

Become a member of the House of Peers, the General was called into the presence of the King. This favour did not make him unfaithful to old recollections. So many immortal days were too deeply engraved in his mind! He could not forget our victories, or him who had conducted them, or those who had obtained them! He had often taken so glorious a part in them! Courage does not disinherit herself. In like manner the brave soldiers who were persecuted by men whom they had eclipsed on the field of battle always found in their General a devoted protector. His purse, his credit were open to them. Never did he repel the unfortunate. Those who had none of the privileges which the standard gives, participated in his benefits; it was sufficient if they were in distress. Misfortune was something sacred in his eyes.

The state of inactivity into which on a sudden he had fallen, after a life of alarms and fatigue, hastened to a fatal termination the wounds with which he was covered. His health was gone; he soon ended the term assigned him by Nature. He beheld death without emotion, ordered himself to be put in a position so as to front the enemy, whom he had always looked in the face, and expired, offering up his prayers for France and his family.

DOCUMENTS

ILLUSTRATIVE OF THE MEMOIRS.

Letter from General Rapp to the Duke of Wurtemberg.

June 14th, 1813.

COLONEL Richemont has communicated to me the letter which your Royal Highness honoured him with, the ..... of this month. I learn with pain that the very conciliatory proposals made, in my name, by M. Richemont, have not been accepted, and that discussions have arisen on points which appeared to afford no room for any debate whatever.

I must observe to your Royal Highness, generally, that the armistice was not demanded by the Emperor Napoleon, which supposes that all the articles ought to be construed favourably to the French army; but since the intentions of the treaty are disputed, I see no other means of attaining the object of your Royal Highness, and my own, than by proposing to your Excellency to leave, as regards the limits, things in their present state, and to inform the commissioners appointed by articles 9 and 12 of the armistice, of the difficulties which have arisen in the execution of article 6. I therefore beg your Highness to name, conjointly with myself, two officers who shall be instructed to repair to those commissioners, and who can speedily bring a report of the solution we are to expect.

I also consent that the article relative to supplies be only settled provisionally, that is to say, that if your Royal Highness would not take upon yourself to allow us 30,000 rations of victuals, reckoning from the day of the armistice, which, according to the returns of the force of the garrison, is necessary, Colonel Richemont will be able to settle with the Russian commissioners, the quantities which shall be supplied to us on account, to be deducted from the amount which shall be definitively appointed by the commissioners of the armistice, to whom it will be referred, as well as the article of limits.

The officer who brought the armistice would have been able to notify at the Imperial head-quarters the discussions which have arisen, if his instructions did not oblige him to delay his departure till after the first distribution which is to be made to the garrison by the directions of the General commanding the blockade.

I should have greatly desired that we could have come to an understanding, on the execution of the treaty, as I have reason to fear that false inferences may be drawn from the delay of this officer, as to the good understanding which the armistice supposes to exist between us; a contingency which I should the more lament, as it appears to me that your Highness might have acceded to the proposals of Colonel Richemont, which I should most certainly have done in your place, without fearing the least reproach for it from my sovereign.

(Signed,) COUNT RAPP.

ANSWER.

Sulmin, June 15th, 1813.

I RECEIVED the letter which your Excellency did me the honour to write to me, dated the 14th of June, and I must frankly confess that it is my duty to enter into the fullest explanation of the cause of the misunderstandings which exist relative to the literal execution of the articles of the truce.

This treaty having laid down fixed principles, in order to avoid every subject of dispute, it appears to me, that it would be infinitely more simple and natural to adhere strictly to it. I confess to your Excellency that it is with sincere pain that I agree to depart from it according to your proposition. It appears to me that by this arrangement, which you wish, both of us, to a certain degree, exceed the limits of our powers, and that it would be much better to settle between us the line of neutrality according to the literal sense of the armistice. Nevertheless, to avoid all farther discussion, I consent to let things remain on their present footing: I will even order the commanders of my advanced posts to come to an understanding with yours about making some arrangements, which may be agreeable to your Excellency, in respect to sentinels and piquets, to prevent any collision between our light troops.

Respecting what concerns the article of provisions, the commission assembled for that purpose has already commenced its sittings, and I hope that Colonel Richemont will soon be able to announce that this article has been definitively settled.

As to what regards the two officers whom your Excellency would send to the commissioners appointed definitively to settle all the difficulties which appear to arise respecting the stipulations of the truce, I must observe, that it is not in my power to grant them the necessary passports: the article of provisions, which will be forthwith settled, will allow, in the course of a few days, Captain Planat to undertake this commission.

Be persuaded, moreover, General, that accustomed, in the course of twenty-five years' service to fulfil with exactness the orders of my sovereign, I should have acted in a very different manner, if I had agreed to the propositions which have been made to me by Colonel Richemont, and which deviated so essentially from the articles of a truce, the simple and natural expressions of which leave no room for the least discussion.

Your Excellency, moreover, will always find me ready to do whatever may be agreeable to you, and which at the same time may not be inconsistent with my duty. I shall eagerly seize all the opportunities that I can to convince you that nothing equals the high consideration with which I have the honour to be, &c.

(Signed,) ALEXANDER, DUKE OF WURTEMBERG.

Letter from the Duke of Wurtemberg to his Excellency Count Rapp.

From my head-quarters, July 12, 1813.

(Received on the 14th, though the Duke was but two leagues from Dantzic.)

GENERAL,

A MESSENGER, who has just arrived from head-quarters, brings me an order for suspending the allowances which have been hitherto made to the garrison of Dantzic. The corps of Volunteers under the orders of the Prussian Major Lutzow having been attacked, during the continuance of the truce, without the least cause, is announced to me as the reason which has caused this determination, and which is not to be varied from until this affair shall be definitively settled.

In communicating the orders which I have received to you, I announce at the same time that this affair, which will probably soon be settled, does not however change the other articles of the truce, which are to remain in full force.

I have the honour be, &c.

(Signed,) ALEXANDER, DUKE OF WURTEMBERG,

General of Cavalry.

ANSWER.

Dantzic, July 14, 1813.

Monsieur le Duc,

From the commencement of the arrangements agreed upon between us, in consequence of the armistice, I have seen, with much pain, that your Royal Highness does not fulfil them with that exactness which such stipulations demand.

I have perceived, in the delay of all the deliveries, a secret war which was destroying in detail the spirit of the armistice. In spite of my continual protests, a great part of the provisions has been left in arrear; you have not even supplied what is due at present, and it is in this state of things that I receive, to-day, the 14th, the letter from your Highness, dated the 12th, which informs me that you have orders to suspend the provisions. This suspension has actually taken place these four days past, that is to say, since the 10th; and as our correspondence may reach each other in two hours, I will not conceal from your Highness with what sentiments I must look at the difference between the date and the arrival of your despatch.

The conditions of an armistice, my Lord Duke, are alike binding on both the parties; and as soon as one of them allows himself to annul one of the principal and most essential clauses, the armistice is from that moment broken, and he puts himself in a state of war against the other. It is in this light, that I consider from henceforth the declaration you have made; and although your

ILLUSTRATIVE DOCUMENTS. 411

Highness informs me that the other articles of the truce shall remain, you must perceive that I cannot accept such modifications but by the orders of my sovereign. It only remains to me, then, to beg you to acquaint me whether the six days which are to precede the recommencement of hostilities are to be reckoned from the 12th at one o'clock in the morning, or from the 14th at twelve.

I must declare to you, that I account you responsible for the rupture of an armistice that was concluded between our sovereigns, and that I cannot listen to any evasive explication until after the reception of all the provisions which are due to me.

(Signed,) COUNT RAPP.

Letter from the Duke of Wurtemberg to General Count Rapp.

From my head-quarters, July 15, 1813.

I HAVE just received the letter which you have addressed to me, and I cannot conceal from your Excellency that I have been more than ordinarily surprised at its contents.

It would be absolutely useless again to repeat to your Excellency what MM. Generals Borozdin and Jelebtzou have not failed to observe to you repeatedly, that is to say, that the momentary delays which the garrison of Dantzic has experienced in being revictualled have only been occasioned by the sudden change of the arrangement that was proposed and demanded by your Excellency, of buying the provisions by your own commissaries, which has necessarily produced the greatest embarrassment; the Prussian commissaries having excused themselves on the state of entire destitution of the provinces contiguous to Dantzic, which have been already charged for so long a time with the provisioning of my troops. If, as I have several times requested, there had been at my head-quarters, conformably to the stipulations of the truce, a French commissary permanently, he would have been able to convince himself of the extreme embarrassment that the Prussian commissaries have felt in procuring waggons, and the necessary provisions for revictualling Dantzic, and for the maintenance of my own troops; so that it is not the army forming the blockade which has thrown obstacles in the way of revictualling the place. Moreover, it is only my sovereign, the august Emperor Alexander, to whom I must render an account of my actions.

. . . .
. . . .

I now come to an article of far greater importance, since it may be attended with the most serious consequences; for it appears, according to the letter of your Excellency, that you are decided on recommencing hostilities on your own authority, whilst the places, Stettin and Custrin, are also temporarily deprived, as well as Dantzic, of the provisions stipulated for in the armistice. I hope, however, that you will seriously consider what you are about to do, and I render you responsible for all the measures you may take, and which may prevent the belligerent powers from coming to an adjustment of their differences.

I send you an exact copy of the letter which I received from the Commander-in-chief of all the armies, Barclay de Tolly; you will see, that far from there being any thoughts of recommencing hostilities, I am expressly prohibited from doing so.

If, in spite of all my observations, which I have had formally certified by my Generals, commanders of corps, you do not think fit to wait patiently till the affair of the legion of Lutzow, which has caused the temporary cessation of the revictualling of Dantzic, (of which the arrears, by the way, are only suspended,) and of the other fortresses, is amicably settled, and you attack my forces, I will prove to you that my brave Russians do not stand in dread of the menaces of any one, and that they are moreover ready to shed their blood for the cause of all sovereigns and all nations.

(Signed,) ALEXANDER, DUKE of WURTEMBERG.

ANSWER.

Dantzic, July 16, 1813.

I RECEIVED the letter which your Royal Highness did me the honour to write to me on the 15th of this month. I will not again touch on the different observations which you make on the non-execution of the conditions of the armistice; they have been constantly brought forward, and always victoriously refuted; and therefore present nothing new. General Heudelet, whom I sent to the conference that was demanded by General Borozdin, has made known on my part the only expedient for a provisional arrangement which could again take place between us.

In a letter of the 14th instant, I intreated your Royal Highness to appoint at what precise time the six days between the rupture and the commencement of hostilities were to begin; to this I have had no positive answer. I must, therefore, acquaint you, that as the letter of your Royal Highness, dated the 12th, only reached me on the 14th at noon, and I can consider your positive and official refusal to continue the supplies as nothing else than a rupture of the armistice, hostilities will recommence on the 20th; I owe this determination to the Emperor and to my corps d'armée. Six guns fired from the different forts of Dantzic, at noon, shall leave no doubt on this subject. I beg your Royal Highness not to consider as a threat the obligation which I am under to interpret the violation of one of the articles of the treaty as a formal declaration, annulling the armistice; I know the brave Russian troops, whom I have often fought with, and I know that they are worthy to be opposed to our own.

Here, my Lord, my letter would close, were I not compelled to make a remark to your Royal Highness on some expressions of your letter of the 15th, that I also am only accountable to my sovereign for my determinations; that, as for what your Highness calls the cause of all sovereigns and all nations, these are very extraordinary phrases in the letter of a prince, who knows better

ILLUSTRATIVE DOCUMENTS. 415

than any one that the Emperor Alexander, his sovereign, was engaged during five years, in our alliance against the despotism of a maritime power, which would make all the Continent tributary to it; and that his august brother, the King of Wurtemberg, has been for a long time past one of the most staunch supporters of this same cause.

(Signed,) COUNT RAPP.

Letter from the Duke of Wurtemberg to General Rapp.

From my head-quarters, July 17, 1813.

GENERAL,

I SHOULD have nothing more to add to the letter which I wrote to your Excellency, dated the 15th of July, if the formal declaration of war which you make to me, as from one power to another, did not oblige me still to make a few important remarks, before the commencement of hostilities which you are about to undertake.

I will observe to you, then, (although it is absolutely impossible for me, officially, to accept the declaration, that you are about to begin hostilities, and though I must declare you, once more, responsible for all the consequences that this event may produce) that if, in spite of my observations, you, nevertheless, persist in a determination which, as I believe, will not even be approved by the Emperor Napoleon, the period for the rupture which you fix for the 20th of July at mid-day, is contrary to the 2d and 3d articles of the armistice; since, after the 20th of July, the term of the expiration of the truce, hostilities should not take place, according to article 9th, till six days after the 20th of July, which will bring us to the 26th of the month; and it would be really singular for us to be the only two chiefs of corps on the theatre of war to recommence hostilities.

I am convinced, that with a little patience we shall soon hear that the affairs of the Cabinets are taking a different turn. What would be then the regret of your Excellency if, by too much precipitation, you should once more create difficulties between the two Courts, of which my own has nothing to reproach itself with, since it was very natural that it should for the time take measures of retaliation, after it had learnt the destruction of the corps of Lutzow in the midst of the armistice;—as it is not possible to bring to life the men so destroyed, while it will, on the other hand, be very possible to furnish the garrison of Dantzic with the provisions in arrear.

I now close my letter, General, compelled to make an observation or two on the last phrases in yours, which have appeared to me extremely strange. All Europe, and, I dare say, France also, is perfectly acquainted with the reasons which caused the rupture of the peace that was signed at Tilsit. It also knows the dictatorial tone which the ambassador Count Lauriston assumed in the heart of the capital of Peter the Great. The august Emperor Alexander was compelled, by such an excess of audacity, to appeal to his sword; he was obliged to surround himself with his valiant soldiers to open the churches, and to confide himself to a generous and faithful people, who have proved to him what may be done by a nation happy in its own territory, but who have not hesitated a moment to arm themselves in defence of their honour and of their sovereign.

As to what concerns my brother, the King of Wurtemberg, whom your Excellency calls one of the most staunch supporters of the cause which you defend, I can assure your Excellency that a Russian General-in-chief does not think himself inferior in any respect to a King of the Confederation, since it only depends on the Emperor Alexander to elevate me to that dignity, if he thinks fit; and then I shall be king like any other; I should, however, premise one small condition, that is, that it should not be at the expense of any power, or any person.

(Signed,) ALEXANDER, DUKE of WURTEMBERG.

CAPITULATION OF DANTZIC.

CAPITULATION of the fortress of Dantzic under special conditions, concluded between their Excellencies Lieutenant-general Borozdin, Major-general Welljaminoff, in quality of chief of the staff, and the Colonels of Engineers, Manfredi and Pullet, intrusted with full powers by his Royal Highness the Duke of Wurtemberg, Commander-in-chief of the troops besieging Dantzic, on one part;

And their Excellencies Count Heudelet, general of division, the General of Brigade d'Hericourt, Adjutant-general; and Colonel Richemont intrusted with full powers from his Excellency Count Rapp, aide-de-camp of the Emperor, Commander-in-chief of the 10th corps d'armée, on the other part.

ARTICLE I. The troops forming the garrison of Dantzic, and of the forts and redoubts thereunto belonging, shall leave the town with their arms and baggage on the 1st of January, 1814, at ten o'clock in the morning, by the gate of Oliwa, and shall lay down their arms before the battery of Gottes-Engel, if by that period the blockade of the garrison of Dantzic is not raised by a corps d'armée, equivalent in force to the besieging army, or if a treaty concluded between the belligerent powers shall not by that time have fixed the fate of the city of Dantzic. The officers shall retain their swords, in consideration of the vigorous defence and distinguished conduct of the garrison. The company of the Imperial guard, and a battalion of six hundred men, shall retain their arms, and shall take with them two six-pounders, with the ammunition waggons belonging to them. Twenty-five horsemen shall also preserve their arms and their horses.

ART. II. The forts of Weichselmunde, the Holm, and the intermediate works shall, together with the keys of the outer gate of Oliwa, be given up to the combined army, on the morning of the 24th Dec. 1813.

ART. III. Immediately on the signature of the present capitulation, the fort La Corte, that of Neufahrwasser, with its dependencies, and the left bank of the

ILLUSTRATIVE DOCUMENTS. 419

Vistula, as far as the height of the redoubt Gudin, and the line of redoubts extending from this last-mentioned work on the Zigangenberg, as well as the Mowenkrugschantz shall be surrendered in their present condition, without any deterioration, into the hands of the besieging army. The bridge which at present connects the *tête-du-pont* of Fahrwasser with the fort of Weichselmunde, shall be removed and placed at the mouth of the Vistula, between Neufahrwasser and the Nowenkrugschantz.

ART. IV. The garrison of Dantzic shall be prisoners of war, and shall be escorted to France. The governor, Count Rapp, formally engages that neither officers nor soldiers shall serve again, until their perfect exchange, against any of the powers now at war with France. There shall be drawn up an exact muster-roll of the names of the generals, officers, and soldiers composing the garrison of Dantzic, without any exception. There shall be two copies of this roll. Each of the generals and officers shall sign a promise and give his word of honour not to serve against Russia or her allies till his perfect exchange. An exact muster-roll shall be also made of all the soldiers who are actually under arms, and another of those who are sick or wounded.

ART. V. The governor, Count Rapp, engages to accelerate as much as possible the exchange of the individuals forming the garrison of Dantzic, rank for rank, for an equal number of prisoners belonging to the allied powers. But if, contrary to all expectation, this exchange should not take place for want of the necessary number of Russians, Austrians, Prussians, or other prisoners belonging to the courts allied against France, or if the said courts should throw obstacles in the way of it, then at the end of a year and a day, dating from Jan. 1, 1814, new style, the individuals forming the garrison of Dantzic shall be released from the formal obligation contracted in Art. IV. of the present capitulation, and may be again employed by their government.

ART. VI. The Polish troops and others belonging to the garrison shall be at full liberty to follow the lot of the French army, and in that case shall be treated in the same manner, excepting those troops whose sovereigns may be in alliance with the coalition against his Majesty the Emperor Napoleon, who shall be forwarded to the states or armies of their sovereigns, according to the orders which they shall receive from them, and which orders they shall send officers or messengers to request, immediately after the signature of the present capitulation. The Polish and other officers shall give each his word of honour in writing not to serve against the allied powers till his perfect exchange, conformably to the explanation given by Art. V.

ART. VII. All prisoners, of whatever nation they may be, who belong to the powers at war with France, and who are at present in Dantzic, shall be set at liberty without exchange, and sent to the Russian advanced posts by the gate Peters-Hagen, on the morning of the 12th of December, 1813.

ART VIII. The sick and wounded belonging to the

garrison shall be treated in the same manner, and with the same care as those of the allied powers; they shall be sent back to France after their perfect recovery, under the same conditions as the rest of the troops forming the garrison of Dantzic. A commissary of war, and medical officers shall be left with these invalids to attend to them and to claim their removal.

ART. IX. As soon as a certain number of individuals belonging to the troops of the allied powers shall have been exchanged for an equal number of individuals belonging to the garrison of Dantzic, then the latter may consider themselves free from their preceding engagement, contracted formally in Art. IV. of the present capitulation.

ART. X. The troops of the garrison of Dantzic, with the exception of those who, according to the terms of Art. VI. are to receive orders from their sovereigns, shall proceed by ordinary marches in four columns, at two days march distance one from the other, and according to the route annexed, and shall be escorted to the advanced posts of the French army. The garrison of Dantzic shall be supplied on its march according to the statement annexed. The 1st column shall begin its march the 2d Jan. 1814; the 2d on the 4th Jan. and so on.

ART. XI. All Frenchmen being non-combatants, and not in the service of the army, may follow, if they think fit, the troops of the garrison; but they cannot claim the rations fixed for the soldiery: they are, moreover, at liberty to dispose of the property which may be recognized as belonging to them.

Art. XII. On the 12th December, 1813, shall be delivered up to the commissioner appointed by the besieging army, all the cannon, mortars, &c. &c., arms, military stores, plans, drawings, sketches, the military chests, all the magazines of every description, the pontoons, all effects belonging to the engineer corps, to the marine, to the artillery, to the train, to the waggon department, &c. &c. without any exception; and a duplicate inventory shall be made of them, which shall be forwarded to the chief of the staff of the combined army.

Art. XIII. The generals, officers of the staff, and other officers, shall retain their baggage, and the horses they are entitled to under the regulations of the French army, and shall receive the necessary forage during their march.

Art. XIV. All details respecting the means of conveyance to be furnished, whether for the sick and wounded, or for the corps and officers, shall be regulated by the heads of the staff of the two armies.

Art. XV. There shall be reserved to the senate of Dantzic, the right of urging on the Emperor Napoleon all its rights to the liquidation of such debts as may exist on any part, and his Excellency the governor engages to give those to whom the debts have been contracted, acknowledgments certifying the justice of their claims, but under no pretext shall hostages be retained on account of these debts.

Art. XVI. Hostilities of all kinds shall cease on both sides from the signature of the present treaty.

ART. XVII. Every article on which a doubt may arise shall always be interpreted in favour of the garrison.

ART. XVIII. Four exact copies of the present capitulation shall be made, two in the Russian, and two in the French language, to be transmitted in duplicate to the two Generals-in-chief.

ART. XIX. After the signature of these official documents the governor, General Count Rapp, shall be at liberty to send a courier to his government; he shall be accompanied to the advanced posts of the French army by a Russian officer.

Done and agreed to at Langfuhr, this 29th of November, 1813.

(Signed,)

The General of Division Count HEUDELET, General d'HERICOURT, Colonel RICHEMONT, Lieutenant-General Chevalier BOROZDIN, Major-General WELJAMINOFF, in quality of Head of the Staff, the Colonel of Engineers MANFREDI, Colonel of Engineers PULLET.

Seen and approved

COUNT RAPP.

Letter from the Duke of Wurtemberg to General Rapp.

From my head-quarters at Pelouken, December 23, 1813.
11 o'clock at night.

GENERAL,

I am bound to inform you that I have just received a despatch from his Imperial Majesty, which acquaints me, that the capitulation concluded between your Excellency and myself has been approved by the Emperor; excepting the part which concerns the return of the garrison to France. Although it does not belong to me to examine whether an apprehension lest the garrison of Dantzic might be forced, like that of Thorn, to resume active service before it should be perfectly exchanged, and after it should have passed the Rhine, may have had its weight, I am nevertheless obliged to acquaint your Excellency with the precise will of his Majesty, being at the same time persuaded that none of the Generals or Officers, forming part of the brave garrison of Dantzic, would permit themselves in any case to be wanting to their engagements, of which I myself would be willingly the guarantee. His Majesty has also formally authorized me to declare to you, General, that the garrison shall not be sent into the distant provinces of Russia, if your Excellency gives up the fortress without further injury, according to the terms of the capitulation. You may choose for your particular abode and for that of the Generals and Officers, any one of the towns of Revel, Pleskow, Zaliega and Orel, to remain there till the garrison is exchanged. Besides, it is understood of itself, that the Generals and Officers will preserve all the advantages which have been secured to them under the capitulation. As to what concerns the Polish troops who are at present in Dantzic, the pleasure of his Majesty is, that they be sent quietly to their homes on quitting the fortress, and in like manner the German troops.

I must believe, General, that your Excellency certainly will not hesitate to consent to these arrangements, since it is to be believed that the war will not last a year, and then every one will immediately return to his own country; and I am so much the more persuaded that your Excellency will take this determination, because in the opposite case I should not be able to spare you, or your garrison, any of the inevitable rigours which a perfectly useless resistance would carry in its train, the infallible consequence of which would be transportation of the garrison to the most distant provinces of the Russian empire, without the possibility of their enjoying the least of those advantages which are now perfectly secured to them; together with all the conveniences necessary for the route stipulated for in the capitulation.

If, however, your Excellency, contrary to all expectation, should take a determination as unexpected as prejudicial to the interests of the garrison, I will then restore to you, the day after to-morrow, Saturday, at noon, all the works which have been surrendered to the besieging army, except the fort of Neufahrwasser, since the supreme will of his Majesty is that your Excellency should previously send out of the fortress all the German troops at present in Dantzic with their arms and baggage, as the Confederation of the Rhine exists no longer, and all the states which composed it have become our allies; and in this case Neufahrwasser also shall be given up to you immediately and without the smallest difficulty. I will send also to Dantzic by the gate of Oliwa, all the stragglers as soon as they shall have returned; and in the event in question, hostilities shall recommence the day after they are given up, at nine o'clock in the morning.

(Signed) The Duke of WURTEMBERG.

P. S. I beg your Excellency to be so good as to let me have your answer to-morrow morning. If General Heudelet or any other of the Generals were sent to my head-quarters, it would infinitely facilitate the conclusion of an affair which may terminate to your satisfaction.

I have written on this subject to his Majesty by a Courier.

ANSWER.

MY LORD,

I made a capitulation with your Royal Highness:— to-day you announce to me that, without having any respect for it, the Emperor Alexander orders that the garrison of Dantzic shall be sent into Russia as prisoners of war, instead of returning to France.

The 10th Corps d'Armée leaves it to Europe, to history, to posterity, to decide on so extraordinary an infraction of the faith of treaties, against which I solemnly protest.

In consequence of these sacred principles, I have the honour to inform your Royal Highness that, holding strictly to the text of a capitulation, which I must not consider as annihilated because it is violated, I will execute it punctually; and that I am ready this very day to give up to the troops of your Highness, the forts of Weichselmunde, Napoleon, and the Holm, as well as all the magazines, and to leave the fortress with my garrison on the 1st of January next.

At that period, force, and the abuse of power, may drag us to Russia, to Siberia, or wherever they please. We shall submit to suffer, to die even if it be necessary, victims of our confidence in a solemn treaty. The Emperor Napoleon and France are powerful enough, sooner or later, to avenge us.

In this state of things, my Lord, there remains no arrangement for me to make with your Royal Highness; referring myself entirely to the capitulation of the 29th of November, which, I repeat, may be infringed, but cannot be annihilated.

(Signed,)   COUNT RAPP.

Dantzic, December 23, 1813.

Letter from Count Rapp to the Duke of Wurtemberg.

My Lord,

My aide-de-camp delivered to me yesterday the letter which your Royal Highness has done me the honour to address to me.

By your return of the letter which you received from me, I imagine your Royal Highness imputes to me exasperated feelings. Your Highness does not render me justice: I have been a soldier twenty-two years; I am habituated to good and to evil fortune.

Your Highness does me the honour to say, that it was quite to be expected that the Emperor Alexander should have the power of ratifying, or not ratifying, the capitulation. Either your Highness was furnished with full powers or you were not; under the last supposition my conduct would have been very different from what it has been.

Marshal Kalkreuth, after a very short defence, obtained a very honourable capitulation. I even recollect that the Emperor Napoleon, who was not twenty leagues from the fortress, was dissatisfied with it, but he would not put his commander-in-chief in an unpleasant position by annulling the capitulation. It was impossible to perform it with more fidelity and delicacy than it was executed with, by Marshal Lefebvre and myself. Marshal Kalkreuth is still living, and has preserved the remembrance of our proceedings. There are Prussian officers at your head-quarters who can also bear witness to them.

Your Highness does me the honour to say that his Majesty orders that all things shall be put upon their previous footing, if I wish to recommence hostilities. Your Highness knows perfectly well that the advantages were at the time of entering on the capitulation on our side, for you had constantly made us offers which you pretended to be favourable; you know that now it is quite the contrary: this assertion stands in no need of proofs.

Besides, my Lord, it is you who have always proposed to me to enter into an arrangement to stop the effusion of blood; offering, as the fundamental condition, our return to France. The correspondence of your Highness attests this fact.

Your Highness knows well in what situation we are placed, and that it is altogether impossible, in all respects, to prolong our defence. The choice which you leave me becomes perfectly illusory.

I pray your Highness to cause to be occupied to-day Weichselmunde, the Holm, and the intermediate works. I have only left in them small detachments to prevent waste. I desire also that your Highness will send commissaries to receive inventories of our magazines of all kinds. I attach importance to this, that there may be no complaints, and that we may not be reproached with having deteriorated any thing; not in the fear of going to Russia with fewer conveniences, which your Highness insists on in your letter, but through the desire of religiously fulfilling all my engagements

I have the honour again to declare to your Highness, that the garrison of Dantzic will leave the fortress on the 1st of January, in the morning, in execution of Art. I. of the capitulation of November 29; to which I entirely adhere, and to which it is quite useless to add any other arrangement. Circumstances will, after the evacuation, place us entirely at the disposal of your Highness.

I have the honour, &c.

COUNT RAPP.

TO THE SAME.

December 26, 1813.

MY LORD,

General Manfredi has delivered to me your Royal Highness's letter of yesterday, the 25th instant. Having had already the honour to treat with you on the first articles of this letter, the last is the only one that seems to require an answer. Your Royal Highness declares to me that you cannot allow me to leave Dantzic without a previous arrangement. On my part, thinking it impossible to open again the capitulation of November 29, approved of by your Royal Highness and by me, I have the honour to declare that, having no means of prolonging my defence, I put myself from the 31st of December at your disposal, together with the troops under my orders. This arrangement, my Lord, is very simple: it is for your Royal Highness to regulate the fate of the garrison.

I content myself with recommending to your generosity, the soldiers, especially those who, by their infirmities and wounds, more particularly claim my solicitude.

I recommend to you also the non-combatants, the women, the children, and the Frenchmen, resident in Dantzic.

(Signed,) COUNT RAPP.

THE END.

www.ingramcontent.com/pod-product-compliance
Lightning Source LLC
Chambersburg PA
CBHW060830190426
43197CB00039B/2536